John Walkenbach's
101 Excel® 2013 Tips, Tricks & Timesavers

by John Walkenbach

WILEY

101 Excel® 2013 Tips, Tricks & Timesavers

Published by
John Wiley & Sons, Inc.
111 River Street
Hoboken, NJ 07030-5774
www.wiley.com

For general information on our other products and services, please contact our Customer Care Department within the U.S. at 877-762-2974, outside the U.S. at 317-572-3993, or fax 317-572-4002.

For technical support, please visit www.wiley.com/techsupport.

Wiley also publishes its books in a variety of electronic formats. Some content that appears in print may not be available in electronic books.

Library of Congress Control Number: 2013936846

ISBN: 978-1-118-64218-4; ISBN: 978-1-118-64232-0 (ebk); ISBN: 978-1-118-65106-3 (ebk); ISBN: 978-1-118-65114-8 (ebk)

Manufactured in the United States of America

10 9 8 7 6 5 4 3 2 1

About the Author

John Walkenbach is a leading authority on spreadsheet software, and principal of J-Walk and Associates Inc., a one-person consulting firm based in southern Arizona. John is the author of more than 50 spreadsheet books and has written more than 300 articles and reviews for a variety of publications, including *PC World*, *InfoWorld*, *PC Magazine*, *Windows*, and *PC/Computing*. John also maintains a popular website (*The Spreadsheet Page*, `http://spreadsheetpage.com`) and is the developer of several Excel utilities, including the Power Utility Pak, an award-winning add-in for Excel. John graduated from the University of Missouri and earned a Masters and PhD from the University of Montana.

Publisher's Acknowledgments

We're proud of this book; please send us your comments at `http://dummies.custhelp.com`. For other comments, please contact our Customer Care Department within the U.S. at 877-762-2974, outside the U.S. at 317-572-3993, or fax 317-572-4002.

Some of the people who helped bring this book to market include the following:

Acquisitions, Editorial, and Media Development

Senior Project Editor: Mark Enochs

Acquisitions Editor: Katie Mohr

Copy Editor: Melba Hopper

Technical Editor: Mike Talley

Editorial Manager: Leah Michael

Vertical Websites Project Manager:
Laura Moss-Hollister

Supervising Producer: Rich Graves

Vertical Websites Associate Producers:
Josh Frank, Marilyn Hummel, Douglas Kuhn,
Shawn Patrick

Editorial Assistant: Annie Sullivan

Sr. Editorial Assistant: Cherie Case

Composition Services

Project Coordinator: Katherine Crocker

Layout and Graphics: Melanee Habig

Proofreader: Melissa Cossell

Indexer: BIM Indexing & Proofreading Services

Publishing and Editorial for Technology Dummies

Richard Swadley, Vice President and Executive Group Publisher

Andy Cummings, Vice President and Publisher

Mary Bednarek, Executive Acquisitions Director

Mary C. Corder, Editorial Director

Publishing for Consumer Dummies

Diane Graves Steele, Vice President and Publisher

Composition Services

Debbie Stailey, Director of Composition Services

▶ Table of Contents

Part II: Formatting

Part III: Formulas

Part V: Tables and Pivot Tables

Part VI: Charts and Graphics

INTRODUCTION

Excel is a very popular program. Millions of people throughout the world use it on a regular basis. But it's a safe bet that the vast majority of users have yet to discover some of the amazing things this product can do. If I've done my job, you'll find enough useful information in this book to help you use Excel on a new level.

What You Should Know

This book isn't a beginner's guide to Excel. Rather, it's a book for those who already use Excel but realize that they have a lot more to learn. This book contains 101 tips and tricks that I've learned over the years, and I'm certain that about 99 percent of all Excel users will find something new and useful in these pages.

If you have absolutely no experience with Excel, this book might not be the best choice for you. To get the most out of this book, you should have some background in using Excel. Specifically, I assume that you know how to accomplish the following tasks with Excel:

- ➤ Create workbooks, insert worksheets, save files, and perform other basic tasks.
- ➤ Navigate through a workbook.
- ➤ Use the Excel Ribbon and dialog boxes.
- ➤ Use basic Windows features, such as file management and copy-and-paste techniques.

What You Should Have

To use this book, you need a copy of Microsoft Excel 2013 for Windows. If you use an older version of Excel, some of the tips won't apply.

As far as hardware goes for the computer you use to run Excel, the faster, the better. And, of course, the more memory in your system, the happier you'll be.

Conventions in This Book

Take a minute to skim this section and become familiar with some of the typographic conventions used throughout this book.

Formula listings

Formulas usually appear on a separate line in monospace font. For example, I might list the following formula:

```
=VLOOKUP(StockNumber,PriceList,2,False)
```

Excel supports a special type of formula known as an *array formula*. When you enter an array formula, press Ctrl+Shift+Enter (not just Enter). Excel encloses an array formula in curly braces to remind you that it's an array formula.

Note **Don't type the curly braces for an array formula. Excel puts them in automatically.**

Key names

Names of keys on the keyboard appear in normal type: for example, Alt, Home, PgDn, and Ctrl. When you need to press two or more keys simultaneously, the keys are connected with a plus sign: Press Ctrl+G to display the Go To dialog box.

The Ribbon

Excel 2013 features the Ribbon user interface, which was introduced in Excel 2007.

When you need to select a command by using the Ribbon, I describe the command by using the tab name, the group name, and the command name: for example, Choose Home➜Alignment➜Wrap Text. This command translates to "Click the Home tab, locate the Alignment group, and then click the Wrap Text button."

Some commands use a drop-down Ribbon control. For example: Home➜Styles➜Conditional Formatting➜New Rule. In this case, you need to click the down-pointing arrow on the Conditional Formatting control in order to access the New Rule command.

Many commands begin with the word File. Clicking the File tab takes you to the Backstage View.

Functions, procedures, and named ranges

The names of the Excel worksheet functions appear in all uppercase letters: for example, "Use the SUM function to add the values in column A."

Unless you're dealing with text inside quotation marks, Excel isn't sensitive to case. In other words, both the following formulas produce the same result:

```
=SUM(A1:A50)
=sum(a1:a50)
```

Excel, however, converts the characters in the second formula to uppercase.

Mouse conventions

The mouse terminology in this book is all standard fare: pointing, clicking, right-clicking, dragging, and so on. You know the drill.

What the icons mean

Throughout this book, icons appear in the left margin to call your attention to points that are particularly important.

Note

I use Note icons to tell you that something is important — perhaps a concept that can help you master the task at hand or something fundamental for understanding subsequent material.

Caution

I use Caution icons when the operation I'm describing can cause problems if you're not careful.

Cross-Ref

I use the Cross-Reference icon to refer you to other tips that have more to say on a particular topic.

How This Book Is Organized

To provide some semblance of order, I grouped these tips and tricks into six parts:

- ➤ Part I: Workbooks and Files
- ➤ Part II: Formatting
- ➤ Part III: Formulas
- ➤ Part IV: Working with Data
- ➤ Part V: Tables and Pivot Tables
- ➤ Part VI: Charts and Graphics

How to Use This Book

This book really isn't intended to be read from cover to cover, as you would read a novel — but I'm sure that some people will do so. More likely, you'll want to use it as a reference book and consult it when necessary. If you're faced with a challenging task, you may want to check the index first to see whether the book specifically addresses your problem. The order of the parts and tips is arbitrary. Most readers will probably skip around and pick up useful tidbits here and there.

There are also an additional 30 bonus tips that you'll find at `www.dummies.com/go/101excel 2013tips`.

About the Power Utility Pak Offer

Toward the back of this book is a coupon that you can redeem for a discounted copy of my award-winning Power Utility Pak — a collection of useful Excel utilities, plus many new worksheet functions.

You can also use this coupon to purchase the complete VBA source code for a nominal fee. Studying the code is an excellent way to pick up some useful programming techniques. You can take the product for a test drive by downloading the trial version from my website at `http://spreadsheetpage.com`.

Note

Power Utility Pak version 7 requires the Windows version of Excel 2007 or later.

PART I

Workbooks and Files

In this part, you'll find tips and tricks covering some of the basics of Excel, including Protected View and AutoRecover, as well as working with the Quick Access toolbar and charging Excel's color scheme.

Tips and Where to Find Them

Changing the Look of Excel

With Excel 2013, what you see isn't necessarily what you have to live with. This tip describes several ways to change the look of Excel. Some changes affect only the appearance. Other options allow you to hide various parts of Excel to make more room for displaying your data — or maybe because you prefer a less-cluttered look.

Cosmetic changes

When the preview version of Microsoft Office 2013 became available, there was a minor uproar about its appearance. Compared to previous versions, the applications looked "flat" and many complained about the overall white color.

When the final version was released, Microsoft added two alternative Office themes: light gray and dark gray. To switch to a different theme, choose File➜Options to display the Excel Options dialog box. Click the General tab and use the Office Theme drop-down list (see Figure 1-1). The theme choice affects the appearance of the title bar, row and column borders, task panes, the taskbar, and a few other items. The theme you choose applies to all other Office 2013 applications.

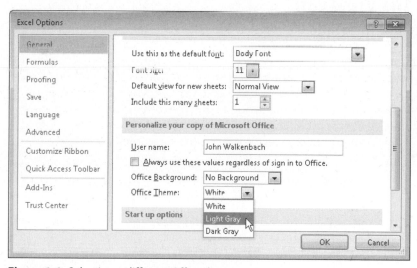

Figure 1-1: Selecting a different Office theme.

Figure 1-1 shows another option: Office Background. Use this drop-down list to select a background image that appears in the Excel title bar. Fortunately, one of the options is No Background.

Hiding the Ribbon

To hide the Ribbon, click the Ribbon Display Options drop-down menu in the Excel title bar. You'll see the choices shown in Figure 1-2.

Figure 1-2: Choosing how the Ribbon works.

Using options on the View tab

The View tab, shown in Figure 1-3, has three groups of commands that determine what you see onscreen.

➤ **Workbook Views group:** These options control the overall view. Most of the time, you'll use Normal view. Page Layout view is useful if you require precise control over how the pages are laid out. Page Break Preview also shows page breaks, but the display isn't nearly as nice. The status bar has icons for each of these views. Custom Views enable you to create named views of worksheet settings (for example, a view in which certain columns are hidden).

➤ **Show group:** The four checkboxes in this group control the visibility of the Ruler (relevant only in Page Layout view), the Formula bar, worksheet gridlines, and row and column headings.

➤ **Zoom group:** These commands enable you to zoom the worksheet in or out. Another way to zoom is to use the Zoom slider on the status bar.

Figure 1-3: Controls on the View tab.

Hiding other elements

To hide other elements, you must make a trip to the Advanced tab of the Excel Options dialog box (choose File→Options). Figure 1-4 shows workbook display options and worksheet display options. These options are self-explanatory.

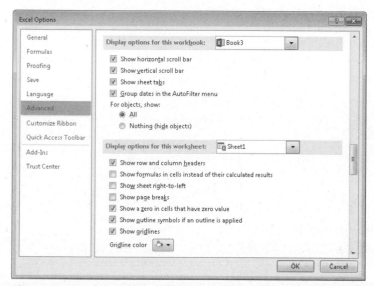

Figure 1-4: Display options on the Advanced tab of the Excel Options dialog box.

Hiding the status bar

You can also hide the status bar, at the bottom of the Excel window. Doing so, however, requires VBA code.

1. Press Alt+F11 to display the Visual Basic Editor.

2. Press Ctrl+G to display the Immediate window.

3. Type this statement and press Enter:

```
Application.DisplayStatusBar = False
```

The status bar will be removed from all open workbook windows. To redisplay the status bar, repeat those instructions, but specify True in the statement.

Customizing the Quick Access Toolbar

If you find that you continually need to switch Ribbon tabs because a frequently used command never seems to be on the Ribbon that's displayed, this tip is for you. The Quick Access toolbar is always visible, regardless of which Ribbon tab is selected. After you customize the Quick Access toolbar, your frequently used commands will always be one click away.

Note

> The only situation in which the Quick Access toolbar is not visible is when the title bar is hidden (by choosing Auto-Hide the Ribbon from the Ribbon Display Options drop-down list in the title bar).

About the Quick Access toolbar

By default, the Quick Access toolbar is located on the left side of the Excel title bar, and it includes three tools:

➤ **Save:** Saves the active workbook.

➤ **Undo:** Reverses the effect of the last action.

➤ **Redo:** Reverses the effect of the last undo.

Commands on the Quick Access toolbar always appear as small icons, with no text. When you hover your mouse pointer over an icon, you see the name of the command and a brief description.

As far as I can tell, the number of icons that you can add to your Quick Access toolbar is limitless. But regardless of the number of icons, the Quick Access toolbar always displays a single line of icons. If the number of icons exceeds the Excel window width, it displays an additional icon at the end: More Controls. Click the More Controls icon, and the hidden Quick Access toolbar icons appear in a pop-up window.

Adding new commands to the Quick Access toolbar

You can add a new command to the Quick Access toolbar in three ways:

➤ Click the Quick Access toolbar drop-down control, which displays a down-pointing arrow and is located on the right side of the Quick Access toolbar (see Figure 2-1). The list contains several commonly used commands. Select a command from the list, and Excel adds it to your Quick Access toolbar.

➤ Right-click any control on the Ribbon and choose Add to Quick Access Toolbar. The control is added to your Quick Access toolbar, positioned after the last control.

➤ Use the Quick Access Toolbar tab of the Excel Options dialog box. A quick way to access this dialog box is to right-click any Quick Access toolbar or Ribbon control and choose Customize Quick Access Toolbar.

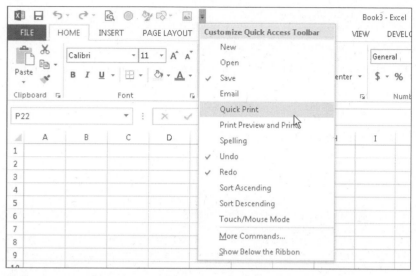

Figure 2-1: The Quick Access toolbar drop-down menu is one way to add a new command to the Quick Access toolbar.

Figure 2-2 shows the Quick Access Toolbar tab of the Excel Options dialog box. The left side of the dialog box displays a list of Excel commands, and the right side shows the commands that are now on the Quick Access toolbar. Above the command list on the left is a drop-down control that lets you filter the list. Select an item from the drop-down list, and the list displays only the commands for that item.

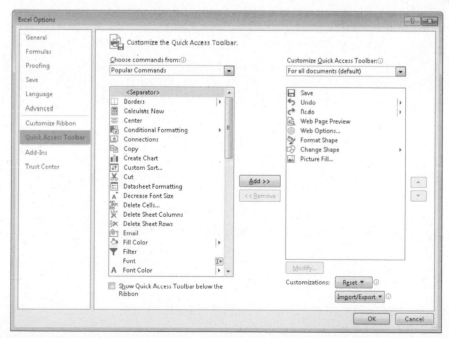

Figure 2-2: Use the Quick Access Toolbar tab in the Excel Options dialog box to customize the Quick Access toolbar.

Some of the items in the drop-down list are described here:

> ➤ **Popular Commands:** Displays commands that Excel users commonly use.

> ➤ **Commands Not in the Ribbon:** Displays a list of commands that you cannot access from the Ribbon.

> ➤ **All Commands:** Displays a complete list of Excel commands.

> ➤ **Macros:** Displays a list of all available macros.

> ➤ **File Tab:** Displays the commands available in the back stage window.

> ➤ **Home Tab:** Displays all commands that are available when the Home tab is active.

In addition, the drop-down list contains an item for every other tab.

Sometimes, you need to do some guessing to find a particular command. For example, if you want to add the command that displays the Excel Options dialog box, you can find it listed as Options, not Excel Options.

Note

Some commands simply aren't available. For example, I'd like the Quick Access toolbar to display the command to toggle the "dashed line" page break display on a worksheet. The only way to issue that command is to display the Advanced tab of the Excel Options dialog box and then scroll down until you find the Show Page Breaks checkbox. No command for doing so can be added to the Quick Access toolbar.

To add an item to your Quick Access toolbar, select it from the list on the left and click Add. If you add a macro to your Quick Access toolbar, you can click the Modify button to change the text and choose a different icon for the macro.

Notice the drop-down control above the list on the right. This lets you create a Quick Access toolbar that's specific to a particular workbook, which is most useful when you add workbook-specific macro commands to the Quick Access toolbar. Most of the time, you'll use the setting labeled For All Documents (Default).

The only time you ever need to use the Quick Access Toolbar tab of the Excel Options dialog box is when you want to add a command that's not on the Ribbon or add a command that executes a macro. In all other situations, it's much easier to locate the command on the Ribbon, right-click the command, and choose Add to Quick Access Toolbar.

Only you can decide which commands to put on your Quick Access toolbar. In general, if you find that you use a particular command frequently, it should probably be on your Quick Access toolbar.

Performing other Quick Access toolbar actions

Here are some other things you can do with your Quick Access toolbar:

➤ **Rearrange the Quick Access toolbar icons.** If you want to change the order of your Quick Access toolbar icons, you can do so on the Customization tab of the Excel Options dialog box. Select the command and then use the up- and down-arrow buttons on the right to move the icon.

➤ **Display the Quick Access toolbar below the ribbon.** To change the position of the Quick Access toolbar, choose the down-pointing arrow control and select Show below the Ribbon.

➤ **Remove Quick Access toolbar icons.** The easiest way to remove an icon from your Quick Access toolbar is to right-click the icon and choose Remove from Quick Access Toolbar. You can also use the Quick Access Toolbar tab of the Excel Options dialog box. Just select the command in the list on the right and click the Remove button.

➤ **Share your Quick Access toolbar.** Use the Import/Export button to save a file that contains your Quick Access toolbar customization. You can then share this file with others. Unfortunately, this file also contains any Ribbon customizations that you might have made (see Tip 3). In other words, you can't share your Quick Access toolbar without also sharing your Ribbon customizations.

➤ **Reset the Quick Access toolbar.** If you want to return the Quick Access toolbar to its default state, display the Quick Access Toolbar tab in the Excel Options dialog box and click the Reset button and choose Reset Only Quick Access Toolbar. All your customizations disappear, and the Quick Access toolbar then displays its three default commands.

Customizing the Ribbon

Tip 2 describes how to customize the Quick Access toolbar by adding Ribbon commands, but some users prefer to make some changes to the Ribbon itself.

You can customize the Ribbon in these ways:

➤ Add a new tab.

➤ Add a new group to tab.

➤ Add commands to a group.

➤ Remove groups from a tab.

➤ Remove commands from custom groups.

➤ Change the order of the tabs.

➤ Change the order of the groups within a tab.

➤ Change the name of a tab.

➤ Change the name of a group.

➤ Reset the Ribbon to remove all customizations.

That's a fairly comprehensive list of customization options, but you *cannot* do some actions:

➤ You cannot remove built-in tabs — but you *can* hide them.

➤ You cannot add commands to built-in groups.

➤ You cannot remove commands from built-in groups.

➤ You cannot change the order of commands in a built-in group.

Note

Unfortunately, you can't customize the Ribbon (or Quick Access toolbar) by using VBA macros. However, developers can write RibbonX code and store it in workbook files. When the file is open, the Ribbon is modified to display new commands. Writing RibbonX is relatively complicated and is the subject of several complete books.

How to customize the Ribbon

You customize the Ribbon in the Customize Ribbon tab of the Excel Options dialog box (see Figure 3-1). The quickest way to display this dialog box is to right-click anywhere in the Ribbon and choose Customize the Ribbon.

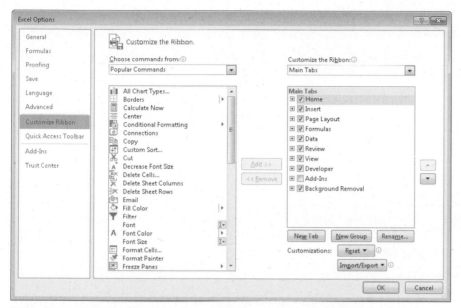

Figure 3-1: The Customize Ribbon tab of the Excel Options dialog box.

Customizing the Ribbon is very similar to customizing the Quick Access toolbar, which is described in Tip 2. The only difference is that you need to decide where to put the command within the Ribbon. Here's the general procedure:

1. Right-click any part of the Ribbon, and choose Customize the Ribbon. Excel displays the Customize Ribbon tab of the Excel Options dialog box.

2. Use the drop-down list on the left (labeled Choose Command From) to display various groups of commands.

3. Locate the command you want in the list box on the left and select it.

4. Use the drop-down list on the right (labeled Customize the Ribbon) to choose a group of tabs.

    Main Tabs refers to the tabs that are always visible; Tool Tabs refers to the context tabs that appear when a particular object is selected.

5. In the list box on the right, select the tab and the group where you want to put the command.

    You must click the "plus sign" controls to expand the hierarchical lists. Remember that you cannot add commands to built-in groups, so you may need to use the New Tab or New Group buttons to add a tab or group.

6. Click the Add button to add the selected command from the left to the group on the right.

When you are finished making your Ribbon changes, click OK to close the Excel Options dialog box.

New tabs and groups are given generic names, so you'll probably want to give them more meaningful names. Use the Rename button to rename the selected tab or group. You can also rename built-in tabs and groups.

Although you cannot remove a built-in tab, you can hide the tab by unchecking the check box next to its name.

Figure 3-2 shows a part of a customized Ribbon. In this case, I added a group to the View tab. The new Text To Speech group has five commands. I inserted this new group between the Zoom and the Window groups.

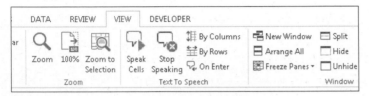

Figure 3-2: The View tab, with a new group added.

Understanding Protected View

There's an excellent chance that you've already encountered an Excel feature known as Protected View. Although it may seem like Excel is trying to keep you from opening your own files, Protected View is all about protecting you from malware.

Malware refers to something that can harm your system. Hackers have figured out several ways to manipulate Excel files so that harmful code can execute. Protected View essentially prevents these types of attacks by opening a file in a protected environment (sometimes called a *sandbox*).

If you open an Excel workbook that you downloaded from the web, you'll see a colorful message above the Formula bar (see Figure 4-1). In addition, Excel's title bar displays the text *[Protected View]*.

Figure 4-1: This message tells you the workbook was opened in Protected View.

If you're certain that the file is safe, click Enable Editing. If you don't enable editing, you'll be able to view the contents of the workbook, but you won't be able to make any changes to it.

If the workbook contains macros, you'll see another message after you enable editing: *Security Warning. Macros Have Been Disabled.* If you're sure that the macros are harmless, click Enable Content.

What causes Protected View?

Protected View kicks in for the following:

- ➤ Files downloaded from the Internet
- ➤ Attachments opened from Outlook
- ➤ Files that open from potentially unsafe locations, such as your Temporary Internet Files folder
- ➤ Files that are blocked by File Block Policy (a feature that allows administrators to define potentially dangerous files)
- ➤ Files that were digitally signed, but the signature has expired

You have some control over how Protected View works. To change the settings, choose File➜Options and click Trust Center. Then click the Trust Center Settings button and click the Protected View tab in the Trust Center dialog box. Figure 4-2 shows the options. By default, all three options are checked.

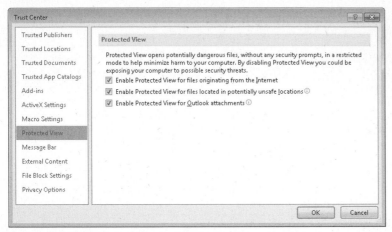

Figure 4-2: Change the Protected View settings in the Trust Center dialog box.

If you want to explicitly open a file in Protected View, choose File➔Open to display the Open dialog box. Select your file and then click the arrow to the right of the Open button. One of the options displayed is Open in Protected View.

If you enable editing in a workbook that opened in Protected View and then save the workbook, it will no longer open in Protected View.

Printing and copying

In some situations, you don't care about working with the document. You just want to print it. Unfortunately, it's not even possible to print a workbook unless you exit Protected View. Choose File➔Print and then click the Enable Printing button to exit Protected View.

Note that you can *copy* worksheet data from a Protected View document and paste it to another workbook. Formulas are not copied, but the current formula results are.

Forcing a file to open in Normal view

If you download a workbook and you're absolutely certain that it's safe, you can force it to open in Normal view. After downloading the workbook:

1. Right-click the workbook name (or icon) and choose Properties from the shortcut menu.

   The Properties dialog box appears.

2. Click the General tab (see Figure 4-3).

3. Click the Unblock button.

4. Click OK to close the Properties dialog box.

After performing these steps, the workbook will open in Excel in Normal view (not Protected View).

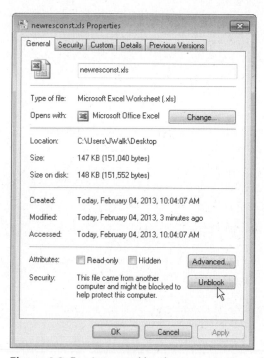

Figure 4-3: Forcing a workbook to open in Normal view.

Understanding AutoRecover

If you've used computers for any length of time, you've probably lost some work. You forgot to save a file, or maybe the power went out and your unsaved work was lost. Or maybe you were working on something and didn't think it was important, so you closed it without saving — and later realized that it *was* important. The AutoRecover feature in Excel can make these types of "doh!" moments less frequent.

As you work in Excel, your work is periodically saved, automatically. It happens in the background, so you don't even know that it's happening. You have the ability to access these autosaved versions of your work — even workbooks that you never explicitly saved.

This feature consists of two components:

➤ Versions of a workbook are saved automatically, and you can view them.

➤ Workbooks that you close without saving are saved as draft versions.

Recovering versions of the current workbook

To see whether any previous versions of the current workbook are available, choose File➜Info. The section labeled Versions lists the available old versions (if any) of the current workbook. Figure 5-1 shows that two autosaved versions of the active workbook are available.

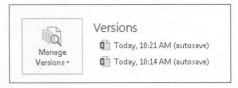

Figure 5-1: Two autosaved versions of this workbook are available.

You can open an autosaved version by clicking its name. Remember that opening an autosaved version *won't* automatically replace the current version of your workbook. Therefore, you can decide whether the autosaved version is preferable to the current version. Or you can just copy some information that may have been accidentally deleted and paste it into your current workbook.

When you close the workbook, the autosaved versions are deleted.

Recovering unsaved work

When you close a workbook without saving your changes, Excel asks whether you want to save your changes. If that unsaved workbook has an autosaved version, the dialog box informs you of that fact, as shown in Figure 5-2.

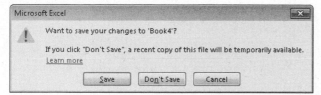

Figure 5-2: If you close a workbook without saving, Excel tells you whether an autosaved version will be available.

To recover a workbook that you closed without saving, choose File➜Info➜Manage Versions and choose Recover Unsaved Workbooks. You see a list of all unsaved versions of your workbooks. You can open them and (hopefully) recover something that you needed. These drafts are also listed in the recent file list, which displays when you choose File➜Recent.

Draft versions of unsaved workbooks are deleted after four days or until you edit the file.

Note

You can choose how AutoRecover works in the Save tab of the Excel Options dialog box. For example, you can change the autosave time interval (the default is 10 minutes), turn off autosave for a particular workbook, or disable this feature for all workbooks.

Using a Workbook in a Browser

Microsoft's Office Web Apps enable you to create, view, and edit workbooks directly in a browser. The experience isn't exactly the same as using the desktop version of Excel, but it's very similar. A key advantage is that you can access your workbooks from any location, and Excel need not be installed on the computer you use.

Note

This tip assumes that you have a Microsoft SkyDrive account (free) and are logged in. You can also use SharePoint.

After creating a workbook, choose File➜Save As and choose a location on your SkyDrive. This action saves your workbook on the cloud, and also saves a copy in your local SkyDrive folder. The two versions are synched.

Open your web browser and navigate to skydrive.com. Locate the workbook and click it. The workbook appears in the Excel Web App. Figure 6-1 shows a workbook displayed in the Google Chrome browser. As you can see, it's remarkably similar to the desktop version of Excel.

The Excel Web App is lacking some features, compared to the desktop version. For example, the following are not supported by the Excel Web App:

➤ Macros

➤ Add-ins

➤ Data validation

➤ Comments

➤ Shapes and other inserted objects

Some features, such as worksheet protection, prevent the workbook from being opened.

Cloud computing is a great idea, and it could be a significant part of the future of computing. But it can also be frustrating because you're at the mercy of your Internet provider and Microsoft. What if you need to get some work done, and the file you need is on the cloud? The message shown in Figure 6-2 could be frustrating.

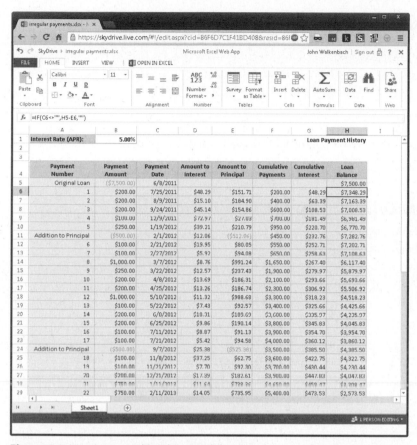

Figure 6-1: Viewing a workbook in a web browser.

Figure 6-2: The downside to storing your work in the cloud.

Saving to a Read-Only Format

If you need to share information in a workbook with someone — and be assured that the information remains intact and isn't altered — you have several choices.

Send a printed copy

Printing a workbook on paper is the low-tech approach. If the recipient is not nearby, this option may also require some type of delivery service.

Send an electronic copy in the form of a PDF file

PDF files (for Portable Document Format) is a common file format, and just about everyone has software installed that displays PDF files.

To save a workbook as a PDF file, choose File→Export→Create PDF/XPS Document and click the Create PDF/XPS button to display the Publish as PDF or XPS dialog box. Click the Options button for additional options:

- ➤ Choose the pages
- ➤ Specify what to save (the current range selection, the selected sheet(s), or the entire workbook
- ➤ Save document properties and accessibility information

For best results, use Excel's Page Layout view (View→Workbook View→Page Layout) before saving, so you'll see exactly how the pages will break. Figure 7-1 shows Adobe Reader displaying an Excel workbook that was saved as a PDF file.

Note

Excel provides another option: XPS format (for XML Paper Specification). This is Microsoft's format. When exporting from Excel, it's limited to a single worksheet, and it doesn't support images. An XPS viewer is installed with Windows. This format is not widely used.

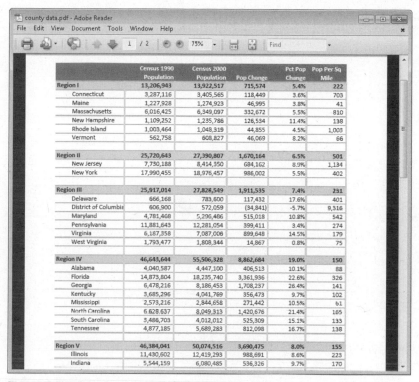

Figure 7-1: Adobe Reader displaying a PDF file created from an Excel workbook.

Send an MHTML file

Many Excel users don't know about this file format. An MHTML faithfully renders an Excel workbook in a single file that can be opened with many browsers, including Internet Explorer, Opera, and Mozilla Firefox (extension required). Choose File→Save As to display the Save As dialog box. Then select Single File Web Page (*.mht, *.mhtl) from the Save As Type drop-down menu.

Figure 7-2 shows a workbook that was saved as an MHTML file, displayed in the Internet Explorer browser. Note the worksheet tabs displayed along the bottom.

If you need to send a read-only, non-alterable workbook, the MHTML format is probably your best choice (assuming that the recipient has a browser that supports this format).

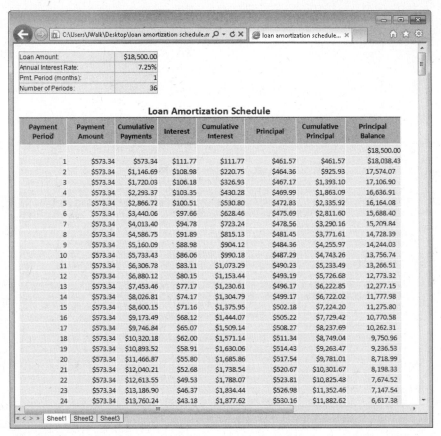

Figure 7-2: An Excel workbook saved as an MHTML file and displayed in a web browser.

Generating a List of Filenames

This tip describes how to retrieve a list of filenames in a folder and display them in a worksheet.

This technique uses an Excel 4 XLM macro function in a named formula. It's useful because it's a relatively simple way of getting a list of filenames into a worksheet — something that normally requires a complex VBA macro.

Start with a new workbook and then follow these steps to create a named formula:

1. Choose Formulas➜Define Name to display the New Name dialog box.

2. Type **FileList** in the Name field.

3. Enter the following formula in the Refers To field (see Figure 8-1):

   ```
   =FILES(Sheet1!$A$1)
   ```

4. Click OK to close the New Name dialog box.

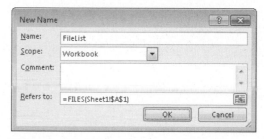

Figure 8-1: Using the New Name dialog box to create a named formula.

Note that the FILES function is not a normal worksheet function. Rather, it's an old XLM style macro function that is intended to be used on a special macro sheet. This function takes one argument (a directory path and a file specification) and returns an array of filenames in that directory that match the file specification.

A normal worksheet formula cannot use these old XLM functions, but named formulas can.

After defining the named formula, enter a directory path and file specification into cell A1. For example:

```
E:\Backup\Excel\*.xl*
```

Then this formula displays the first file found:

```
=INDEX(FileList, 1)
```

If you change the second argument to 2, it displays the second file found, and so on.

Figure 8-2 shows an example. The path and file specification is in cell A1. Cell A2 contains this formula, copied down the column:

```
=INDEX(FileList,ROW()-1)
```

The ROW function, as used here, generates a series of consecutive integers: 1, 2, 3, and so on. These integers are used as the second argument for the INDEX function. Note that cell A21 (and cells below it) displays an error. That's because the directory has only 19 files, and the formula is attempting to display files that don't exist.

When you change the directory or filespec in cell A1, the formulas update to display the new filenames.

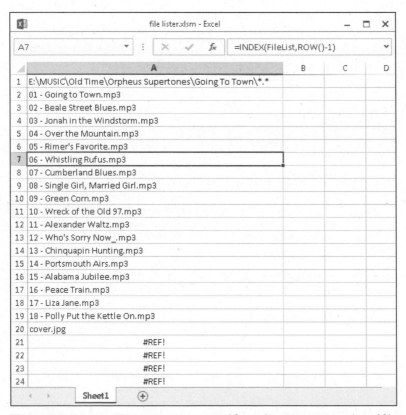

	A	B	C	D
1	E:\MUSIC\Old Time\Orpheus Supertones\Going To Town*.*			
2	01 - Going to Town.mp3			
3	02 - Beale Street Blues.mp3			
4	03 - Jonah in the Windstorm.mp3			
5	04 - Over the Mountain.mp3			
6	05 - Rimer's Favorite.mp3			
7	06 - Whistling Rufus.mp3			
8	07 - Cumberland Blues.mp3			
9	08 - Single Girl, Married Girl.mp3			
10	09 - Green Corn.mp3			
11	10 - Wreck of the Old 97.mp3			
12	11 - Alexander Waltz.mp3			
13	12 - Who's Sorry Now_.mp3			
14	13 - Chinquapin Hunting.mp3			
15	14 - Portsmouth Airs.mp3			
16	15 - Alabama Jubilee.mp3			
17	16 - Peace Train.mp3			
18	17 - Liza Jane.mp3			
19	18 - Polly Put the Kettle On.mp3			
20	cover.jpg			
21	#REF!			
22	#REF!			
23	#REF!			
24	#REF!			

Figure 8-2: Using an XLM macro in a named formula can generate a list of filenames in a worksheet.

Note

If you use this technique, you must save the workbook as a macro-enabled file (with an *.xlsm or *.xls extension).

Generating a List of Sheet Names

Oddly, Excel doesn't provide a direct way to generate a list of sheet names in a workbook. This tip describes how to generate a list of all the sheets in a workbook. Like the previous tip ("Generating a List of Filenames"), this tip uses an Excel 4 XLM macro function in a named formula.

Start with a workbook that has lots of worksheets or chart sheets. Then follow these steps to create a list of the sheet names:

1. Insert a new worksheet to hold the list of sheet names.

2. Choose Formulas➜Define Name to display the New Name dialog box.

3. Type **SheetList** in the Name field.

4. Enter the following formula in the Refers To field (see Figure 9-1):

```
=REPLACE(GET.WORKBOOK(1),1,FIND("]",GET.WORKBOOK(1)),"")
```

5. Click OK to close the New Name dialog box.

Figure 9-1: Using the New Name dialog box to create a named formula.

Note that this formula uses the GET.WORKBOOK function — which is not a normal worksheet function. Rather, it's an old XLM-style macro function intended for use on a special macro sheet. Using an argument of 1 returns an array of sheet names, and each name is preceded by the workbook name. The REPLACE and FIND functions remove the workbook name from the sheet names.

To generate the sheet names, enter this formula in cell A1, and then copy it down the column:

```
=INDEX(SheetList,ROW())
```

Figure 9-2 shows this formula in the range A1:A10. The workbook has seven sheets, so the formula returns a #REF! error when it attempts to display a nonexistent sheet name. To eliminate this error, modify the formula as follows:

```
=IFERROR(INDEX(SheetList,ROW()),"")
```

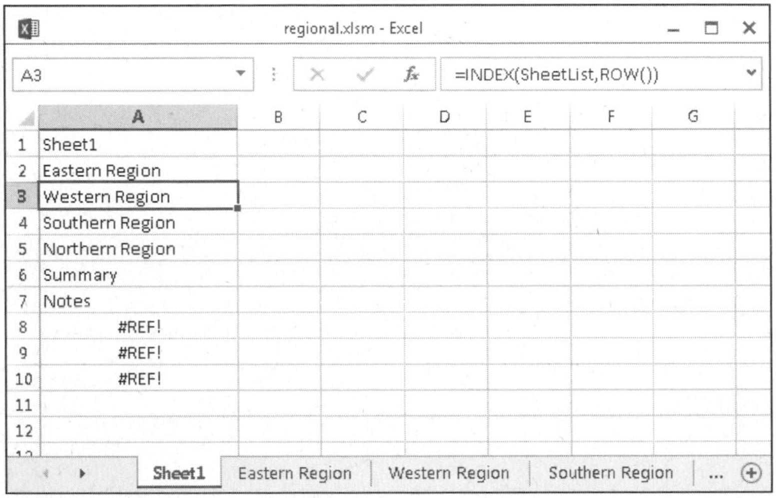

Figure 9-2: Using a formula to display a list of sheet names.

The list of sheet names will adjust if you add sheets, delete sheets, or rename sheets — but the adjustment doesn't happen automatically. To force the formulas to update, press Ctrl+Alt+F9. If you want the sheet names to adjust automatically when the workbook is calculated, edit the named formula to make it "volatile."

```
=REPLACE(GET.WORKBOOK(1),1,FIND("]",GET.WORKBOOK(1)),"")&T(NOW())
```

What good is a list of sheet names? Figure 9-3 shows a table of contents created by using the HYPERLINK function. The formula in cell B1 is

```
=HYPERLINK("#"&A1&"!A1","Go to sheet")
```

Clicking a hyperlink activates the worksheet and selects cell A1. Unfortunately, Excel doesn't support hyperlinking to a chart sheet, so you get an error if a hyperlink points to a chart sheet.

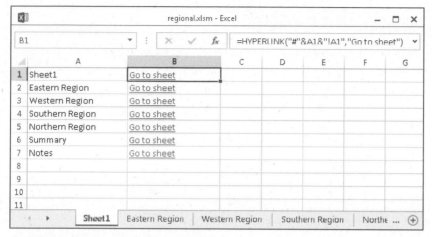

Figure 9-3: Creating a list of hyperlinks.

Note

If you use this technique, you must save the workbook as a macro-enabled file (with an *.xlsm or *.xls extension).

Using Document Themes

Over the years, I've seen hundreds of Excel workbooks that were created by others. A significant percentage of these workbooks have one thing in common: They are ugly!

In an effort to help users create more professional-looking documents, Microsoft designers (starting with Office 2007) incorporated the concept of Office *document themes*. Using themes is an easy (and almost foolproof) way to specify the colors and fonts and a variety of graphical effects in a document. Best of all, changing the entire look of your document is a breeze. A few mouse clicks is all it takes to apply a different theme and change the look of your workbook.

Importantly, the concept of themes is incorporated into other Office applications. Therefore, a company can easily create a standard look for all its documents.

Elements within Excel that are controlled by document themes are

➤ Cells and ranges that use theme colors (as opposed to standard colors)

➤ Tables

➤ Charts

➤ Conditional formatting (but not always)

➤ Sparkline graphics

➤ Pivot tables

➤ PivotTable slicers and timelines

➤ Shapes

➤ SmartArt

➤ WordArt

➤ Sheet tab colors

Figure 10-1 shows a worksheet that contains various Excel elements. These items all use the default theme, which is known as Office Theme.

Figure 10-2 shows the same worksheet after applying a different document theme. The different theme changes the fonts, colors (which may not be apparent in the figure), and graphical effects for the SmartArt diagram.

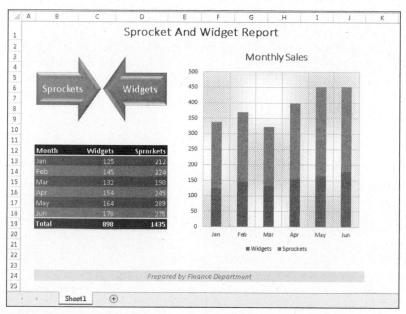

Figure 10-1: The elements in this worksheet use default formatting.

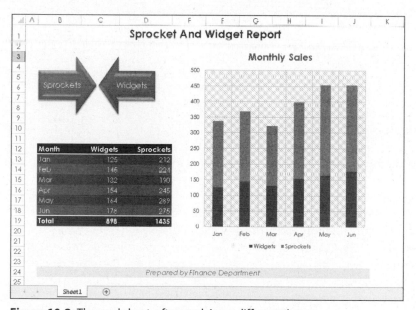

Figure 10-2: The worksheet, after applying a different theme.

Applying a theme

Figure 10-3 shows the theme choices that appear when you choose Page➜Layout➜Themes. This display is a live preview. As you move your mouse over the theme choices, the active worksheet displays the theme. When you see a theme you like, click it to apply the theme to all worksheets in the workbook.

A theme applies to the entire workbook. You cannot use different themes on different worksheets within a workbook.

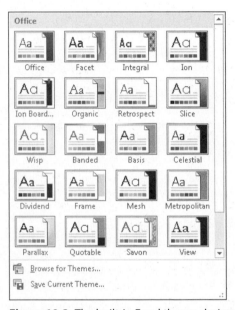

Figure 10-3: The built-in Excel theme choices.

When you specify a particular theme, you find that the gallery choices for various elements reflect the new theme. For example, the chart styles that you can choose from vary, depending on which theme is active.

Note

Because themes use different fonts and font sizes, changing to a different theme can affect the layout of your worksheet. For example, after you apply a new theme, a worksheet that printed on a single page may spill over to a second page. Therefore, you may need to make some adjustments after you apply a new theme. For best results, decide on a theme before you do too much work on the file.

Customizing a theme

Office 2013 includes quite a few themes. If that's not enough, you can modify them and even create your own themes.

Notice that the Page Layout→Themes group contains three other controls: Colors, Fonts, and Effects. You can use these controls to change just one of the three components of a theme. For example, if you like the Urban theme but prefer different fonts, apply the Urban theme and then specify your preferred font set by using the Page Layout→Themes→Fonts control.

Each theme uses two fonts (one for headers and one for the body), and in some cases, these two fonts are the same. If none of the theme choices is suitable, choose Page Layout→Themes→Fonts→ Create New Theme Fonts to specify the two fonts you prefer (see Figure 10-4). When you use the Home→Fonts→Font command, the two fonts from the current theme are listed first in the drop-down list.

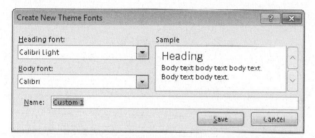

Figure 10-4: Use this dialog box to specify two fonts for a theme.

Use the Page Layout→Themes→Colors command to select a different set of colors. Also, if you're so inclined, you can even create a custom set of colors by choosing Page Layout→Themes→Colors→ Customize Colors. This command displays the dialog box shown in Figure 10-5. Note that each theme consists of 12 colors. Four of the colors are for text and backgrounds, six are for accents, and two are for hyperlinks. The first ten are the colors that appear in theme color selector controls. As you specify different colors, the Preview panel in the dialog box is updated.

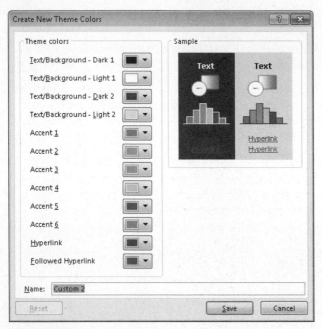

Figure 10-5: If you're feeling creative, you can specify a set of custom colors for a theme.

Theme effects operate on graphical elements, such as SmartArt, shapes, and charts. You can't customize theme effects.

If you customize a theme by using different fonts or colors, you can save the new theme by choosing Page Layout→Themes→Save Current Theme. Your customized themes appear in the theme list in the Custom category. Other Office applications, such as Word and PowerPoint, can use these theme files.

Understanding Excel Compatibility Issues

The most recent version of Excel is known as Excel 2013, and it's version 15. Microsoft's version numbering is a bit misleading because they've only released 12 versions of Excel for Windows. The first version was Excel 2, and they skipped right over versions 6 and 13.

Besides Excel 2013, three other versions of Excel for Windows are still widely used: Excel 2003, Excel 2007, and Excel 2010.

If you create workbooks only for Excel 2013 users, you can skip this tip because you don't have to be concerned with compatibility. But if you create workbooks for those who use an earlier version, you need to understand compatibility.

The Excel 2013 file formats

The current Excel file formats (all of which were introduced in Excel 2007) are

> ➤ .xlsx: A workbook file that doesn't contain macros

> ➤ .xlsm: A workbook file that contains macros

> ➤ .xltx: A workbook template file that doesn't contain macros

> ➤ .xltm: A workbook template file that contains macros

> ➤ .xlsa: An add-in file

> ➤ .xlsb: A binary file that's similar to the old .xls format but able to accommodate the new features

> ➤ .xlsk: A backup file

With the exception of .xlsb, these are all "open" XML files, which means that the file format is not proprietary and other applications can read and write these types of files.

Note

The XML files are actually zip-compressed text files. If you rename one of these files to have a .zip extension, you can examine the contents using any of several zip file utilities — including the zip file support built into Windows. Taking a look at the innards of an Excel workbook is an interesting exercise for curious-minded users.

The Office Compatibility Pack

Normally, those who use a version prior to Excel 2007 can't open workbooks saved in the newer Excel file formats. But, fortunately, Microsoft has released a free Compatibility Pack for Office 2003 and Office XP.

If an Office 2003 or Office XP user installs the Compatibility Pack, he can open files created in Office 2007 or later and save files in the newer format. The Office programs that are affected are Excel,

Word, and PowerPoint. This software doesn't endow the older versions with any new features — it just gives them the capability to open and save files in the new format.

To download the Compatibility Pack from Microsoft, search the web for *Office Compatibility Pack.*

It's important to understand the limitations regarding version compatibility. Even though your colleague is able to open your file, there is no guarantee that everything will function correctly or look the same.

Checking compatibility

If you save your workbook to an older file format (such as .xls, for versions prior to Excel 2007), Excel automatically runs the Compatibility Checker. The Compatibility Checker identifies the elements of your workbook that will result in a loss of functionality or fidelity (cosmetics).

Figure 11-1 shows the Compatibility Checker dialog box. Click the Select Versions to Show button to limit the compatibility-checking to a specific version of Excel.

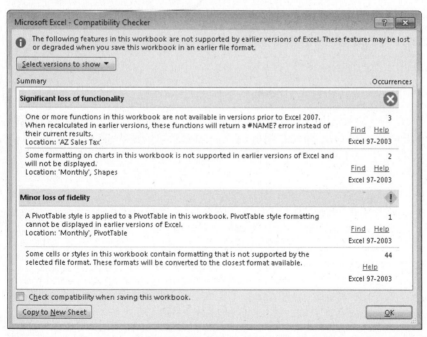

Figure 11-1: The Compatibility Checker is a useful tool for those who share workbooks with other people.

The bottom part of the Compatibility Checker lists the potential compatibility problems. To display the results in a more readable format, click the Copy to New Sheet button.

Keep in mind that compatibility problems also can occur with Excel 2007 and Excel 2010, even though these versions use the same file format as Excel 2013. You can't expect features that are new to Excel 2013 to work in earlier versions. For example, if you add slicers to table (a new feature in Excel 2013) and send it to a colleague who uses Excel 2010, the slicers won't be displayed. In addition, formulas that use any of the new worksheet functions will return an error. The Compatibility Checker identifies these types of problems.

Where to Change Printer Settings

If you want to print a copy of a worksheet with no fuss and bother, use the Quick Print option. One way to access this command is to choose File→Print (which displays the Print pane of Backstage view) and then click the Print button.

However, if the default print settings aren't good enough, you must make some adjustments. A little tweaking of the print settings can often improve your printed reports.

Unfortunately, Excel has no one-stop location for adjusting print setting. You can adjust print settings in three places:

➤ The Print settings screen in Backstage view, which opens when you choose File→Print.

➤ The Page Layout tab of the Ribbon.

➤ The Page Setup dialog box, which opens when you click the dialog launcher in the lower-right corner of the Page Layout→Page Setup group on the Ribbon. You can also access the Page Setup dialog box from the Print settings screen in Backstage view.

Table 12-1 summarizes the locations where you can make various types of print-related adjustments in Excel 2013.

Table 12-1: Where to Change Printer Settings

Setting	Print Settings Screen	Page Layout Tab of Ribbon	Page Setup Dialog Box
Number of copies	X		
Printer to use	X		
What to print	X		
Specify worksheet print area		X	X
1-sided or 2-sided	X		
Collated	X		
Orientation	X	X	X
Paper size	X	X	X
Adjust margins	X	X	X
Specify manual page breaks		X	
Specify repeating rows and/or columns			X
Set print scaling		X	X
Print or hide gridlines		X	X
Print or hide row and column headings		X	X

continued

Table 12-1: Where to Change Printer Settings *(continued)*

Setting	Print Settings Screen	Page Layout Tab of Ribbon	Page Setup Dialog Box
Specify the first page number			X
Center output on page			X
Specify repeating rows or columns			X
Specify header/footers and options			X
Specify how to print cell comments			X
Specify page order			X
Specify black-and-white output			X
Specify how to print error cells			X
Launch dialog box for printer-specific settings	X		X

This table might make printing seem more complicated than it really is. The key point to remember is this: If you can't find a way to make a particular adjustment, it's probably available from the Page Setup dialog box.

PART II

Formatting

Excel has lots of formatting options to make your work look good. In this part, you'll find tips that cover formatting numbers, copying formatting, and other topics.

Tips and Where to Find Them

Working with Merged Cells

Merging cells is a simple concept: Join two or more cells to create a larger single cell. To merge cells, just select them and choose Home→Alignment→Merge & Center. Excel combines the selected cells and displays the contents of the upper-left cell, centered.

Merging cells is usually done as a way to enhance the appearance of a worksheet. Figure 13-1, for example, shows a worksheet with four sets of merged cells: C2:I2, J2:P2, B4:B8, and B9:B13. The merged cells in column B also use vertical text.

▲	A	B	C	D	E	F	G	H	I	J	K	L	M	N	O	P	Q
1																	
2			Week 1							Week 2							
3			1	2	3	4	5	6	7	8	9	10	11	12	13	14	
4		Group 1	90	97	32	0	63	82	29	16	29	28	31	87	5	42	
5			14	88	79	16	38	2	86	26	37	20	49	97	35	58	
6			18	43	63	30	34	47	10	51	38	47	61	67	40	61	
7			22	67	18	38	40	25	18	47	81	10	1	71	70	58	
8			42	64	64	17	8	94	81	61	18	76	18	7	94	4	
9		Group 2	93	70	84	62	29	12	79	46	62	11	38	76	53	81	
10			15	88	38	67	8	42	9	37	59	71	67	55	4	30	
11			2	74	34	64	27	28	81	96	6	77	21	93	83	75	
12			79	50	80	94	13	14	32	95	51	3	94	48	69	34	
13			5	89	5	29	9	12	55	95	4	31	43	91	89	37	
14																	
15																	

Figure 13-1: This worksheet has four sets of merged cells.

Remember that merged cells can contain only one piece of information: a single value, text, or a formula. If you attempt to merge a range of cells that contains more than one nonempty cell, Excel prompts you with a warning that only the data in the upper-leftmost cell will be retained.

To unmerge cells, just select the merged area and click the Merge and Center button again.

Other merge actions

Notice that the Merge and Center button is a drop-down menu. If you click the arrow, you see three additional commands:

➤ **Merge Across:** Lets you select a range and then creates multiple merged cells — one for each row in the selection.

➤ **Merge Cells:** Works just like Merge and Center, except that the content of the upper-left cell is not centered. (It retains its original horizontal alignment.)

➤ **Unmerge Cells:** Unmerges the selected merged cell.

Wrapping text in merged cells is an easy way to display lengthy text. To make text wrap in merged cells, select the merged cells and choose Home➜Alignment➜Wrap Text. Use the vertical and horizontal alignment controls in Home➜Alignment group to adjust the text position.

Figure 13-2 shows a worksheet in which 171 cells have been merged (19 rows and 9 columns). The text in the merged cells uses the Wrap Text option.

	A	B	C	D	E	F	G	H	I	J	K
1											
2											
3		Four score and seven years ago our fathers brought forth on this continent a new nation, conceived in liberty, and dedicated to the proposition that all men are created equal.									
5											
6		Now we are engaged in a great civil war, testing whether that nation, or any nation, so conceived and so dedicated, can long endure. We are met on a great battle-field of that war. We have come to dedicate a portion of that field, as a final resting place for those who here gave their lives that that nation might live. It is altogether fitting and proper that we should do this.									
11											
12		But, in a larger sense, we can not dedicate, we can not consecrate, we can not hallow this ground. The brave men, living and dead, who struggled here, have consecrated it, far above our poor power to add or detract. The world will little note, nor long remember what we say here, but it can never forget what they did here. It is for us the living, rather, to be dedicated here to the unfinished work which they who fought here have thus far so nobly advanced. It is rather for us to be here dedicated to the great task remaining before us—that from these honored dead we take increased devotion to that cause for which they gave the last full measure of devotion—that we here highly resolve that these dead shall not have died in vain—that this nation, under God, shall have a new birth of freedom—and that government of the people, by the people, for the people, shall not perish from the earth.									
22											
23											

Figure 13-2: Here 171 cells are merged into one.

Potential problems with merged cells

Many Excel users have a deep-seated hatred of merged cells. They avoid using this feature and urge everyone else to also avoid merged cells. But if you understand the limitations and potential problems, there's no reason to completely avoid using merged cells.

Here are a few things to keep in mind:

➤ You can't use merged cells in a table (created by choosing Insert➔Tables➔Table). This is understandable because data in a table must be consistent in terms of rows and columns. Merging cells in a table will destroy that consistency.

➤ Normally, you can double-click a column header or row header to autofit the data in the column or row, but that feature doesn't work if the row or column contains merged cells. Instead, you need to adjust the column width or row height manually.

➤ Merged cells can also affect sorting and filtering. That's another reason why merged cells aren't allowed in tables. If you have a range of data that you will sort or filter, avoid using merged cells.

➤ Finally, merged cells can cause problems with VBA macros. For example, if the cells in A1:D1 are merged, a VBA statement such as the following will actually select four columns (not at all what the programmer intended):

```
Columns("B:B").Select
```

Locating all merged cells

To find out whether a worksheet contains merged cells, follow these steps:

1. Press Ctrl+F to open the Find and Replace dialog box.

2. Check to be sure the Find What field is empty.

3. Click the Options button to expand the dialog box.

4. Click the Format button to open the Find Format dialog box, where you specify the formatting to find.

5. In the Find Format dialog box, choose the Alignment tab and place a check mark next to Merged Cells.

6. Click OK to close the Find Format dialog box.

7. In the Find and Replace dialog box, click Find All.

Excel displays a list of all merged cells in the worksheet (see Figure 13-3). Click an address in the list, and the merged cell is activated.

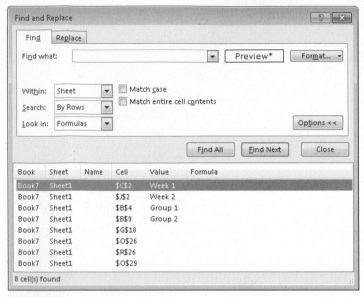

Figure 13-3: Finding all merged cells in a worksheet.

Unmerging all merged cells

Here's a quick way to unmerge all merged cells in a worksheet:

1. Select all cells in the worksheet.

   A quick way to do so is to click the triangle at the intersection of the row headers and column headers.

2. Click the Home tab.

3. If the Merge & Center command is highlighted, click it.

Note

In Step 3, if the Merge & Center command isn't highlighted, there are no merged cells. If you click the command when all cells are selected, all 17,179,869,184 cells in the worksheet will be merged.

Alternatives to merged cells

In some cases, you can use Excel's Center Across Selection command as an alternative to merged cells. This command is useful for centering text across several columns.

1. Enter the text to be centered in a cell.

2. Select the cell that has the text and additional cells to the right of it.

3. Press Ctrl+1 to display the Format Cells dialog box.

4. In the Format Cells dialog box, choose the Alignment tab.

5. In the Text Alignment section, choose the Horizontal drop-down and select Center Across Selection.

6. Click OK to close the Format Cells dialog box.

The text is centered across the selected cells.

Another alternative to merging cells is to use a text box. This is particular useful for text that must be displayed vertically. Figure 13-4 shows an example of a text box that displays vertical text. To add a text box, choose Insert➔Text➔Text Box, draw the box on the worksheet, and then enter the text. Use the text formatting tools on the Home tab to adjust the text; use the tools in the Drawing Tools➔ Format context tab to make other modifications (for example, to hide the text box outline).

*? How To Clear a Text Box
Use Home → Ed. T → Clear*

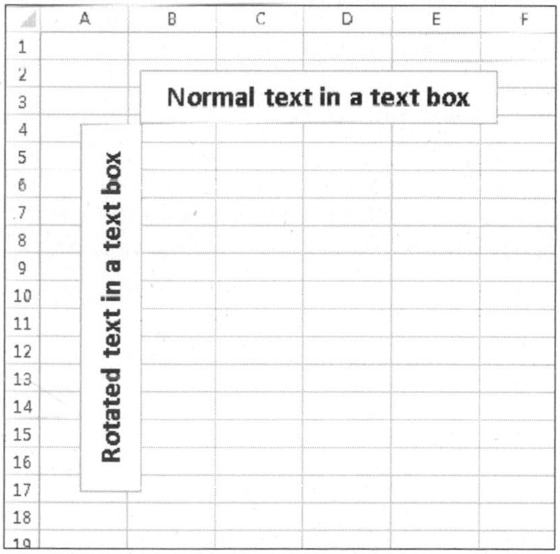

Figure 13-4: Using a text box as an alternative to merged cells.

Indenting Cell Contents

As you probably know, Excel (by default) left-aligns text and right-aligns numbers. Most of the time, that's exactly how you want data to be aligned.

But if a column of text is to the right of a column of numbers, the information can be difficult to read. Figure 14-1 shows an example. All the data in this table uses the default alignment. The table would be more legible if there were a larger gap between the numbers and the text.

	A	B	C	D	E
1	Employee Number	Employee	Hire Code	Location	
2	1439	Tami Harris	1002	California	
3	934	Carrie Bell	1002	Oregon	
4	1157	Robin Wood	1002	California	
5	892	Wilbur Jenkins	1002	Oregon	
6	1330	Frederick Perez	1002	Washington	
7	965	Joseph Jordan	1205	Washington	
8	1249	Michael Waters	1205	Oregon	
9	1490	Gregory Burns	1002	Oregon	
10	1404	Norma Moore	1308	Oregon	
11	1157	Holly Diaz	1002	Washington	
12	949	Joan Campbell	1308	California	
13	1354	Emma West	1002	California	
14	1057	Linda Rodriguez	1205	Washington	
15	1405	Hazel Leonard	1205	California	
16	1458	Marion Davis	1205	Oregon	
17	1057	Frank Jones	1002	Washington	
18					

Figure 14-1: The legibility of this table can be improved by indenting the text.

Many users don't realize that Excel can indent data — either from the left or from the right. Unfortunately, the command to indent is not on the Ribbon. You need to select the cells and then use the Alignment tab of the Format Cells dialog box (see Figure 14-2). A quick way to access this dialog box is to click the dialog launcher icon in the lower-right corner of the Home➜Alignment group.

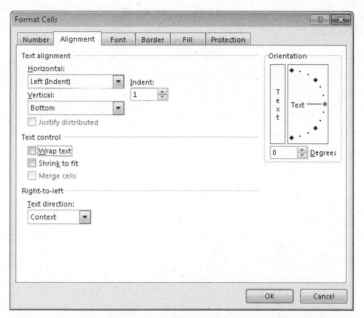

Figure 14-2: The Alignment tab of the Format Cells dialog box.

Use the Indent spinner to specify the size of the indenting. Usually, 1 is sufficient, but feel free to experiment. Then use the Horizontal drop-down list to choose the location for the indent: either Left (Indent) or Right (Indent). Click OK, and the text adjusts.

Figure 14-3 shows the original table after indenting the text. Much more legible!

	Employee Number	Employee	Hire Code	Location
2	1439	Tami Harris	1002	California
3	934	Carrie Bell	1002	Oregon
4	1157	Robin Wood	1002	California
5	892	Wilbur Jenkins	1002	Oregon
6	1330	Frederick Perez	1002	Washington
7	965	Joseph Jordan	1205	Washington
8	1249	Michael Waters	1205	Oregon
9	1490	Gregory Burris	1002	Oregon
10	1404	Norma Moore	1308	Oregon
11	1157	Holly Diaz	1002	Washington
12	949	Joan Campbell	1308	California
13	1354	Emma West	1002	California
14	1057	Linda Rodriguez	1205	Washington
15	1405	Hazel Leonard	1205	California
16	1450	Marion Davis	1205	Oregon
17	1057	Frank Jones	1002	Washington
18				

Figure 14-3: Indenting the text makes the table easier to read.

Using Named Styles

Throughout the years, one of the most underused features in Excel has been named styles. Named styles make it very easy to apply a set of predefined formatting options to a cell or range. In addition to saving time, using named styles helps to ensure a consistent look across your worksheets.

A style can consist of settings for up to six different attributes (which correspond to the tabs in the Format Cells dialog box):

➤ Number format

➤ Alignment (vertical and horizontal)

➤ Font (type, size, and color)

➤ Borders

➤ Fill (background color)

➤ Protection (locked and hidden)

The real power of styles is apparent when you change a component of a style. All cells that have been assigned that named style automatically incorporate the change. Suppose that you apply a particular style to a dozen cells scattered throughout your worksheet. Later, you realize that these cells should have a font size of 14 points rather than 12 points. Rather than change each cell, simply edit the style definition. All cells with that particular style change automatically.

Using the Style gallery

Excel comes with dozens of predefined styles, and you apply these styles in the Style gallery (located in the Home➜Styles group). Figure 15-1 shows the predefined styles in the Style gallery. To apply a style to the selected cell or range, just click the style. Notice that this gallery provides a preview. When you hover your mouse over a style, it's temporarily applied to the selection so that you can see the effect. To make it permanent, just click the style.

After you apply a style to a cell, you can apply additional formatting to it by using any formatting method discussed in this chapter. Formatting modifications that you make to the cell don't affect other cells that use the same style.

To maximize the value of styles, it's best to avoid additional formatting. Rather, consider creating a new style (explained later in this tip).

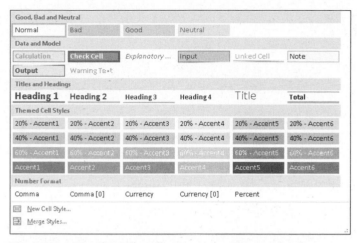

Figure 15-1: Use the Style gallery to work with named styles.

Modifying an existing style

To change an existing style, activate the Style gallery, right-click the style you want to modify, and choose Modify from the shortcut menu. Excel displays the Style dialog box, shown in Figure 15-2. In this example, the Style dialog box shows the settings for the Normal style, which is the default style for all cells. (The style definitions vary, depending on which document theme is active.)

Figure 15-2: Use the Style dialog box to modify named styles.

Cells, by default, use the Normal style. Here's a quick example of how you can use styles to change the default font used throughout your workbook:

1. Choose Home➜Styles➜Cell Styles.

   Excel displays the list of styles for the active workbook.

2. Right-click Normal in the Styles list and choose Modify.

   The Style dialog box opens with the current settings for the Normal style.

3. Click the Format button.

   The Format Cells dialog box opens.

4. Click the Font tab and choose the font and size that you want as the default.

5. Click OK to return to the Style dialog box.

6. Click OK again to close the Style dialog box.

The font for all cells that use the Normal style changes to the font that you specified. You can change any formatting attributes for any style.

Creating new styles

In addition to using the built-in Excel styles, you can create your own styles. This flexibility can be quite handy because it enables you to apply your favorite formatting options very quickly and consistently.

To create a new style from an existing formatted cell, follow these steps:

1. Select a cell and apply all the formatting that you want to include in the new style.

   You can use any of the formatting that's available in the Format Cells dialog box.

2. After you format the cell to your liking, activate the Style gallery and choose New Cell Style.

   The Style dialog box opens, along with a proposed generic name for the style. Note that Excel displays the words "By Example" to indicate that it's basing the style on the current cell.

3. Enter a new style name in the Style Name box.

   The check boxes show the current formats for the cell. By default, all check boxes are checked.

4. If you don't want the style to include one or more format categories, remove the check marks from the appropriate boxes.

5. Click OK to create the style and close the dialog box.

After you perform these steps, the new custom style is available in the Style gallery. Custom styles are available only in the workbook in which they were created. To copy your custom styles, see the section that follows.

Note

The Protection option in the Styles dialog box controls whether users can modify cells for the selected style. This option is effective only if you also turn on worksheet protection, by choosing Review➜Changes➜Protect Sheet.

Merging styles from other workbooks

It's important to understand that custom styles are stored with the workbook in which they were created. If you created some custom styles, you probably don't want to go through all the work to create copies of those styles in each new Excel workbook. A better approach is to merge the styles from a workbook in which you previously created them.

To merge styles from another workbook, open both the workbook that contains the styles you want to merge and the workbook into which you want to merge styles. From the workbook into which you want to merge styles, activate the Style gallery and choose Merge Styles. The Merge Styles dialog box opens with a list of all open workbooks. Select the workbook that contains the styles you want to merge and click OK. Excel copies styles from the workbook you selected into the active workbook.

You may want to create a master workbook that contains all your custom styles so that you always know from which workbook to merge styles.

Creating Custom Number Formats

Although Excel provides a good variety of built-in number formats, you may find that none of them suits your needs. In such a case, you can probably create a custom number format. You do so on the Number tab of the Format Cells dialog box (see Figure 16-1). The easiest way to display this dialog box is to press Ctrl+1. Or click the dialog box launcher in the Home➜Number group. (The dialog box launcher is the small icon to the right of the word *Number*.)

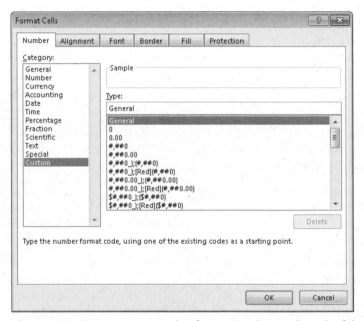

Figure 16-1: Create custom number formats on the Number tab of the Format Cells dialog box.

Many Excel users — even advanced users — avoid creating custom number formats because they think that the process is too complicated. In reality, custom number formats tend to *look* more complex than they are.

You construct a number format by specifying a series of codes as a number format string. To enter a custom number format, follow these steps:

1. Press Ctrl+1 to display the Format Cells dialog box.

2. Click the Number tab and select the Custom category.

3. Enter your custom number format in the Type field.

   See Tables 16-1 and 16-2 for examples of codes you can use to create your own, custom number formats.

4. Click OK to close the Format Cells dialog box.

Parts of a number format string

A custom format string enables you to specify different format codes for four categories of values: positive numbers, negative numbers, zero values, and text. You do so by separating the codes for each category with a semicolon. The codes are arranged in four sections, separated by semicolons:

```
Positive format; Negative format; Zero format; Text format
```

The following general guidelines determine how many of these four sections you need to specify:

➤ If your custom format string uses only one section, the format string applies to all values.

➤ If you use two sections, the first section applies to positive values and zeros, and the second section applies to negative values.

➤ If you use three sections, the first section applies to positive values, the second section applies to negative values, and the third section applies to zeros.

➤ If you use all four sections, the last section applies to text stored in the cell.

The following example of a custom number format specifies a different format for each of these types:

```
[Green]General;[Red]-General;[Black]General;[Blue]General
```

This example takes advantage of the fact that colors have special codes. A cell formatted with this custom number format displays its contents in a different color, depending on the value. When a cell is formatted with this custom number format, a positive number is green, a negative number is red, a zero is black, and text is blue. By the way, using the Excel conditional formatting feature is a much better way to apply color to cells based on their content.

Note

When you create a custom number format, don't overlook the Sample box in the Number tab of the Format Cells dialog box. This box displays the value in the active cell by using the format string in the Type field. Be sure to test your custom number formats by using the following data: a positive value, a negative value, a zero value, and text. Often, creating a custom number format takes several attempts. Each time you edit a format string, it's added to the list. When you finally get the correct format string, open the Format Cells dialog box one more time and delete your previous attempts.

Custom number format codes

Table 16-1 briefly describes the formatting codes available for custom formats.

Table 16-1: Codes Used to Create Custom Number Formats

Code	What It Does
General	Displays the number in General format.
#	Serves as a digit placeholder that displays only significant digits and doesn't display insignificant zeros.
0 (zero)	Serves as a digit placeholder that displays insignificant zeros if a number has fewer digits than there are zeros in the format.
?	Serves as a digit placeholder that adds spaces for insignificant zeros on either side of the decimal point so that decimal points align when formatted with a fixed-width font; also used for fractions that have varying numbers of digits.
.	Displays the decimal point.
%	Displays a percentage.
,	Displays the thousands separator.
E- E+ e- e+	Displays scientific notation.
$ – + / ( ) : space	Displays the actual character.
\	Displays the next character in the format.
*	Repeats the next character to fill the column width.
_ (underscore)	Leaves a space equal to the width of the next character.
"text"	Displays the text inside the double quotation marks.
@	Serves as a text placeholder.
[color]	Displays the characters in the specified color and can be any of the following text strings (not case-sensitive): Black, Blue, Cyan, Green, Magenta, Red, White, or Yellow.
[COLOR n]	Displays the corresponding color in the color palette, where *n* is a number from 0 to 56.
[condition value]	Enables you to set your own criteria for each section of a number format.

Table 16-2 describes the codes used to create custom formats for dates and times.

Table 16-2: Codes Used in Creating Custom Formats for Dates and Times

Code	What It Displays
M	The month as a number without leading zeros (1–12)
mm	The month as a number with leading zeros (01–12)
mmm	The month as an abbreviation (Jan–Dec)
mmmm	The month as a full name (January–December)
mmmmm	The first letter of the month (J–D)
d	The day as a number without leading zeros (1–31)
dd	The day as a number with leading zeros (01–31)
ddd	The day as an abbreviation (Sun–Sat)
dddd	The day as a full name (Sunday–Saturday)
yy or yyyy	The year as a two-digit number (00–99) or as a four-digit number (1900–9999)
h or hh	The hour as a number without leading zeros (0–23) or as a number with leading zeros (00–23)
m or mm	The minute as a number without leading zeros (0–59) or as a number with leading zeros (00–59)
s or ss	The second as a number without leading zeros (0–59) or as a number with leading zeros (00–59)
[ ]	Hours greater than 24 or minutes or seconds greater than 60
AM/PM	The hour using a 12-hour clock or no AM/PM indicator if the hour uses a 24-hour clock

Using Custom Number Formats to Scale Values

If you work with large numbers, you may prefer to display them scaled to thousands or millions rather than display the entire number. For example, you may want to display a number like 132,432,145 in millions: 132.4.

The way to display scaled numbers is to use a custom number format. The actual unscaled number, of course, will be used in calculations that involve that cell. The formatting affects only how the number is displayed. To enter a custom number format, press Ctrl+1 to display the Format Cells dialog box. Then click the Number tab and select the Custom category. Put your custom number format in the Type field.

Table 17-1 shows examples of number formats that scale values in millions.

Table 17-1: Examples of Displaying Values in Millions

Value	Number Format	Display
123456789	#,###,,	123
1.23457E+11	#,###,,	123,457
1000000	#,###,,	1
5000000	#,###,,	5
−5000000	#,###,,	−5
0	#,###,,	(blank)
123456789	#,###.00,,	123.46
1.23457E+11	#,###.00,,	123,457.00
1000000	#,###.00,,	1.00
5000000	#,###.00,,	5.00
−5000000	#,###.00,,	−5.00
0	#,###.00,,	.00
123456789	#,###,,"M"	123M
1.23457E+11	#,###,,"M"	123,457M
1000000	#,###,,"M"	1M
−5000000	#,###,,"M"	−5M
123456789	#,###.0,,"M"_);(#,###.0,,"M)";0.0"M"_)	123.5M
1000000	#,###.0,,"M"_);(#,###.0,,"M)";0.0"M"_)	1.0M
−5000000	#,###.0,,"M"_);(#,###.0,,"M)";0.0"M"_)	(5.0M)
0	#,###.0,,"M"_);(#,###.0,,"M)";0.0"M"_)	0.0M

Table 17-2 shows examples of number formats that scale values in thousands.

Table 17-2: Examples of Displaying Values in Thousands

Value	Number Format	Display
123456	#,###,	123
1234565	#,###,	1,235
−323434	#,###,	−323
123123.123	#,###,	123
499	#,###,	(blank)
500	#,###,	1
500	#,###.00,	.50

Table 17-3 shows examples of number formats that display values in hundreds.

Table 17-3: Examples of Displaying Values in Hundreds

Value	Number Format	Display
546	0"."00	5.46
100	0"."00	1.00
9890	0"."00	98.90
500	0"."00	5.00
−500	0"."00	−5.00
0	0"."00	0.00

Creating a Bulleted List

Word-processing software, such as Microsoft Word, makes it very easy to create a bulleted list of items. Excel doesn't have a feature that creates bulleted lists, but it's easy to fake it.

Using a bullet character

You can generate a bullet character by pressing Alt, and typing **0149** on the numeric keypad. If your keyboard lacks a numeric keypad, press the Function key and type numbers using the normal keys.

Figure 18-1 shows a list in which each item is preceded with a bullet character and a space. The cells use wrap-text formatting. Items that occupy more than one line are not indented. In a bulleted list, multiple lines are usually indented so they line up with the first line.

	A	B	C
1		• Schedule a planning meeting with the Survey Team	
2		• Develop the questionnaire	
3		• Print and mail questionnaires	
4		• Receive Responses	
5		• Data entry and analysis	
6		• Write Report	
7		• Distribute draft report to the survey team members	
8		• Make revisions, if necessary	
9		• Distribute the final report to the Board of Directors	
10			
11			

Figure 18-1: Inserting a bullet character before each item.

Figure 18-2 shows a second attempt. This approach requires two columns. Column A holds the bullet character, formatted so the bullet is top-aligned and right-aligned. The text is in column B.

Figure 18-2 also shows an alternative, a numbered list. The cells that contain the numbers use this custom number format, which displays a decimal point, but no decimal places:

```
General". "
```

Note   You can, of course, use any character you like for the bullet. Use Insert→Symbols→ Symbol to display (and insert) characters from any font that's installed on your system.

▲	A	B	C	D	E	F
1		• Schedule a planning meeting with the Survey Team			1. Schedule a planning meeting with the Survey Team	
2		• Develop the questionnaire			2. Develop the questionnaire	
3		• Print and mail questionnaires			3. Print and mail questionnaires	
4		• Receive Responses			4. Receive Responses	
5		• Data entry and analysis			5. Data entry and analysis	
6		• Write Report			6. Write Report	
7		• Distribute draft report to the survey team members			7. Distribute draft report to the survey team members	
8		• Make revisions, if necessary			8. Make revisions, if necessary	
9		• Distribute the final report to the Board of Directors			9. Distribute the final report to the Board of Directors	
10						

Figure 18-2: Using an additional column for the bullet characters, or for numbers.

Using SmartArt

Another way to create a bulleted list in Excel is to use SmartArt. Choose Insert➜Illustrations➜ SmartArt, and choose the diagram style from the dialog box.

Figure 18-3 shows a "Vertical Bullet List" SmartArt diagram. This object is free-floating and can easily be moved and resized. The example shown here uses minimal formatting, but you have lots of control over the appearance of SmartArt.

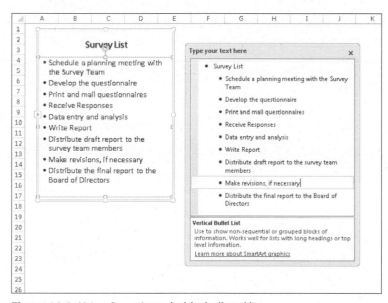

Figure 18-3: Using SmartArt to hold a bulleted list.

Shading Alternate Rows Using Conditional Formatting

When you create a table (using Insert→Tables→Table), you have the option of formatting the table in such a way that alternate rows are shaded. Alternate row shading can make your spreadsheets easier to read.

This tip describes how to use conditional formatting to obtain alternate row shading for any range of data. It's a dynamic technique: If you add or delete rows within the conditional formatting area, the shading is updated automatically.

Displaying alternate row shading

Figure 19-1 shows an example. Here's how to apply shading to alternate rows:

1. Select the range to format.

2. Choose Home→Conditional Formatting→New Rule.

   The New Formatting Rule dialog box appears.

3. For the rule type, choose Use a Formula to Determine Which Cells to Format.

4. Enter the following formula in the box labeled Format Values Where This Formulas Is True:

   ```
   =MOD(ROW(),2)=0
   ```

5. Click the Format button.

   The Format Cells dialog box appears.

6. In the Format Cells dialog box, click the Fill tab and select a background fill color.

7. Click OK to close the Format Cells dialog box, and click OK again to close the New Formatting Rule dialog box.

This conditional formatting formula uses the ROW function (which returns the row number) and the MOD function (which returns the remainder of its first argument divided by its second argument). For cells in even-numbered rows, the MOD function returns *0*, and cells in that row are formatted.

For alternate shading of columns, use the COLUMN function instead of the ROW function.

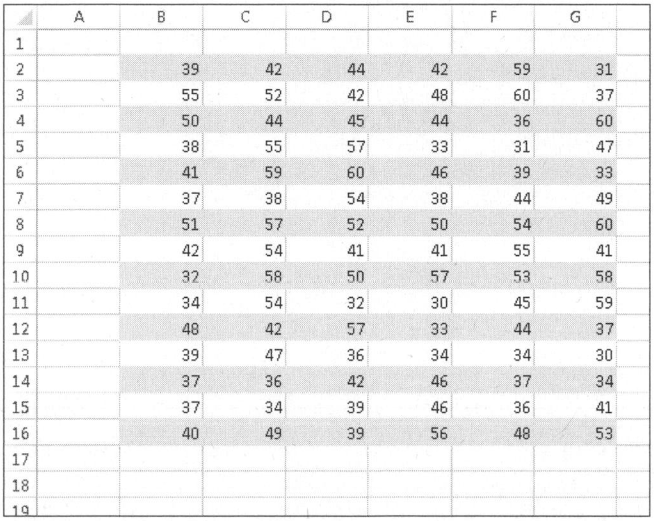

	A	B	C	D	E	F	G
1							
2		39	42	44	42	59	31
3		55	52	42	48	60	37
4		50	44	45	44	36	60
5		38	55	57	33	31	47
6		41	59	60	46	39	33
7		37	38	54	38	44	49
8		51	57	52	50	54	60
9		42	54	41	41	55	41
10		32	58	50	57	53	58
11		34	54	32	30	45	59
12		48	42	57	33	44	37
13		39	47	36	34	34	30
14		37	36	42	46	37	34
15		37	34	39	46	36	41
16		40	49	39	56	48	53
17							
18							
19							

Figure 19-1: Using conditional formatting to apply formatting to alternate rows.

Creating checkerboard shading

The following formula is a variation on the example in the preceding section. It applies formatting to alternate rows and columns, creating a checkerboard effect. Figure 19-2 shows the result.

```
=MOD(ROW(),2)=MOD(COLUMN(),2)
```

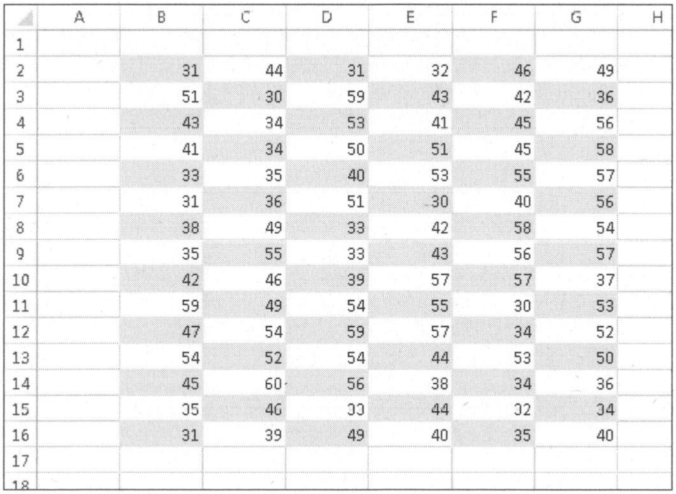

	A	B	C	D	E	F	G	H
1								
2		31	44	31	32	46	49	
3		51	30	59	43	42	36	
4		43	34	53	41	45	56	
5		41	34	50	51	45	58	
6		33	35	40	53	55	57	
7		31	36	51	30	40	56	
8		38	49	33	42	58	54	
9		35	55	33	43	56	57	
10		42	46	39	57	57	37	
11		59	49	54	55	30	53	
12		47	54	59	57	34	52	
13		54	52	54	44	53	50	
14		45	60	56	38	34	36	
15		35	46	33	44	32	34	
16		31	39	49	40	35	40	
17								
18								

Figure 19-2: Conditional formatting produces this checkerboard effect.

Shading groups of rows

Here's another row shading variation. The following formula shades alternate groups of rows. It produces four rows of shaded rows, followed by four rows of unshaded rows, followed by four more shaded rows, and so on. Figure 19-3 shows an example.

```
=MOD(INT((ROW()-1)/4)+1,2)
```

For different sized groups, change the 4 to some other value. For example, use this formula to shade alternate groups of two rows:

```
=MOD(INT((ROW()-1)/2)+1,2)
```

◢	A	B	C	D	E	F	G	H
1		52	52	33	44	56	51	
2		52	51	58	46	35	34	
3		32	46	36	52	58	36	
4		43	47	56	53	37	42	
5		37	60	44	31	49	38	
6		39	58	44	56	41	41	
7		42	48	53	33	49	60	
8		38	49	51	38	46	50	
9		38	54	57	43	55	39	
10		51	57	30	55	42	55	
11		32	40	37	53	53	57	
12		35	60	48	32	31	50	
13		59	34	37	51	46	58	
14		56	35	60	48	58	51	
15		53	40	60	34	48	36	
16		59	60	40	52	59	43	
17		45	32	60	59	49	56	
18		48	44	41	59	55	43	
19		49	55	52	55	46	43	
20		44	45	48	31	57	31	
21		44	30	46	56	48	44	
22		42	54	47	44	60	46	
23		54	39	40	43	59	40	
24		36	50	38	32	54	54	
25								
26								

Figure 19-3: Conditional formatting produces these groups of alternate shaded rows.

Formatting Individual Characters in a Cell

Excel cell formatting isn't an all-or-none proposition. In some cases, you might find it helpful to be able to format individual characters within a cell.

Note　**This technique is limited to cells that contain text. It doesn't work if the cell contains a value or a formula.**

To apply formatting to characters within a text string, select those characters first. You can select them by clicking and dragging your mouse on the Formula bar, or you can double-click the cell and then click and drag the mouse to select specific characters directly in the cell. A more efficient way to select individual characters is to press F2 first and then use the arrow keys to move between characters and use the Shift+arrow keys to select characters.

When the characters are selected, use formatting controls to change the formatting. For example, you can make the selected text bold, italic, or a different color; you can even apply a different font. If you right-click, the Mini Toolbar appears, and you can use those controls to change the formatting of the selected characters.

Figure 20-1 shows a few examples of cells that contain individual character formatting.

Unfortunately, two useful formatting attributes are not available on the Ribbon or on the Mini Toolbar: superscript and subscript formatting. If you want to apply superscripts or subscripts, open the Font tab in the Format Cells dialog box. Just press Ctrl+1 after you select the text to format.

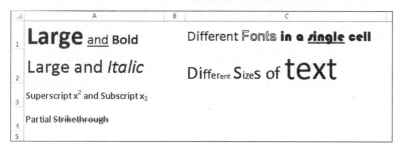

Figure 20-1: Examples of individual character formatting.

Using the Format Painter

You've probably seen that little Format Painter paint brush icon in the Home➜Clipboard group. It's an easy way to copy cell formatting — and it's actually more versatile than you might think.

When you use the Format Painter, *every* aspect of the source range's formatting is copied, including number formats, borders, cell merging, and conditional formatting.

Painting basics

Here's how to use the Format Painter tool in its basic form:

1. Select a cell that contains the formatting that you want to duplicate.

2. Choose Home➜Clipboard➜Format Painter.

   The mouse cursor displays a paintbrush to remind you that you're in Format Painter mode (see Figure 21-1).

3. Drag the mouse over another range.

4. Release the mouse button, and the formatting is copied.

In Step 2, you can right-click the selected cell and choose the Format Painter icon from the Mini Toolbar.

Note that the Format Painter is mouse-centric. You cannot use the keyboard to do your painting.

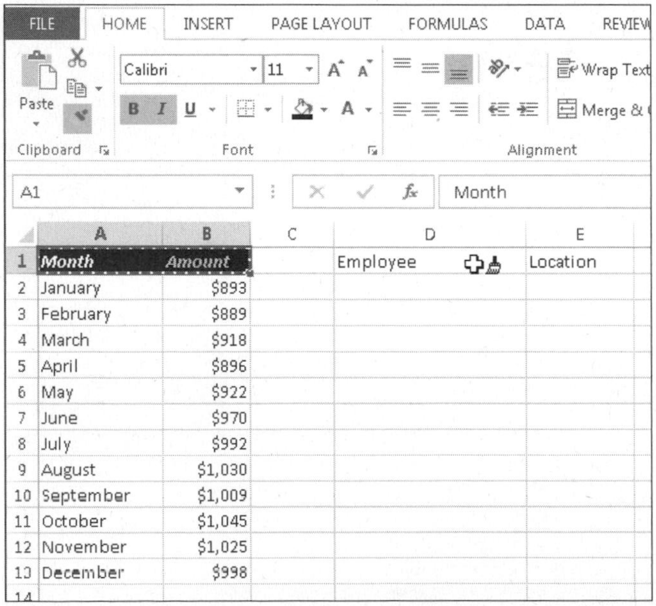

Figure 21-1: Copying cell formatting by using the Format Painter.

Format Painter variations

In Step 1 in the preceding section, if you select a *range* of cells, you can paint another range by clicking a single cell. The formatting is copied to a range that's the same size as the original selection.

In Step 2, if you *double-click* the Format Painter button, Excel remains in Format Painter mode until you cancel it. This enables you to copy the format to multiple ranges of cells. To get out of Format Painter mode, press Esc or click the Format Painter button again.

You can also use the Format Painter to remove all formatting from a range and return the range to its pristine state. Start by selecting an unformatted cell. Then click the Format Painter button and drag it over the range.

The Format Painter also works with complete rows and columns. If you start by selecting one or more complete rows, the Format Painter also copies row height. The same thing occurs with column widths if you start by selecting one or more columns.

This feature even works with complete worksheets. For example, if you want to remove all formatting from a worksheet, select an unformatted cell, click the Format Painter button, and then click the "select all" button at the intersection of the row and column borders.

You can also use the Format Painter with shapes and other objects such as pictures. Just select the object, click the Format Painter button, and click another object. Figure 21-2 shows an example of copying shape formats using the Format Painter.

 Although the Format Painter is versatile, it doesn't work with charts.

Note

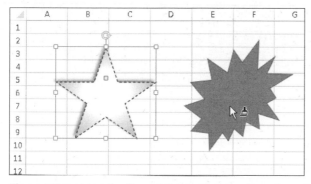

Figure 21-2: Using the Format Painter to copy shape formatting.

Finally, the Format Painter is a handy tool, but it doesn't perform any actions that can't be done via other methods. For example, you can copy a range, select another range, and use the Home→Clipboard→Paste→Formatting (R) command to paste the formatting only.

Inserting a Watermark

A *watermark* is an image (or text) that appears on a printed page. A watermark can be a faint company logo or a word, such as *DRAFT*.

Excel doesn't have an official command to print a watermark, but you can add a watermark by inserting a picture in the page header or footer. Here's how to do it:

1. Locate an image on your hard drive that you want to use for the watermark.

2. Choose View→Workbook Views→Page Layout View to enter Page Layout view.

3. Click the center section of the header.

4. Choose Header & Footer Tools→Header & Footer Elements→Picture.

   The Insert Picture dialog box appears.

5. Click Browse and locate and select the image you picked in Step 1 (or locate a suitable image from other sources listed); then click Insert to insert the image.

6. Click outside the header to see your image.

7. To center the image vertically on the page, click the center section of the header and press Enter a few times before the &[Picture] code**.**

   You'll need to experiment to determine the number of carriage returns required to push the image into the body of the document.

8. If you need to adjust the image (for example, to make it lighter), click the center section of the header and then choose Header & Footer Tools→Header & Footer Elements→Format Picture; use the Image controls on the Picture tab of the Format Picture dialog box to adjust the image.

   You may need to experiment with the settings to make sure that the worksheet text is legible.

Figure 22-1 shows an example of a header image (a copyright symbol) used as a watermark. You can create a similar effect with plain text in the header (for example, the word DRAFT).

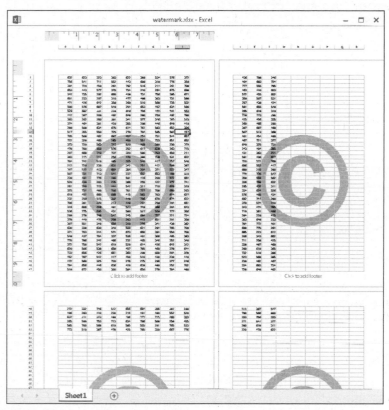

Figure 22-1: Displaying a watermark on a page.

Showing Text and a Value in a Cell

If you need to display a number and text in a single cell, Excel gives you three options:

> ➤ Concatenation
>
> ➤ The TEXT function
>
> ➤ A custom number format

Assume that cell A1 contains a value, and in a cell somewhere else in your worksheet, you want to display the text *Total:* along with that value. It looks something like this:

```
Total: 594.34
```

You could, of course, put the text *Total:* in the cell to the left. This section describes the three methods for accomplishing this task using a single cell.

Using concatenation

The following formula concatenates the text *Total:* with the value in cell A1:

```
="Total: "&A1
```

This solution is the simplest, but it has a problem. The result of the formula is text, rather than a numeric value. Therefore, the cell cannot be used in a numeric formula. Also, the numeric portion will display with no formatting. For example, the formula might return

```
Total: 1594.34320933
```

Using the TEXT function

Another solution uses the TEXT function, which displays a value by using a specified number format:

```
=TEXT(A1,"""Total: ""$#,0.00")
```

This formula returns something like this:

```
Total: $1,594.34
```

The second argument for the TEXT function is a number format string — the same type of string that you use when you create a custom number format. Because the number portion is formatted, this approach looks good. But besides being a bit unwieldy (because of the extra quotation marks), this formula suffers from the same problem mentioned in the previous section: The result is not numeric.

Using a custom number format

If you want to display text and a value — and still be able to use that value in a numeric formula — the solution is to use a custom number format.

To add text, just create the number format string as usual and put the text within quotation marks. For this example, the following custom number format does the job:

```
"Total: "$#,0.00
```

Even though the cell displays text, Excel still considers the cell contents to be a numeric value. Therefore, you can use this cell in other formulas that perform calculations.

Avoiding Font Substitution for Small Point Sizes

When you specify a font size smaller than eight points, you may notice that the numbers in a column no longer line up correctly. That's because Excel uses a different (non-proportional) font for small text. Normally, each numeric character takes the same amount of horizontal space — that's why numbers line up so nicely. But with a proportional font, numeric characters vary in width. The "1" character is more narrow than the "0" character, for example.

Figure 24-1 shows a worksheet with columns of numbers in varying font sizes. Notice that everything is fine until the point size is smaller than 8 points. In column E (7 points), the "1" character take up less space. In column F (6 points), the "5" and "7" characters also take up less space.

	A	B	C	D	E	F	G
1	Calibri 11-pt	Calibri 10-pt	Calibri 9-pt	Calibri 8-pt	Calibri 7-pt	Calibri 6-pt	
2	00000000	00000000	00000000	00000000	00000000	00000000	
3	11111111	11111111	11111111	11111111	11111111	11111111	
4	22222222	22222222	22222222	22222222	22222222	22222222	
5	33333333	33333333	33333333	33333333	33333333	33333333	
6	44444444	44444444	44444444	44444444	44444444	44444444	
7	55555555	55555555	55555555	55555555	55555555	55555555	
8	66666666	66666666	66666666	66666666	66666666	66666666	
9	77777777	77777777	77777777	77777777	77777777	77777777	
10	88888888	88888888	88888888	88888888	88888888	88888888	
11	99999999	99999999	99999999	99999999	99999999	99999999	
12							

font substitution.xlsx - Excel

Sheet3

Figure 24-1: Various font sizes, with font substitution enabled.

Font substitution also occurs when you zoom the worksheet, using the Zoom slider in the status bar. Sometimes zooming out causes values to appear as a series of hash marks (#####). The point at which the font is changed seems to vary, depending on the size of the original font. For the default 11-point font, zooming below 75% causes Excel to switch to a different font.

You can instruct Excel to stop this font substitution for small font sizes, but doing so requires editing the Windows registry.

Note

Editing the registry can be dangerous if you don't understand what you're doing; always create a backup before you make any changes. If you're not comfortable editing the registry, find someone who is — or just don't implement this tip.

1. Close Excel.

2. Click the Windows Start button and run regedit.exe, the Registry Editor program.

3. In the Registry Editor, navigate to this registry key:

   ```
   HKEY_CURRENT_USER\Software\Microsoft\Office\15.0\Excel\Options
   ```

4. With that registry key selected, choose Edit➜New➜DWORD.

   The entry will be named New Value #1.

5. Right-click the entry and choose Rename. Specify **FontSub** for the entry name.

6. Double-click the FontSub entry.

   The Edit DWORD dialog box appears.

7. Specify 0 as the Value Data (the Base, Hexadecimal, or Decimal doesn't matter), as shown in Figure 24-2.

8. Click OK to close the Edit DWORD dialog box.

9. Choose File➜Exit to quit Registry Editor.

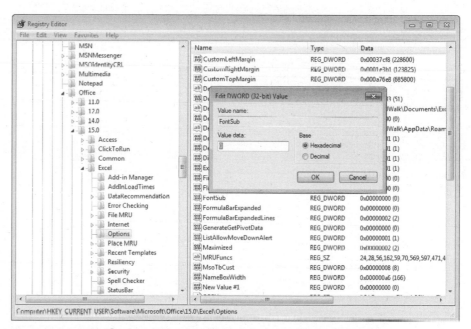

Figure 24-2: Using Registry Editor to add a new value to the Windows registry.

When you restart Excel, you'll find that Excel no longer uses font substitution for small fonts. When font substitution is disabled, small text will be a bit more difficult to read, but the numbers will continue to line up, and you won't see the #### display when you zoom out.

Figure 24-3 shows the worksheet in Figure 24-1, after disabling font substitution.

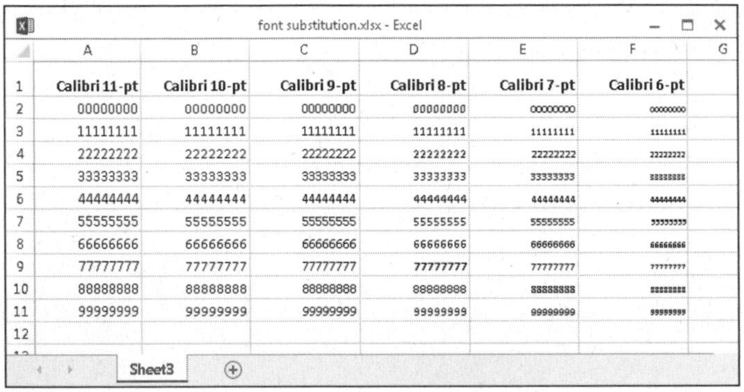

	A	B	C	D	E	F	G
1	**Calibri 11-pt**	**Calibri 10-pt**	**Calibri 9-pt**	**Calibri 8-pt**	**Calibri 7-pt**	**Calibri 6-pt**	
2	00000000	00000000	00000000	00000000	00000000	00000000	
3	11111111	11111111	11111111	11111111	11111111	11111111	
4	22222222	22222222	22222222	22222222	22222222	22222222	
5	33333333	33333333	33333333	33333333	33333333	33333333	
6	44444444	44444444	44444444	44444444	44444444	44444444	
7	55555555	55555555	55555555	55555555	55555555	55555555	
8	66666666	66666666	66666666	66666666	66666666	66666666	
9	77777777	77777777	77777777	77777777	77777777	77777777	
10	88888888	88888888	88888888	88888888	88888888	88888888	
11	99999999	99999999	99999999	99999999	99999999	99999999	
12							

Sheet3

Figure 24-3: Various font sizes, with font substitution disabled.

Updating Old Fonts

When you install Microsoft Office, several new fonts are added to your system, and these new fonts are used when you create a new workbook. The exact fonts that are used as defaults vary, depending on which document theme is in effect.

 See Tip 10 for more information about using document themes.
Cross-Ref

If you use the default Office theme, a newly created Excel workbook uses two new fonts: Cambria (for headings) and Calibri (for body text). When you open a workbook that was saved in a version prior to Excel 2007, the old fonts (probably Arial) aren't updated. The difference in appearance between a worksheet that uses the old fonts and a worksheet that uses the new fonts is dramatic. When you compare an Excel 2003 worksheet with an Excel 2013 worksheet, the latter is much more readable and appears less cramped.

Figure 25-1 shows a workbook that was created in Excel 2003.

	A	B	C	D	E	F
				Natural Increase	Net International	Net Internal
3	State	Births	Deaths	(Births - Deaths)	Migration	Migration
4	Florida	211,499	171,890	39,609	107,303	177,734
5	California	523,578	238,007	285,571	288,051	(94,861)
6	Texas	373,855	143,888	229,967	135,010	15,998
7	Arizona	88,164	44,124	44,030	34,266	61,200
8	Georgia	135,487	66,406	69,081	38,914	31,785
9	Nevada	32,399	17,552	14,847	13,501	44,718
10	North Carolina	118,831	73,644	45,187	31,395	25,100
11	Virginia	99,299	57,552	41,747	27,462	28,412
12	Washington	76,952	45,019	31,933	27,216	5,687
13	Maryland	73,876	45,592	28,284	22,204	8,266
14	Tennessee	78,895	56,655	22,240	10,057	19,942
15	Pennsylvania	140,937	132,031	8,906	21,201	7,841
16	Oregon	43,966	32,305	11,661	14,755	13,300
17	South Carolina	55,751	38,725	17,026	6,997	19,735
18	New Jersey	114,525	76,525	38,000	59,067	(33,225)
19	Missouri	76,122	57,441	18,681	8,623	7,871
20	Wisconsin	67,278	48,376	18,902	9,427	4,981
21	Connecticut	41,565	30,560	11,005	15,542	(1,234)
22	Kentucky	55,140	40,755	14,385	5,416	8,592
23	Idaho	20,184	10,016	10,168	2,907	10,132
24	Indiana	84,242	57,197	27,045	11,147	1,019
25	Colorado	67,319	30,077	37,242	22,766	(10,611)
26	Maine	13,023	12,912	111	952	9,862
27	New Mexico	26,701	14,700	12,001	5,567	5,074
28	Arkansas	39,292	29,486	9,806	4,363	5,255

state population data.xls [Compatibility Mode] - Excel

Figure 25-1: This Excel 2003 workbook uses Arial 10-point font as the normal font.

To update the fonts in a workbook that was created in a previous version of Excel, follow these steps:

1. Press Ctrl+N to create a new, blank workbook.

2. Activate the workbook that uses the fonts to be updated.

3. Choose Home➜Styles➜Merge Styles

   The Merge Styles dialog box appears.

4. In the Merge Styles dialog box, select the workbook that you created in Step 1 and click OK.

   Excel asks whether you want to merge styles that have the same names.

5. Reply by clicking the Yes button.

This procedure updates the fonts used in all cells except those that have additional formatting, such as a different font size, bold, italic, colored text, or a shaded background. To change the font in these cells, follow these steps:

1. Select any single cell.

2. Choose Home➜Editing➜Find & Select➜Replace, or press Ctrl+H.

   The Find and Replace dialog box appears.

3. Make sure that the two Format buttons are visible. If these buttons aren't visible, click the Options button to expand the dialog box.

4. Click the upper Format button to display the Find Format dialog box.

5. Click the Font tab.

6. In the Font list, select the name of the font that you're replacing (probably Arial, the old default font) and then click OK to close the Find Format dialog box.

7. Click the lower Format button to display the Replace Format dialog box.

8. Click the Font tab.

9. In the Font list, select the name of the font that will replace the old font (probably Calibri) and then click OK to close the Replace Format dialog box.

10. In the Find and Replace dialog box, click Replace All to replace the old font with the new font.

Figure 25-2 shows the Excel 2003 workbook after updating the font.

	A	B	C	D	E	F
				Natural Increase	**Net International**	**Net Internal**
3	**State**	**Births**	**Deaths**	**(Births - Deaths)**	**Migration**	**Migration**
4	Florida	211,499	171,890	39,609	107,303	177,734
5	California	523,578	238,007	285,571	288,051	(94,861)
6	Texas	373,855	143,888	229,967	135,010	15,998
7	Arizona	88,154	44,124	44,030	34,266	61,200
8	Georgia	135,487	66,406	69,081	38,914	31,785
9	Nevada	32,399	17,552	14,847	13,501	44,718
10	North Carolina	118,831	73,644	45,187	31,395	25,100
11	Virginia	99,299	57,552	41,747	27,462	28,412
12	Washington	76,952	45,019	31,933	27,216	5,687
13	Maryland	73,876	45,592	28,284	22,204	8,266
14	Tennessee	78,895	56,655	22,240	10,057	19,942
15	Pennsylvania	140,937	132,031	8,906	21,201	7,841
16	Oregon	43,966	32,305	11,661	14,755	13,300
17	South Carolina	55,751	38,725	17,026	6,997	19,735
18	New Jersey	114,525	76,525	38,000	59,067	(33,225)
19	Missouri	76,122	57,441	18,681	8,623	7,871
20	Wisconsin	67,278	48,376	18,902	9,427	4,981
21	Connecticut	41,565	30,560	11,005	15,542	(1,234)
22	Kentucky	55,140	40,755	14,385	5,416	8,592
23	Idaho	20,184	10,016	10,168	2,907	10,132
24	Indiana	84,242	57,197	27,045	11,147	1,019
25	Colorado	67,319	30,077	37,242	22,766	(10,611)
26	Maine	13,023	12,912	111	952	9,862
27	New Mexico	26,701	14,700	12,001	5,567	5,074
28	Arkansas	38,292	28,486	9,806	4,363	5,255

Figure 25-2: This Excel workbook uses Calibri 11-point font as the normal font.

PART III

Formulas

The ability to create formulas is what makes a spreadsheet. In this part, you'll find formula-related tips that can make your workbooks more powerful than ever.

Tips and Where to Find Them

Resizing the Formula Bar

In earlier versions of Excel, editing a cell that contains a lengthy formula or lots of text often obscures the worksheet. Figure 26-1 shows Excel 2003 when a cell that contains lengthy text is selected. Notice that many of the cells are covered up by the expanded Formula bar. Beginning with Excel 2007, this problem is corrected.

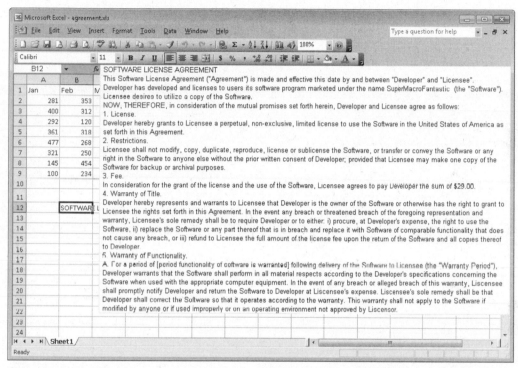

Figure 26-1: In older versions of Excel, editing a lengthy formula or a cell that contains lots of text often obscures the worksheet.

The Excel 2013 Formula bar displays a small arrow on the right; click the arrow, and the Formula bar expands. You can also drag the bottom border of the Formula bar to change its height. Also useful is a shortcut key combination: Ctrl+Shift+U. Pressing this key combination toggles the height of the Formula bar to show either one row or the previous size. If the expanded Formula bar isn't tall enough to display all of the text in the active cell, a scrollbar displays to the right of the Formula bar.

Figure 26-2 shows an example of the resized Formula bar. As you can see, increasing the height of the Formula bar doesn't obscure the information in the worksheet. Instead, the worksheet information is displayed below the Formula bar. You can make the formula bar almost as tall as the workbook window (one worksheet row always remains visible).

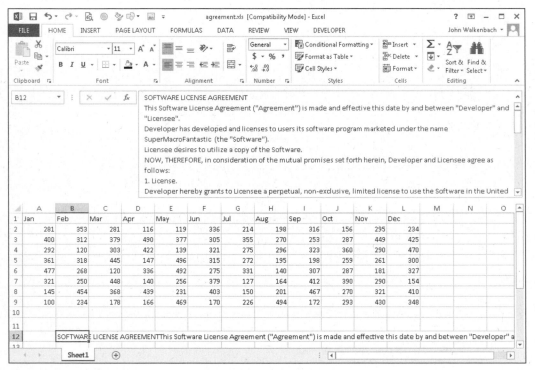

Figure 26-2: Changing the height of the formula bar makes it much easier to edit lengthy formulas and text, and you can still view all cells in your worksheet.

You can also resize the width of the Formula bar. Click and drag the three dots to the right of the Name box. When the Name box gets wider, the Formula bar gets narrower.

Monitoring Formula Cells from Any Location

If you have a large spreadsheet model, you might find it helpful to monitor the values in a few key cells as you change various input cells. The Watch Window feature makes this task very simple. Using the Watch Window, you can keep an eye on any number of cells, regardless of which worksheet or workbook is active. Using this feature can save time and eliminate scrolling and switching among worksheet tabs and workbook windows.

About the Watch Window

To display the Watch Window, choose Formulas➜Formula Auditing➜Watch Window. To watch a cell, click the Add Watch button in the Watch Window and then specify the cell in the Add Watch dialog box. When the Add Watch dialog box opens, you can add multiple cells by selecting a range or by pressing Ctrl and clicking individual cells.

For each cell, the Watch Window displays the workbook name, the worksheet name, the cell name (if it has one), the cell address, the current value, and the formula (if it has one).

Excel remembers the cells in a Watch Window, even between sessions. If you close a workbook that contains cells being monitored in the Watch Window, those cells are removed from the Watch Window. But if you reopen that workbook, the cells are displayed again.

Figure 27-1 shows the Watch Window, with several cells being monitored.

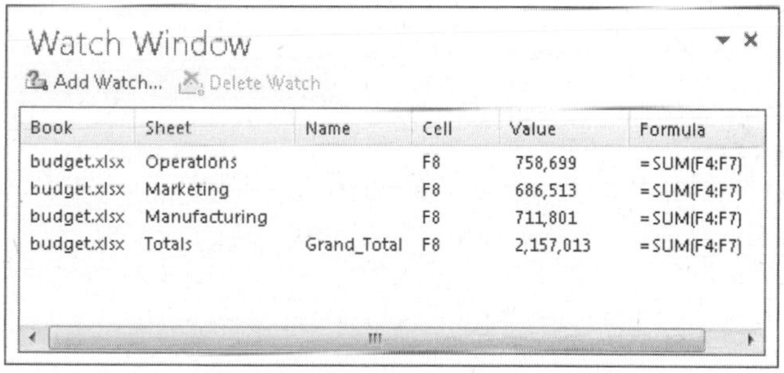

Book	Sheet	Name	Cell	Value	Formula
budget.xlsx	Operations		F8	758,699	=SUM(F4:F7)
budget.xlsx	Marketing		F8	686,513	=SUM(F4:F7)
budget.xlsx	Manufacturing		F8	711,801	=SUM(F4:F7)
budget.xlsx	Totals	Grand_Total	F8	2,157,013	=SUM(F4:F7)

Figure 27-1: Using the Watch Window to monitor the value of formula cells.

Customizing the Watch Window

The Watch Window is a task pane, and you can customize the display by doing any of the following:

➤ Click and drag a border to change the size of the task pane.

➤ Drag the task pane to an edge of an Excel workbook window, and it becomes docked rather than free floating.

➤ Click and drag the borders in the header to change the width of the columns displayed. By dragging a column border all the way to the left, you can hide the column.

➤ Click one of the headers to sort the contents by that column.

Navigating with the Watch Window

You can also use the Watch Window as a navigational aid. If you find that you often need to switch among worksheets, add a cell for each worksheet to the Watch Window. To activate a cell displayed in the Watch Window, double-click it in the Watch Window.

Note

Unfortunately, in Excel 2013, this navigational technique works only with the active workbook. In other words, double-clicking a Watch Window item that points to a cell in a different workbook will not activate the workbook. I don't know if this is by design or if it's a bug in Excel 2013.

Learning Some AutoSum Tricks

Just about every Excel user knows about the AutoSum button. This command is so popular that it's available in two Ribbon locations: in the Home→Editing group and in the Formulas→Function Library group.

Just activate a cell and click the button, and Excel analyzes the data surrounding the active cell and proposes a SUM formula. If the proposed range is correct, click the AutoSum button again (or press Enter), and the formula is inserted. If you change your mind, press Esc.

Be careful if the range to be summed contains any blank cells. A blank cell will cause Excel to mis-identify the complete range. If Excel incorrectly guesses the range to be summed, just select the correct range to be summed and press Enter.

You can also access AutoSum using your keyboard. Pressing Alt+= has exactly the same effect as clicking the AutoSum button.

The AutoSum button can insert other types of formulas. Notice the little arrow on the right side of that button? Click it, and you see four other functions: AVERAGE, COUNT, MAX, and MIN (see Figure 28-1). Click one of those items, and the appropriate formula is proposed. You also see a More Functions item, which simply displays the Insert Function dialog box — the same one that appears when you choose Formulas→Function Library→Insert Function (or click the fx button to the left of the formula bar).

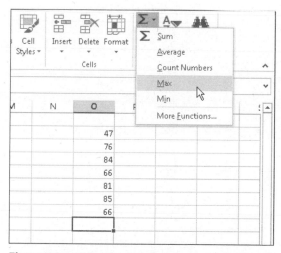

Figure 28-1: Using the AutoSum button to insert other functions.

Note

In some situations (described next), AutoSum creates formulas automatically and doesn't give you an opportunity to review the range to be summed. Don't assume that Excel guessed the range correctly.

Following are some additional tricks related to AutoSum:

➤ If you need to enter a similar SUM formula into a range of cells, select the entire range before you click the AutoSum button. In this case, Excel inserts the functions for you without asking you — one formula in each of the selected cells.

➤ To sum both across and down a table of numbers, select the range of numbers plus an additional column to the right and an additional row at the bottom. Click the AutoSum button, and Excel inserts the formulas that add the rows and the columns. In Figure 28-2, the range to be summed is D4:G15, so I selected an additional row and column: D4:H16. Clicking the AutoSum buttons puts formulas in row 16 and column H.

➤ If you're working with a table (created by choosing Insert➜Tables➜Table), using the AutoSum button after selecting the row below the table inserts a Total row for the table and creates formulas that use the SUBTOTAL function rather than the SUM function. The SUBTOTAL function sums only the visible cells in the table, which is useful if you filter the data.

➤ Unless you applied a different number format to the cell that will hold the SUM formula, AutoSum applies the same number format as the first cell in the range to be summed.

➤ To create a SUM formula that uses only *some* of the values in a column, select the cells to be summed and then click the AutoSum button. Excel inserts the SUM formula in the first empty cell below the selected range. The selected range must be a contiguous group of cells — a multiple selection isn't allowed.

	A	B	C	D	E	F	G	H	I
1									
2									
3				Region-1	Region-2	Region-3	Region-4	Total	
4			January	6,489	6,491	6,023	6,188		
5			February	6,032	6,103	5,583	6,488		
6			March	5,188	6,264	5,428	5,004		
7			April	6,229	5,019	5,283	6,507		
8			May	5,962	5,520	6,154	5,382		
9			June	6,040	5,525	5,508	6,135		
10			July	5,820	5,330	6,448	5,997		
11			August	6,182	5,527	6,229	5,907		
12			September	5,771	5,740	5,688	5,843		
13			October	5,005	5,617	5,713	5,929		
14			November	5,179	5,512	5,149	6,166		
15			December	6,439	5,693	6,062	5,650		
16			Total						
17									
18									

Figure 28-2: Using AutoSum to insert SUM formulas for rows and columns.

Knowing When to Use Absolute and Mixed References

When you create a formula that refers to another cell or range, the cell references are usually relative references. When you copy a formula that uses relative references, the cell references adjust to their new location in a relative manner. Assume this formula (which uses relative references) is in cell A13:

```
=SUM(A1:A12)
```

If you copy the formula to cell B13, the copied formula is

```
=SUM(B1:B12)
```

Most of the time, you want cell references to adjust when you copy formulas. That's why most of the time you use relative references in formulas. But some situations require either absolute or relative references.

Using absolute references

You specify an absolute reference by using two dollar signs (one in front of the column part and one in front of the row part). Here are two examples of formulas that use absolute references:

```
=$A$1
=SUM($A$1:$F$24)
```

An *absolute* cell reference in a formula does not change, even when the formula is copied elsewhere. For example, assume the following formula is in cell B13:

```
=SUM($B$1:$B$12)
```

When you copy this formula to a different cell, the references do not adjust. The copied formula refers to the same cells as the original, and both formulas return the same result.

When do you use an absolute reference? The answer is simple: The only time you even need to *think* about using an absolute reference is if you plan to copy the formula — and you need the copied formula to refer to the same range as the original.

The easiest way to understand this concept is with an example. Figure 29-1 shows a simple worksheet. The formula in cell D2 is

```
=(B2*C2)*$B$7
```

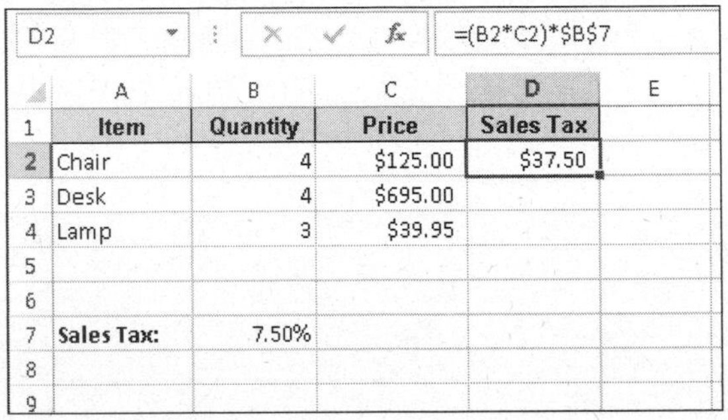

| D2 | ▾ | ⋮ | ✕ | ✓ | *fx* | =(B2*C2)*$B$7 |

	A	B	C	D	E
1	**Item**	**Quantity**	**Price**	**Sales Tax**	
2	Chair	4	$125.00	$37.50	
3	Desk	4	$695.00		
4	Lamp	3	$39.95		
5					
6					
7	**Sales Tax:**	7.50%			
8					
9					

Figure 29-1: Formula references to the sales tax cell should be absolute.

This formula uses relative cell references (B2 * C2) and also an absolute reference to the sales tax cell ($B$7). This formula can be copied to the cells below, and all of the references will be correct. For example, after copying the formula in cell D2, cell D3 contains this formula:

```
=(B3*C3)*$B$7
```

The references to the cells in columns B and C are adjusted, but the reference to cell B7 is not — which is exactly what you want.

Using mixed references

In a *mixed cell reference,* either the column part or the row part of a reference is absolute (and therefore doesn't change when the formula is copied and pasted). Mixed cell references aren't used often, but as you see in this tip, in some situations, using mixed references makes your job much easier.

Here are two examples of mixed references:

```
=$A1
=A$1
```

In the first example, the column part of the reference (A) is absolute, and the row part (1) is relative. In the second example, the column part of the reference is relative, and the row part is absolute.

Figure 29-2 shows a worksheet demonstrating a situation in which using mixed references is the best choice.

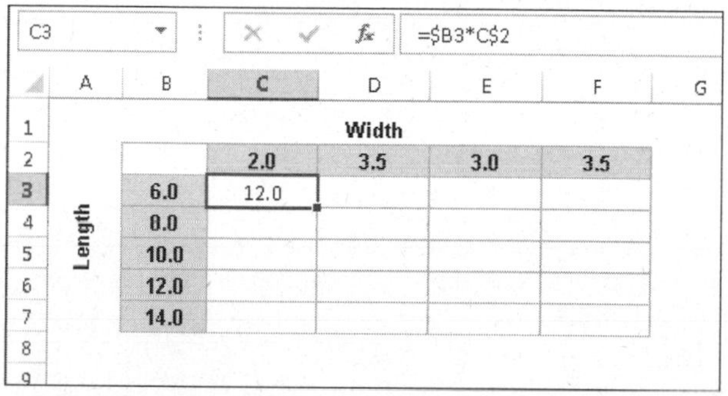

Figure 29-2: Using mixed cell references.

The formulas in the table calculate the area for various lengths and widths of a rectangle. Here's the formula in cell C3:

```
=$B3*C$2
```

Notice that both cell references are mixed. The reference to cell B3 uses an absolute reference for the column ($B), and the reference to cell C2 uses an absolute reference for the row ($2). As a result, this formula can be copied down and across, and the calculations are correct. For example, the formula in cell F7 is

```
=$B7*F$2
```

If C3 used either absolute or relative references, copying the formula would produce incorrect results.

Avoiding Error Displays in Formulas

Sometimes a formula returns an error, such as #REF! or #DIV/0!. Usually, you want to know when a formula error occurs so you can fix it. But in some cases, you might prefer to simply avoid displaying the error messages. Figure 30-1 shows an example.

D2		▼	:	✕	✓	*fx*	=B2/C2	

◢	A	B	C	D	E	F
1	Month	Total Sales	No. Reps	Average		
2	January	7,832,083	12	652,674		
3	February	8,398,338	15	559,889		
4	March	6,823,444	16	426,465		
5	April	9,004,563	16	562,785		
6	May			#DIV/0!		
7	June			#DIV/0!		
8	July			#DIV/0!		
9	August			#DIV/0!		
10	September			#DIV/0!		
11	October			#DIV/0!		
12	November			#DIV/0!		
13	December			#DIV/0!		
14						

Figure 30-1: The formulas in column D display an error if the data is missing.

Column D contains formulas that calculate the average sales volume. For example, cell D2 contains this formula:

```
=B2/C2
```

Using the IFERROR function

As you can see, the formula displays an error if the cells used in the calculation are empty. If you prefer to hide those error values, you can do so by using an IFERROR function. This function takes two arguments: The first argument is the expression that's checked for an error, and the second is the value to return if the formula evaluates to an error.

The formula presented earlier can be rewritten as

```
=IFERROR(B2/C2,"")
```

As you see in Figure 30-2, when this formula is copied down the column, the result is a bit more visually pleasing.

By the way, you can put anything you like as the second argument for the IFERROR function. (It doesn't have to be an empty string.) For example, you can make it a cell reference.

	A	B	C	D	E	F
				=IFERROR(B2/C2,"")		
1	Month	Total Sales	No. Reps	Average		
2	January	7,832,083	12	652,674		
3	February	8,398,338	15	559,889		
4	March	6,823,444	16	426,465		
5	April	9,004,563	16	562,785		
6	May					
7	June					
8	July					
9	August					
10	September					
11	October					
12	November					
13	December					
14						

Figure 30-2: Using an IFERROR function to hide error values.

Note

The IFERROR function was introduced in Excel 2007, so it doesn't work with earlier versions of Excel. If you plan to share your workbook with people who use Excel 2003 or earlier, you'll need to use the ISERROR function — described next.

Using the ISERROR function

The ISERROR function is used with an IF function. For the example presented earlier, use this formula in cell D1:

```
=IF(ISERROR(B2/C2),"",B2/C2)
```

The ISERROR function returns TRUE if its argument evaluates to an error. In such a case, the IF function returns an empty string. Otherwise, the IF function returns the calculated value.

This method of avoiding an error display is a bit more complicated, and it's also less efficient because the formula is actually evaluated two times if it doesn't return an error. Therefore, unless you require compatibility with Excel 2003 or earlier versions, you should use the IFERROR functions.

Creating Worksheet-Level Names

Normally, when you name a cell or range, you can use that name in all worksheets in the workbook. For example, if you create a name, say *RegionTotal*, that refers to the cell M32 on Sheet1, you can use this name in any formula in any worksheet. This name is a workbook-level name (or a global name). By default, all cell and range names are workbook-level names.

Suppose that you have several worksheets in a workbook (one for each region) and you want to use the same name (such as *RegionTotal*) on each sheet. In this case, you need to create worksheet-level names (sometimes referred to as local names).

To define the worksheet-level name *RegionTotal*, activate the worksheet in which you want to define the name and choose Formulas➜Defined Names➜Define Name. The New Name dialog box then appears. In the Names field, enter the name in the Name field and use the Scope drop-down list to select the sheet in which the name is valid. Figure 31-1 shows a worksheet-level name being created.

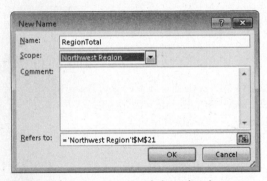

Figure 31-1: Creating a worksheet-level name.

You can also create a worksheet-level name by using the Name box (located to the left of the Formula bar). Select the cell or range you want named, click in the Name box, and type the name, preceded by the sheet name and an exclamation point. Press Enter to create the name. Here's an example of a worksheet-level name:

```
Sheet3!RegionTotal
```

If the worksheet name contains at least one space, enclose the worksheet name in apostrophes, like this:

```
'Northwest Region'!RegionTotal
```

When you write a formula that uses a worksheet-level name on the sheet in which you defined it, you don't need to include the worksheet name in the range name. (The Name box doesn't display the worksheet name, either.) If you use the name in a formula on a *different* worksheet, however, you must use the entire name (sheet name, exclamation point, and name).

If you copy a worksheet that has worksheet-level names, the names are duplicated as worksheet-level names in the new worksheet.

The Name Manager dialog box clearly identifies each name by its scope (see Figure 31-2). If the scope of a name isn't Workbook, the dialog box lists the sheet on which the name is defined.

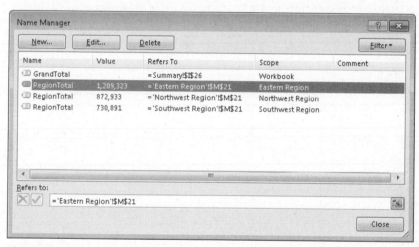

Figure 31-2: The Name Manager makes it easy to distinguish between workbook-level names and worksheet-level names.

Note

Only the worksheet-level names on the current sheet appear in the Name box. Similarly, only worksheet-level names in the current sheet appear in the list when you open the Paste Name dialog box (by pressing F3).

Using Named Constants

This tip describes a useful technique that can remove some clutter from your worksheets: named constants.

Consider a worksheet that generates an invoice and calculates sales tax for a sales amount. The common approach is to insert the sales tax rate value into a cell and then use this cell reference in your formulas. To make things easier, you probably would name this cell something like SalesTax.

You can store your sales tax rate by using a name (and avoid using a cell). Figure 32-1 demonstrates the following steps:

1. Choose Formulas➜Defined Names➜Define Name to open the New Name dialog box.

2. Type the name (in this case, **SalesTax**) into the Name field.

3. Specify Workbook as the scope for the name. If you want the name to be valid only on a particular worksheet, specify the worksheet in the Scope field of the New Name dialog box.

4. Click the Refers To field, delete its contents, and replace it with a simple formula, such as **=7.5%**.

5. Click OK to close the dialog box.

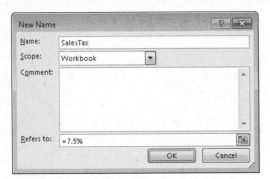

Figure 32-1: Defining a name that refers to a constant.

The preceding steps create a named formula that doesn't use any cell references. To try it out, enter the following formula into any cell:

```
=SalesTax
```

This simple formula returns .075, the result of the formula named SalesTax. Because this named formula always returns the same result, you can think of it as a *named constant*. And you can use this constant in a more complex formula, such as this one:

```
=A1*SalesTax
```

A named constant can also consist of text. For example, you can define a constant for a company's name. You can use the New Name dialog box to create the following formula, named MSFT:

```
="Microsoft Corporation"
```

Then you can use a cell formula, such as this one:

```
="Annual Report: "&MSFT
```

This formula returns the text *Annual Report: Microsoft Corporation*.

Note

Names that don't refer to ranges don't appear in the Name box or in the Go To dialog box (which appears when you press F5). This makes sense because these constants don't reside anywhere tangible. They do, however, appear in the Paste Name dialog box (which appears when you press F3) and in the intellisense drop-down list when you're creating a formula. This does make sense because you use these names in formulas.

As you might expect, you can change the value of the constant at any time by using the Name Manager dialog box (choose Formulas➜Defined Names➜Name Manager). Just click the Edit button to open the Edit Name dialog box. Then change the value in the Refers To field. When you close the dialog box, Excel uses the new value to recalculate the formulas that use this name.

Sending Personalized E-Mail from Excel

This tip describes a method to compose and send short customized e-mail messages from Excel, using the HYPERLINK function.

About the HYPERLINK function

The HYPERLINK function creates a link that, when clicked, activates your default browser and navigates to a web page. The function takes two arguments: the URL and the text that's displayed in the cell. For example, this formula creates a link to my website:

```
=HYPERLINK("http://spreadsheetpage.com","Spreadsheet Page")
```

A URL can also contain an e-mail address. When clicked, the hyperlink opens the new message window of your default e-mail client, with the e-mail address in the "To" field. Here's an example:

```
=HYPERLINK("mailto:support@example.com","Email support")
```

Note

If you don't have a local default e-mail client and rely on a web-based e-mail service (such as Gmail or Hotmail), this technique won't work.

You can also include a subject line. Here's an example of the first argument for the HYPERLINK function that includes an e-mail subject line:

```
"mailto:support@example.com?subject=Help!"
```

In addition, you can include a short default message:

```
"mailto:support@example.com?subject=Help me!&body=I don't understand this."
```

Things get a bit more complicated if you want to include a line break in the message body. If that's the case, you need to "percent encode" the line break by using this code: %0A. Here's an example that inserts two line breaks into the e-mail body:

```
"mailto:support@example.com?subject=Help me!&body=I don't understand
    this.%0A%0AYour customer"
```

Note

Technically, all non-alphanumeric characters should be encoded, including spaces. You can use the ENCODEURL function (introduced in Excel 2013) to encode any text string.

A practical example using HYPERLINK

Figure 33-1 shows a worksheet set up to make it easy to send a brief personalized e-mail from Excel.

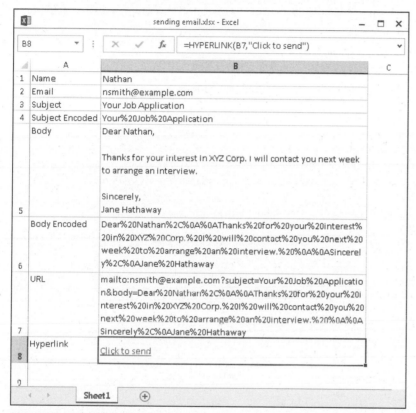

Figure 33-1: The hyperlink in cell B8, when clicked, opens the default e-mail client with a message ready to send.

Here's a description of each cell:

➤ **B1:** The first name of the e-mail recipient.

➤ **B2:** The e-mail address.

➤ **B3:** The subject line for the e-mail address.

➤ **B4:** The subject line, encoded using this formula:

```
=ENCODEURL(B3)
```

➤ **B5:** The body of the message. This cell uses wrap text formatting, and line breaks were entered by using Alt+Enter.

➤ **B6:** The body text, encoded using this formula:

```
=ENCODEURL(B5)
```

➤ **B7:** The first argument for the HYPERLINK function, constructed by concatenating text and cells. The formula is

```
="mailto:"&B2&"?subject="&(B4)&"&body="&B6&""
```

➤ **B8:** This cell contains a formula that uses the HYPERLINK function:

```
=HYPERLINK(B7,"Click to send")
```

Note The length of the text in cell B7 (the first argument for the HYPERLINK function) cannot exceed 255 characters. If the text is too long, cell B8 displays a #VALUE error.

Figure 33-2 shows how it looks when Windows Live Mail is the default e-mail client.

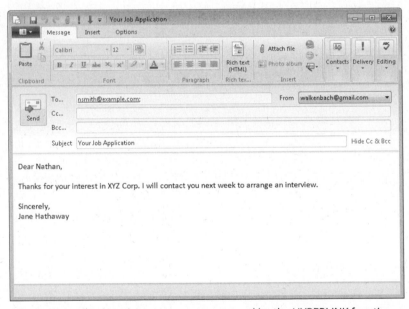

Figure 33-2: This e-mail message was composed by the HYPERLINK function.

Looking Up an Exact Value

The VLOOKUP and HLOOKUP functions are useful if you need to return a value from a table (in a range) by looking up another value.

The classic example of a lookup formula involves an income tax rate schedule (see Figure 34-1). The tax rate schedule shows the income tax rates for various income levels. The following formula (in cell B3) returns the tax rate for the income value in cell B2:

```
=VLOOKUP(B2,D2:F7,3)
```

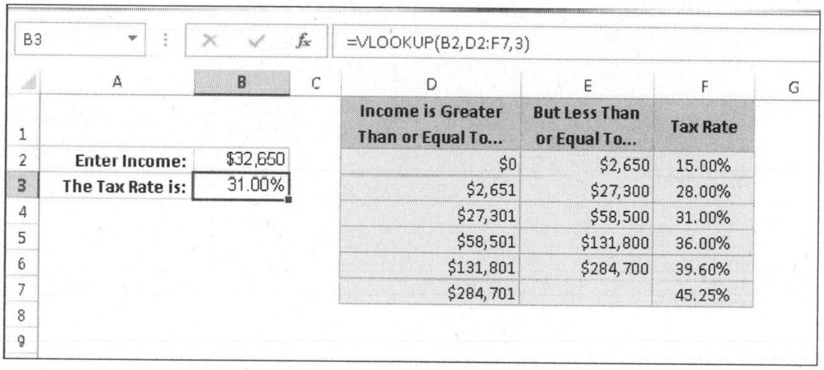

	A	B	C	D	E	F	G
				Income is Greater Than or Equal To...	**But Less Than or Equal To...**	**Tax Rate**	
1							
2	Enter Income:	$32,650		$0	$2,650	15.00%	
3	The Tax Rate is:	31.00%		$2,651	$27,300	28.00%	
4				$27,301	$58,500	31.00%	
5				$58,501	$131,800	36.00%	
6				$131,801	$284,700	39.60%	
7				$284,701		45.25%	
8							
9							

Figure 34-1: Using VLOOKUP to look up a tax rate.

The tax table example demonstrates that VLOOKUP and HLOOKUP don't require an exact match between the value to be looked up and the values in the lookup table. In some cases, though, you might require a perfect match. For example, when looking up an employee number, close doesn't count. You require an exact match for the number.

To look up only an exact value, use the VLOOKUP (or HLOOKUP) function with the optional fourth argument set to FALSE.

Figure 34-2 shows a worksheet with a lookup table that contains employee numbers (column D) and employee names (column E). The formula in cell B2, which follows, looks up the employee number entered in cell B1 and returns the corresponding employee name:

```
=VLOOKUP(B1,D1:E11,2,FALSE)
```

Because the last argument for the VLOOKUP function is FALSE, the function returns a value only if an exact match is found. If the value isn't found, the formula returns #N/A. This is exactly what you want to happen, of course, because returning an approximate match for an employee number makes no sense. Also, notice that the employee numbers in column D aren't in ascending order. If the last argument for VLOOKUP is FALSE, the values don't need to be in ascending order.

B2		:	×	✓	f_x	=VLOOKUP(B1,EmpList,2,FALSE)		

	A	B	C	D	E	F
1	Employee No.:	972		**Employee No.**	**Employee Name**	
2	Employee Name:	Sally Rice		873	Charles K. Barkley	
3				1109	Francis Jenikins	
4				1549	James Brackman	
5				1334	Linda Harper	
6				1643	Louise Victor	
7				1101	Melinda Hindquest	
8				1873	Michael Orenthal	
9				983	Peter Yates	
10				972	Sally Rice	
11				1398	Walter Franklin	
12						

Figure 34-2: This lookup table requires an exact match.

If you prefer to see something other than #N/A when the employee number isn't found, you can use the IFERROR function to test for the #N/A result (using the ISNA function) and substitute a different string. The following formula displays the text "Not Found" rather than #N/A:

```
=IFERROR(VLOOKUP(B2,D1:E11,2,FALSE),"Not Found")
```

The IFERROR function was introduced in Excel 2007, so if your workbook must be compatible with Excel 2003 and earlier versions, use this formula:

```
=IF(ISERROR(VLOOKUP(B2,D1:E11,2,FALSE)),"Not Found",
VLOOKUP(B2,D1:E11,2,FALSE))
```

Performing a Two-Way Lookup

A two-way lookup identifies the value at the intersection of a column and a row. This tip describes two methods to perform a two-way lookup.

Using a formula

Figure 35-1 shows a worksheet with a range that displays product sales by month. To retrieve sales for a particular month and product, the user enters a month in cell B1 and a product name in cell B2.

| B9 | ▼ | ⋮ | ✕ | ✓ | *fx* | =INDEX(Table, MATCH(Month,MonthList,0), MATCH(Product,ProductList,0)) |

	A	B	C	D	E	F	G	H	I
1	Month:	July			**Widgets**	**Sprockets**	**Snapholytes**	**Combined**	
2	Product:	Sprockets		January	2,892	1,771	4,718	9,381	
3				February	3,380	4,711	2,615	10,706	
4	Month Offset:	8		March	3,744	3,223	5,312	12,279	
5	Product Offset:	3		April	3,221	2,438	1,108	6,767	
6	Sales:	3,337		May	4,839	1,999	1,994	8,832	
7				June	3,767	5,140	3,830	12,737	
8				July	5,467	3,337	3,232	12,036	
9	Single-formula -->	3,337		August	3,154	4,895	1,607	9,656	
10				September	1,718	2,040	1,563	5,321	
11				October	1,548	1,061	2,590	5,199	
12				November	5,083	3,558	3,960	12,601	
13				December	5,753	2,839	3,013	11,605	
14				Total	44,566	37,012	35,542	117,120	
15									

Figure 35-1: This table demonstrates a two-way lookup.

To simplify the process, the worksheet uses the named ranges shown in the following minitable.

Name	Refers To
Month	B1
Product	B2
Table	D1:H14
MonthList	D1:D14
ProductList	D1:H1

The following formula (in cell B4) uses the MATCH function to return the position of the Month within the MonthList range. For example, if the month is January, the formula returns 2 because January is the second item in the MonthList range (the first item is a blank cell, D1):

```
=MATCH(Month,MonthList,0)
```

The formula in cell B5 works similarly but uses the *ProductList* range:

```
=MATCH(Product,ProductList,0)
```

The final formula, in cell B6, returns the corresponding sales amount. It uses the INDEX function with the results from cells B4 and B5:

```
=INDEX(Table,B4,B5)
```

You can combine these formulas into a single formula, as shown here:

```
=INDEX(Table,MATCH(Month,MonthList,0),MATCH(Product,ProductList,0))
```

Using implicit intersection

The second method to accomplish a two-way lookup is quite a bit simpler, but it requires that you create a name for each row and column in the table.

A quick way to name each row and column is to select the table and choose Formulas➔Defined Names➔Create from Selection. In the Create Names from Selection dialog box, specify that the names are in the top row and left column (see Figure 35-2). Click OK, and Excel creates the names.

C	D	E	F	G	H	I
		Widgets	Sprockets	Snapholytes	Combined	
	January	2,892	1,771	4,718	9,381	
	February	3,380	4,711	2,615	10,706	
	March	3,744				79
	April	3,221				67
	May	4,839				32
	June	3,767				37
	July	5,467				36
	August	3,154				56
	September	1,718				21
	October	1,548				99
	November	5,083				01
	December	5,753	2,839	3,013	11,605	
	Total	44,566	37,012	35,542	117,120	

Create Names from Selection

Create names from values in the:
- ☑ Top row
- ☑ Left column
- ☐ Bottom row
- ☐ Right column

OK   Cancel

Figure 35-2: Creating range names automatically.

After creating the names, you can use a simple formula to perform the two-way lookup, such as

```
=Sprockets July
```

This formula, which uses the range intersection operator (a space), returns July sales data for Sprockets.

Performing a Two-Column Lookup

Some situations may require a lookup based on the values in two columns. Figure 36-1 shows an example.

B3	▼	:	×	✓	*fx*	{=INDEX(Code, MATCH(Make&Model,Makes&Models,0))}		

◢	A	B	C	D	E	F	G	H
1	**Make:**	Toyota		**Make**	**Model**	**Code**		
2	**Model:**	Sequoia		Chevy	Suburban	C-094		
3	**Code:**	T-871		Chevy	Tahoe	C-823		
4				Ford	Explorer	F-772		
5				Ford	Escape	F-229		
6				Honda	Pilot	I-897		
7				Honda	CR-V	I-900		
8				Jeep	Compass	J-983		
9				Jeep	Grand Cherokee	I-701		
10				Nissan	Suburban	N-231		
11				Toyota	Sequoia	T-871		
12				Toyota	Land Cruiser	T-981		

Figure 36-1: This workbook performs a lookup by using information in two columns (D and E).

The lookup table contains automobile makes and models and a corresponding code for each one. The technique described here allows you to look up the value based on the car's make and model.

The worksheet uses named ranges, as shown in the following minitable.

Range	Name
F2:F12	*Code*
B1	*Make*
B2	*Model*
D2:D12	*Range1*
E2:E12	*Range2*

The following array formula displays the corresponding code for an automobile make and model:

```
=INDEX(Code,MATCH(Make&Model,Range1&Range2,0))
```

When you enter an array formula, press Ctrl+Shift+Enter (not just Enter).

Note

This formula works by concatenating the contents of Make and Model and then searching for this text in an array consisting of the corresponding concatenated text in *Range1* and *Range2*.

An alternative approach is to create a new two-column lookup table, as shown in Figure 36-2. This table contains the same information as the original table, but column H contains the data from columns D and E, concatenated.

	G	H	I	J
1		**Make and Model**	**Code**	
2		ChevySuburban	C-094	
3		ChevyTahoe	C-823	
4		FordExplorer	F-772	
5		FordEscape	F-229	
6		HondaPilot	I-897	
7		HondaCR-V	I-900	
8		JeepCompass	J-983	
9		JeepGrand Cherokee	J-701	
10		NissanSuburban	N-231	
11		ToyotaSequoia	T-871	
12		ToyotaLand Cruiser	T-981	
13				
14				

Figure 36-2: Avoid a two-column lookup by combing two columns into one.

After you create this new table, you can use a simpler formula to perform the lookup:

```
=VLOOKUP(Make&Model,H2:I12,2)
```

Calculating Holidays

Determining the date for a particular holiday can be tricky. Some holidays, such as New Year's Day and Independence Day (U.S.), are no-brainers because they always occur on the same date. For these kinds of holidays, you can simply use the DATE function. For example, to calculate New Year's Day (which always falls on January 1) for a specific year stored in cell A1, you can enter this function:

```
=DATE(A1,1,1)
```

Other holidays are defined in terms of a particular occurrence of a particular weekday in a particular month. For example, Labor Day in the U.S. falls on the first Monday in September.

The formulas that follow all assume that cell A1 contains a year value (for example, 2013). Notice that because New Year's Day, Independence Day, Veterans Day, and Christmas Day all fall on the same days of the year, their dates can be calculated by using the simple DATE function.

Figure 37-1 shows a workbook that contains all of these formulas.

	A	B	C	D	E	F
1	2013	← Enter the year				
2						
3			**U.S. Holiday Calculations**			
4						
5		Holiday	Description	Date	Weekday	
6		New Year's Day	1st Day in January	January 1, 2013	Tuesday	
7		Martin Luther King Jr. Day	3rd Monday in January	January 21, 2013	Monday	
8		Presidents' Day	3rd Monday in February	February 18, 2013	Monday	
9		Easter	Complicated	March 31, 2013	Sunday	
10		Memorial Day	Last Monday in May	May 27, 2013	Monday	
11		Independence Day	4th Day of July	July 4, 2013	Thursday	
12		Labor Day	1st Monday in September	September 2, 2013	Monday	
13		Columbus Day	2nd Monday in October	October 14, 2013	Monday	
14		Veterans Day	11th Day of November	November 11, 2013	Monday	
15		Thanksgiving Day	4th Thursday in November	November 28, 2013	Thursday	
16		Christmas Day	25th Day of December	December 25, 2013	Wednesday	
17						

Figure 37-1: Formulas calculate the dates of holidays for the year in cell A1.

New Year's Day

This holiday always falls on January 1:

```
=DATE(A1,1,1)
```

Martin Luther King Jr. Day

This holiday occurs on the third Monday in January. The following formula calculates Martin Luther King Jr. Day for the year in cell A1:

```
=DATE(A1,1,1)+IF(2<WEEKDAY(DATE(A1,1,1)),7-WEEKDAY(DATE(A1,1,1))
+2,2-WEEKDAY(DATE(A1,1,1)))+((3-1)*7)
```

Presidents' Day

Presidents' Day occurs on the third Monday in February. This formula calculates Presidents' Day for the year in cell A1:

```
=DATE(A1,2,1)+IF(2<WEEKDAY(DATE(A1,2,1)),7-WEEKDAY(DATE(A1,2,1))
+2,2-WEEKDAY(DATE(A1,2,1)))+((3-1)*7)
```

Easter

Calculating the date for Easter is difficult because of the complicated manner in which Easter is determined. Easter Day is the first Sunday after the next full moon occurs after the vernal equinox. I found these formulas to calculate Easter on the web. I have no idea how they work. They don't work if your workbook uses the 1904 date system.

```
=DOLLAR(("4/"&A1)/7+MOD(19*MOD(A1,19)-7,30)*14%,)*7-6
```

This one is slightly shorter, but equally obtuse:

```
=FLOOR("5/"&DAY(MINUTE(A1/38)/2+56)&"/"&A1,7)-34
```

Memorial Day

The last Monday in May is Memorial Day. This formula calculates Memorial Day for the year in cell A1:

```
=DATE(A1,6,1)+IF(2<WEEKDAY(DATE(A1,6,1)),7-WEEKDAY(DATE(A1,6,1))
+2,2-WEEKDAY(DATE(A1,6,1)))+((1-1)*7)-7
```

Notice that this formula calculates the first Monday in June and then subtracts 7 from the result, to return the last Monday in May.

Independence Day

The Independence Day holiday always falls on July 4:

```
=DATE(A1,7,4)
```

Labor Day

Labor Day occurs on the first Monday in September. This formula calculates Labor Day for the year in cell A1:

```
=DATE(A1,9,1)+IF(2<WEEKDAY(DATE(A1,9,1)),7-WEEKDAY(DATE(A1,9,1))
+2,2-WEEKDAY(DATE(A1,9,1)))+((1-1)*7)
```

Columbus Day

The Columbus Day holiday occurs on the second Monday in October. The following formula calculates Columbus Day for the year in cell A1:

```
=DATE(A1,10,1)+IF(2<WEEKDAY(DATE(A1,10,1)),7-WEEKDAY(DATE(A1,10,1))
+2,2-WEEKDAY(DATE(A1,10,1)))+((2-1)*7)
```

Veterans Day

The Veterans Day holiday always falls on November 11:

```
=DATE(A1,11,11)
```

Thanksgiving Day

Thanksgiving Day is celebrated on the fourth Thursday in November. This formula calculates Thanksgiving Day for the year in cell A1:

```
=DATE(A1,11,1)+IF(5<WEEKDAY(DATE(A1,11,1)),7-WEEKDAY(DATE(A1,11,1))
+5,5-WEEKDAY(DATE(A1,11,1)))+((4-1)*7)
```

Christmas Day

Christmas Day always falls on December 25:

```
=DATE(A1,12,25)
```

Calculating a Person's Age

Calculating a person's age is a bit tricky because the calculation depends on not only the current year but also the current day. And then you have to consider the complications resulting from leap years.

In this tip, I present three methods to calculate a person's age. These formulas assume that cell B1 contains the date of birth (for example, 2/16/1952) and that cell B2 contains the current date (calculated with the TODAY function).

Method 1

The following formula subtracts the date of birth from the current date and divides by 365.25. The INT function then eliminates the decimal part of the result:

```
=INT((B2-B1)/365.25)
```

This formula isn't 100 percent accurate because it divides by the average number of days in a year. For example, consider a child who is exactly one year old. This formula returns 0, not 1.

Method 2

A more accurate way to calculate age uses the YEARFRAC function:

```
=INT(YEARFRAC(B2, B1))
```

The YEARFRAC function is normally used in financial calculations, but it works just fine for calculating ages. This function calculates the fraction of the year represented by the number of whole days between two dates. Using the INT function eliminates the fraction and returns an integer that represents full years.

Method 3

The third method for calculating age uses the DATEDIF function. This undocumented function isn't described in the Excel Help system:

```
=DATEDIF(B1,B2,"Y")
```

About the DATEDIF function

The DATEDIF function, which isn't documented in the Excel Help system, is one of the little Excel mysteries. Although the Excel 2000 Help system has an entry for DATEDIF, the function is not documented in earlier or later versions.

The old Lotus 1-2-3 spreadsheet program introduced DATEDIF, and Excel likely included the function for compatibility purposes.

DATEDIF calculates the difference between two dates and expresses the result in terms of months, days, or years. The syntax for the DATEDIF function is

```
=DATEDIF(Date1,Date2,Interval)
```

Date1 and *Date2* are standard dates (or a reference to a cell that contains a date). *Date1* must be earlier (or equal to) *Date2*. The third argument, Interval, is a text string that specifies the unit of time that will be returned.

Valid interval codes are described in this list:

- **m:** The number of complete months between *Date1* and *Date2*.
- **d:** The number of days between *Date1* and *Date2*.
- **y:** The number of complete years between *Date1* and *Date2*.
- **ym:** The number of months between *Date1* and *Date2*. This interval excludes years, so it works as though the two dates are in the same year.
- **yd:** The number of days between *Date1* and *Date2*. This interval excludes years, so it works as though *Date1* and *Date2* are in the same year.
- **md:** The number of days between *Date1* and *Date2*. This interval excludes both month and year, so it works as though *Date1* and *Date2* are in the same month and the same year.

If you're a stickler for accuracy, here's another version:

```
=DATEDIF(B1,B2,"y") & " years, "&DATEDIF(B1,B2,"ym") &
" months, "&DATEDIF(B1,B2,"md") & " days"
```

This function returns a text string, like this:

```
33 years, 8 months, 17 days
```

Working with Pre-1900 Dates

According to Excel, the world began on January 1, 1900. If you work with historical information or do genealogy research, you may have noticed that Excel doesn't recognize pre-1900 dates. For example, if you enter July 4, 1776, into a cell, Excel interprets it as text, not a date.

Unfortunately, the only way to work with pre-1900 dates is to enter the date into a cell as text. The problem, however, is that you can't perform any manipulation on dates recognized as text. For example, you can't change its numeric formatting, you can't determine which day of the week this date occurred on, and you can't calculate the date that occurs seven days later.

Use three columns

To be able to sort by dates that precede 1900, enter the year, month, and day into separate cells. Figure 39-1 shows a simple example.

	A	B	C	D	E
1	**President**	**Year**	**Month**	**Day**	
2	Abraham Lincoln	1809	2	12	
3	Andrew Jackson	1767	3	15	
4	Andrew Johnson	1808	12	29	
5	Barack Obama	1961	8	3	
6	Benjamin Harrison	1833	8	20	
7	Calvin Coolidge	1872	7	4	
8	Chester A. Arthur	1829	10	5	
9	Dwight D. Eisenhower	1890	10	14	
10	Franklin D. Roosevelt	1882	1	30	
11	Franklin Pierce	1804	11	23	
12	George H. W. Bush	1924	6	12	
13	George W. Bush	1946	7	6	
14	George Washington	1732	2	22	
15	Gerald R. Ford	1913	7	14	
16	Grover Cleveland	1837	3	18	
17	Harry S Truman	1884	5	8	
18	Herbert Hoover	1874	8	10	
19	James A. Garfield	1831	11	19	
20	James Buchanan	1791	4	23	
21	James K. Polk	1795	11	2	
22	James Madison	1751	3	16	
23	James Monroe	1758	4	28	
24	Jimmy Carter	1924	10	1	

Figure 39-1: To allow sorting by pre-1900 dates, enter the year, month, and day into separate cells.

To sort the presidents by birthday, first do an ascending sort on column D (day), an ascending sort on column C (month), and finally, an ascending sort on column B (year). The result is shown in Figure 39-2.

Unfortunately, you can't perform other date-related operations for these pre-1900 dates. For example, you cannot perform subtraction to determine ages.

	A	B	C	D	E
1	**President**	**Year**	**Month**	**Day**	
2	George Washington	1732	2	22	
3	John Adams	1735	10	30	
4	Thomas Jefferson	1743	4	13	
5	James Madison	1751	3	16	
6	James Monroe	1758	4	28	
7	Andrew Jackson	1767	3	15	
8	John Quincy Adams	1767	7	11	
9	William Henry Harrison	1773	2	9	
10	Martin Van Buren	1782	12	5	
11	Zachary Taylor	1784	11	24	
12	John Tyler	1790	3	29	
13	James Buchanan	1791	4	23	
14	James K. Polk	1795	11	2	
15	Millard Fillmore	1800	1	7	
16	Franklin Pierce	1804	11	23	
17	Andrew Johnson	1808	12	29	
18	Abraham Lincoln	1809	2	12	
19	Ulysses S. Grant	1822	4	27	
20	Rutherford B. Hayes	1822	10	4	
21	Chester A. Arthur	1829	10	5	
22	James A. Garfield	1831	11	19	
23	Benjamin Harrison	1833	8	20	
24	Grover Cleveland	1837	3	10	

Figure 39-2: The presidents sorted by birthday, after performing three sorts.

Use custom functions

I created an Excel add-in, XDATE, which contains a number of functions written in VBA. These functions enable you to work with dates in the years 0100 through 9999. You can download a free copy from my website: http://spreadsheetpage.com.

The extended date functions are

➤ **XDATE(y,m,d,fmt):** Returns a date for a given year, month, and day. As an option, you can provide a date formatting string.

➤ **XDATEADD(xdate1,days,fmt):** Adds a specified number of days to a date. As an option, you can provide a date formatting string.

➤ **XDATEDIF(xdate1,xdate2):** Returns the number of days between two dates.

➤ **XDATEYEARDIF(xdate1,xdate2):** Returns the number of full years between two dates (useful for calculating ages).

➤ **XDATEYEAR(xdate1):** Returns the year of a date.

➤ **XDATEMONTH(xdate1):** Returns the month of a date.

➤ **XDATEDAY(xdate1):** Returns the day of a date.

➤ **XDATEDOW(xdate1):** Returns the day of the week of a date (as an integer between 1 and 7).

Figure 39-3 shows a worksheet that uses some of these custom functions.

	A	B	C	D	E	F	G	H
1	President	Year	Month	Day	XDATE	XDATEDIF	XDATEYEARDIF	XDATEDOW
2	George Washington	1732	2	22	February 22, 1732	102,617	280	Friday
3	John Adams	1735	10	30	October 30, 1735	101,271	277	Sunday
4	Thomas Jefferson	1743	4	13	April 13, 1743	98,549	269	Saturday
5	James Madison	1751	3	16	March 16, 1751	95,655	261	Tuesday
6	James Monroe	1758	4	28	April 28, 1758	93,055	254	Friday
7	John Quincy Adams	1767	7	11	July 11, 1767	89,694	245	Saturday
8	Andrew Jackson	1767	3	15	March 15, 1767	89,812	245	Sunday
9	Martin Van Buren	1782	12	5	December 5, 1782	84,068	230	Thursday
10	William Henry Harrison	1773	2	9	February 9, 1773	87,654	239	Tuesday
11	John Tyler	1790	3	29	March 29, 1790	81,397	222	Monday
12	James K. Polk	1795	11	2	November 2, 1795	79,353	217	Monday
13	Zachary Taylor	1784	11	24	November 24, 1784	83,348	228	Wednesday
14	Millard Fillmore	1800	1	7	January 7, 1800	77,826	213	Tuesday
15	Franklin Pierce	1804	11	23	November 23, 1804	76,045	208	Friday
16	James Buchanan	1791	4	23	April 23, 1791	81,007	221	Saturday
17	Abraham Lincoln	1809	2	12	February 12, 1809	74,503	203	Sunday
18	Andrew Johnson	1808	12	29	December 29, 1808	74,548	204	Thursday
19	Ulysses S. Grant	1822	4	27	April 27, 1822	69,681	190	Saturday
20	Rutherford B. Hayes	1822	10	4	October 4, 1822	69,521	190	Friday
21	James A. Garfield	1831	11	19	November 19, 1831	66,188	181	Saturday
22	Chester A. Arthur	1829	10	5	October 5, 1829	66,963	183	Monday
23	Grover Cleveland	1837	3	18	March 18, 1837	64,242	175	Saturday
24	Benjamin Harrison	1833	8	20	August 20, 1833	65,548	179	Tuesday

Figure 39-3: Using custom functions to work with pre-1900 dates.

Note The extended date functions don't make any adjustments for changes made to the calendar in 1582. Consequently, working with dates prior to October 15, 1582, may not yield correct results.

Use a different product

A final option is to use a different spreadsheet product that supports pre-1900 dates. Figure 39-4 shows Google Spreadsheet. This (free) product uses the same date serial number system as Excel, but uses negative values for dates prior to 1900. It supports dates from 1583 through 9956.

President	Born	Days Since Birth	Years Since Birth	Day of the Week
George Washington	2/22/1732	102,617	280	Friday
John Adams	10/30/1735	101,271	277	Sunday
Thomas Jefferson	4/13/1743	98,549	269	Saturday
James Madison	3/16/1751	95,655	261	Tuesday
James Monroe	4/28/1758	93,055	254	Friday
John Quincy Adams	7/11/1767	89,694	245	Saturday
Andrew Jackson	3/15/1767	89,812	245	Sunday
Martin Van Buren	12/5/1782	84,068	230	Thursday
William Henry Harrison	2/9/1773	87,654	239	Tuesday
John Tyler	3/29/1790	81,397	222	Monday
James K. Polk	11/2/1795	79,353	217	Monday
Zachary Taylor	11/24/1784	83,348	228	Wednesday
Millard Fillmore	1/7/1800	77,826	213	Tuesday
Franklin Pierce	11/23/1804	76,045	208	Friday
James Buchanan	4/23/1791	81,007	221	Saturday
Abraham Lincoln	2/12/1809	74,503	203	Sunday
Andrew Johnson	12/29/1808	74,548	204	Thursday
Ulysses S. Grant	4/27/1822	69,681	190	Saturday
Rutherford B. Hayes	10/4/1822	69,521	190	Friday
James A. Garfield	11/19/1831	66,188	181	Saturday
Chester A. Arthur	10/5/1829	66,963	183	Monday

Figure 39-4: Google Spreadsheet can handle pre-1900 dates.

Displaying a Live Calendar in a Range

This tip describes how to create a "live" calendar in a range of cells. Figure 40-1 shows an example. If you change the date that's displayed at the top of the calendar, the calendar recalculates to display the dates for the month and year.

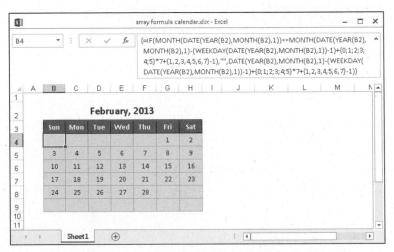

Figure 40-1: This calendar was created with a complex array formula.

To create this calendar in the range B2:H9, follow these steps:

1. Select B2:H2 and then merge the cells by choosing Home➡Alignment➡Merge & Center.

2. Enter a date into the merged range.

   The day of the month isn't important, so change the format of the cell to a custom format that doesn't display the day: mmmm, yyyy.

3. Enter the abbreviated day names in the range B3:H3.

4. Select B4:H9 and then enter the following array formula without the line breaks.

   Note: To enter an array formula, press Ctrl+Shift+Enter (not just Enter):

```
=IF(MONTH(DATE(YEAR(B2),MONTH(B2),1))
<>MONTH(DATE(YEAR(B2),MONTH(B2),1)-
(WEEKDAY(DATE(YEAR(B2),MONTH(B2),1))-1)
+{0;1;2;3;4;5}*7+{1,2,3,4,5,6,7}-1),"",
DATE(YEAR(B2),MONTH(B2),1)-
(WEEKDAY(DATE(YEAR(B2),MONTH(B2),1))-1)
+{0;1;2;3;4;5}*7+{1,2,3,4,5,6,7}-1)
```

5. Select the range B4:H9 and choose Home→Number→More Number formats to display the Number tab of the Format Cells dialog box.

6. In the Format Cells dialog box, choose Custom and enter the following custom number format (which displays the day only) in the Type field:

    ```
    d
    ```

7. Adjust the column widths and format the cells the way you like.

Change the date and year in cell B2, and the calendar updates automatically. After creating this calendar, you can copy the range to any other worksheet or workbook.

Returning the Last Nonblank Cell in a Column or Row

Suppose that you update a worksheet frequently by adding new data to its columns. You might need a way to reference the last value in a particular column (the value most recently entered). This tip presents three ways to accomplish this.

Figure 41-1 shows an example. The worksheet tracks the value of three funds in columns B:D. Notice that the information does not arrive at the same time. The goal is to get the sum of the most recent data for each fund. These values are calculated in the range G4:G6.

	A	B	C	D	E	F	G	H
1	**Month**	**Fund A**	**Fund B**	**Fund C**				
2	January	189.43	83.12	220.33				
3	February	192.50	88.10	221.71		**Latest Values**		
4	March	194.55	87.84	224.57		Fund A	196.27	
5	April	195.88	89.07	224.91		Fund B	93.56	
6	May	193.68	92.38			Fund C	224.91	
7	June	196.27	91.47					
8	July		90.93			Total:	514.74	
9	August		93.56					
10	September							
11	October							
12	November							
13	December							
14								

Figure 41-1: Use a formula to return the last non-empty cell in columns B:D.

Cell counting method

The formulas in G4, G5, and G6 are

```
=INDEX(B:B,COUNTA(B:B))
=INDEX(C:C,COUNTA(C:C))
=INDEX(D:D,COUNTA(D:D))
```

These formulas use the COUNTA function to count the number of non-empty cells in column C. This value is used as the second argument for the INDEX function. For example, in column B the last value is in row 6, COUNTA returns 6, and the INDEX function returns the 6th value in the column.

The preceding formulas work in most, but not all, situations. If the column has one or more empty cells interspersed, determining the last nonblank cell is a bit more challenging because the COUNTA function doesn't count the empty cells.

Array formula method

The following array formula returns the contents of the last non-empty cell in the first 500 rows of column B, even if column B contains blank cells:

```
=INDEX(B:B,MAX(ROW(B:B)*(B:B<>"")))
```

Note   **Press Ctrl+Shift+Enter (not just Enter) to enter an array formula.**

You can, of course, modify the formula to work with a column other than column B. To use a different column, change the four column references from B to whatever column you need.

You can't use this formula, as written, in the same column in which it's working. Attempting to do so generates a circular reference. You can, however, modify it. For example, to use the function in cell B1, change the references so that they begin with row 2 rather than the entire columns. For example, use B2:B1000 to return the last non-empty cell in the range B2:B1000.

The following array formula is similar to the previous formula, but it returns the last non-empty cell in a row (in this case, row 1):

```
=INDEX(1:1,MAX(COLUMN(1:1)*(1:1<>"")))
```

To use this formula for a different row, change the three 1:1 row references to correspond to the correct row number.

Standard formula method

The final method uses a standard (non-array) formula, and is rather cryptic. This formula returns the last non-empty cell in column B:

```
=LOOKUP(2,1/(B:B<>""),B:B)
```

This formula ignores error values, so if the last non-empty cell contains an error (such as #DIV/0!), the formula returns the last non-empty, non-error cell.

The following formula returns the last non-empty, non-error cell in row 1:

```
=LOOKUP(2,1/(1:1<>""),1:1)
```

Various Methods of Rounding Numbers

Rounding numbers is a common task, and Excel provides quite a few functions that round values in various ways.

You must understand the difference between *rounding* a value and *formatting* a value. When you *format* a number to display a specific number of decimal places, formulas that refer to that number use the actual value, which might differ from the displayed value. When you *round* a number, formulas that refer to that value use the rounded number.

Table 42-1 summarizes the Excel rounding functions.

Table 42-1: Excel Rounding Functions

Function	What It Does
CEILING.MATH	Rounds a number up to the nearest specified multiple
DOLLARDE	Converts a dollar price, expressed as a fraction, into a decimal number
DOLLARFR	Converts a dollar price, expressed as a decimal, into a fractional number
EVEN	Rounds up (away from zero) positive numbers to the nearest even integer; rounds down (away from zero) negative numbers to the nearest even integer
FLOOR.MATH	Rounds a number down to the nearest integer or to the nearest specified multiple
INT	Rounds a number down to make it an integer
MROUND	Rounds a number to a specified multiple
ODD	Rounds up (away from zero) numbers to the nearest odd integer; rounds down (away from zero) negative numbers to the nearest odd integer
ROUND	Rounds a number to a specified number of digits
ROUNDDOWN	Rounds down (toward zero) a number to a specified number of digits
ROUNDUP	Rounds up (away from zero) a number to a specified number of digits
TRUNC	Truncates a number to a specified number of significant digits

The following sections provide examples of formulas that use various types of rounding.

Rounding to the nearest multiple

The MROUND function is useful for rounding values to the nearest multiple. For example, you can use this function to round a number to the nearest 5. The following formula returns 135:

```
=MROUND(133,5)
```

Rounding currency values

Often, you need to round currency values. For example, a calculated price might be a number like $45.78923. In such a case, you want to round the calculated price to the nearest penny. This process might sound simple, but you can round this type of value in one of three ways:

➤ Round it up to the nearest penny.

➤ Round it down to the nearest penny.

➤ Round it to the nearest penny (the rounding can be up or down).

The following formula assumes that a dollar-and-cents value is in cell A1. The formula rounds the value to the nearest penny. For example, if cell A1 contains $12.421, the formula returns $12.42.

```
=ROUND(A1,2)
```

If you need to round up the value to the nearest penny, use the CEILING.MATH function. The following formula rounds up the value in cell A1 to the nearest penny (if, for example, cell A1 contains $12.421, the formula returns $12.43):

```
=CEILING.MATH(A1,0.01)
```

To round down a dollar value, use the FLOOR.MATH function. The following formula, for example, rounds down the dollar value in cell A1 to the nearest penny (if cell A1 contains $12.421, the formula returns $12.42):

```
=FLOOR.MATH(A1,0.01)
```

To round up a dollar value to the nearest nickel, use this formula:

```
=CEILING.MATH(A1,0.05)
```

Using the INT and TRUNC functions

On the surface, the INT and TRUNC functions seem similar. Both convert a value to an integer. The TRUNC function simply removes the fractional part of a number. The INT function rounds down a number to the nearest integer, based on the value of the fractional part of the number.

In practice, INT and TRUNC return different results only when using negative numbers. For example, the following formula returns –14.0:

```
=TRUNC(-14.2)
```

The next formula returns –15.0 because –14.2 is rounded down to the next lower integer:

```
=INT(-14.2)
```

The TRUNC function takes an additional (optional) argument that's useful for truncating decimal values. For example, the following formula returns 54.33 (the value truncated to two decimal places):

```
=TRUNC(54.3333333,2)
```

Rounding to n significant digits

In some situations, you may need to round a value to a particular number of significant digits. For example, you may want to express the value 1,432,187 in terms of two significant digits (that is, as 1,400,000). The value 84,356 expressed in terms of three significant digits is 84,300.

If the value is a positive number with no decimal places, the following formula does the job. This formula rounds the number in cell A1 to two significant digits. To round to a different number of significant digits, replace the 2 in this formula with a different number:

```
=ROUNDDOWN(A1,2-LEN(A1))
```

For non-integers and negative numbers, the solution is a bit trickier. The following formula provides a more general solution that rounds the value in cell A1 to the number of significant digits specified in cell A2. This formula works for positive and negative integers and non-integers:

```
=ROUND(A1,A2-1-INT(LOG10(ABS(A1))))
```

For example, if cell A1 contains 1.27845 and cell A2 contains 3, the formula returns 1.28000 (the value, rounded to three significant digits).

Converting Between Measurement Systems

You know the distance from New York to London in miles, but your European office needs the numbers in kilometers. What's the conversion factor?

The Excel CONVERT function can convert between a variety of measurements in these categories:

➤ Area

➤ Distance

➤ Energy

➤ Force

➤ Information

➤ Magnetism

➤ Power

➤ Pressure

➤ Speed

➤ Temperature

➤ Time

➤ Volume (or liquid measure)

➤ Weight and mass

The CONVERT function requires three arguments: the value to be converted, the from-unit, and the to-unit. For example, if cell A1 contains a distance expressed in miles, use this formula to convert miles to kilometers:

```
=CONVERT(A1,"mi","km")
```

The second and third arguments are unit abbreviations, which are listed in the Help system. Some abbreviations are commonly used, but others aren't. And, of course, you must use the *exact* abbreviation. Furthermore, the unit abbreviations are case-sensitive, so the following formula returns an error:

```
=CONVERT(A1,"Mi","km")
```

The CONVERT function is even more versatile than it seems. When using metric units, you can apply a multiplier. In fact, the first example I presented uses a multiplier. The unit abbreviation for the third argument is *m*, for meters. I added the kilo-multiplier (*k*) to express the result in kilometers.

In some situations, the CONVERT function requires some creativity. For example, if you need to convert 100 km/hour into miles/sec, the formula requires two uses of the CONVERT function:

```
=CONVERT(100,"km","mi")/CONVERT(1,"hr","sec")
```

The CONVERT function has been significantly enhanced in Excel 2013 and supports dozens of new measurement units.

If you can't find a particular unit that works with the CONVERT function, perhaps Excel has another function that will do the job. Table 43-1 lists some other functions that convert between measurement units.

Table 43-1: Other Conversion Functions

Function	Description
ARABIC*	Converts an Arabic number to decimal.
BASE*	Converts a decimal number to a specified base.
BIN2DEC	Converts a binary number to decimal.
BIN2OCT	Converts a binary number to octal.
DEC2BIN	Converts a decimal number to binary.
DEC2HEX	Converts a decimal number to hexadecimal.
DEC2OCT	Converts a decimal number to octal.
DEGREES	Converts an angle (in radians) to degrees.
HEX2BIN	Converts a hexadecimal number to binary.
HEX2DEC	Converts a hexadecimal number to decimal.
HEX2OCT	Converts a hexadecimal number to octal.
OCT2BIN	Converts an octal number to binary.
OCT2DEC	Converts an octal number to decimal.
OCT2HEX	Converts an octal number to hexadecimal.
RADIANS	Converts an angle (in degrees) to radians.

* Function is new to Excel 2013.

Counting Nonduplicated Entries in a Range

In some situations, you may need to count the number of nonduplicated entries in a range. Figure 44-1 shows an example. Column A has a list of animals, and the goal is to count the number of different animals in the list. The formula in cell B2 returns 6, which is the number of nonduplicated animals. This formula (an array formula, by the way) is

```
=SUM(1/COUNTIF(A1:A10,A1:A10))
```

To adapt this formula to your own worksheet, just change both instances of A1:A10 to the range address that you're working with.

Note **When you enter an array formula, press Ctrl+Shift+Enter (not just Enter).**

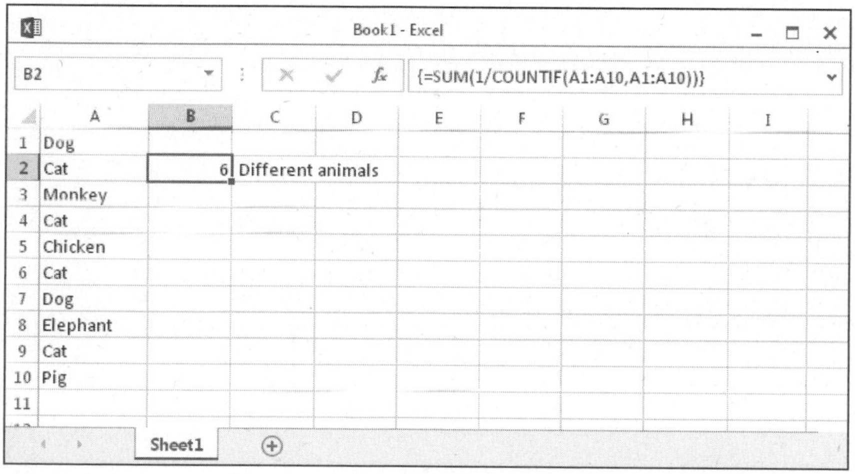

◢	A	B	C	D	E	F	G	H	I
1	Dog								
2	Cat	6	Different animals						
3	Monkey								
4	Cat								
5	Chicken								
6	Cat								
7	Dog								
8	Elephant								
9	Cat								
10	Pig								
11									

Cell B2: `{=SUM(1/COUNTIF(A1:A10,A1:A10))}`

Figure 44-1: Use an array formula to count the number of nonduplicated entries in a range.

This formula is one of those "Internet classics" that is passed around on various websites and newsgroups. Credit goes to David Hager, who first came up with the formula.

The preceding array formula works fine unless the range contains one or more empty cells. The following modified version of this array formula uses the IFERROR function to overcome this problem:

```
=SUM(IFERROR(1/COUNTIF(A1:A10,A1:A10),0))
```

The preceding formulas work with both values and text. If the range contains only numeric values or blank cells (but no text), you can use the following formula (which isn't an array formula) to count the number of nonduplicated values:

```
=SUM(N(FREQUENCY(A1:A10,A1:A10)>0))
```

Using the AGGREGATE Function

One of the most versatile functions available in Excel is AGGREGATE, which was introduced in Excel 2010. You can use this multipurpose function to sum values, calculate an average, count entries, and more. What makes this function useful is that it can (optionally) ignore values in hidden rows and error values. In some cases, you can use AGGREGATE to replace a complex array formula.

The AGGREGATE function takes three arguments, but for some functions, an additional argument is required.

The first argument for the AGGREGATE function is a value between 1 and 19 that determines the type of calculation to perform. The calculation type, in essence, is one of Excel's other functions. Table 45-1 contains a list of these values, with the function it mimics.

Table 45-1: Values for the First Argument of the AGGREGATE Function

Argument Value	Function
1	AVERAGE
2	COUNT
3	COUNTA
4	MAX
5	MIN
6	PRODUCT
7	STDEV.S
8	STDEV.P
9	SUM
10	VAR.S
11	VAR.P
12	MEDIAN
13	MODE.SNGL
14*	LARGE
15*	SMALL
16*	PERCENTILE.INC
17*	QUARTILE.INC
18*	PERCENTILE.EXC
19*	QUARTILE.EXC

* Indicates a function that requires an additional (4th) argument.

The second argument for the AGGREGATE function is an integer between 0 and 7 that specifies how hidden cells and errors are handled. Table 45-2 summarizes these options.

Table 45-2: Values for the Second Argument of the AGGREGATE Function

Option	Behavior
0 or omitted	Ignore nested SUBTOTAL and AGGREGATE functions.
1	Ignore hidden rows, nested SUBTOTAL and AGGREGATE functions.
2	Ignore error values, nested SUBTOTAL and AGGREGATE functions.
3	Ignore hidden rows, error values, nested SUBTOTAL and AGGREGATE functions.
4	Ignore nothing.
5	Ignore hidden rows.
6	Ignore error values.
7	Ignore hidden rows and error values.

The third argument of the AGGREGGATE function is a range reference for the data to be aggregated.

Note

The SUBTOTAL function always ignores data that is hidden, but only if the hiding is a result of filtering a table or contracting an outline. The AGGREGATE function works similarly, but also ignores data in rows that has been hidden manually. Note that this function does not ignore data in hidden columns. In other words, the AGGREGATE function was designed to work only with vertical ranges.

Fortunately, Excel provides "formula autocomplete" assistance when you enter this function in a formula. Figure 45-1 shows the drop-down list of arguments that appears automatically. Choose the argument and press Tab to continue.

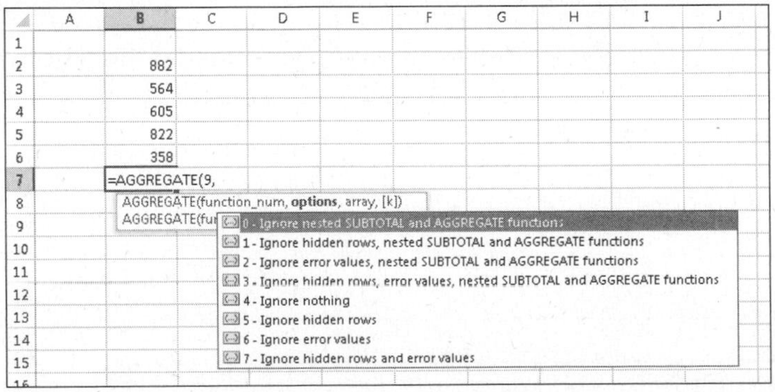

Figure 45-1: Using autocomplete to identify the argument values for AGGREGATE.

Figure 45-2 shows an example of how the AGGREGATE function can be useful. The worksheet contains pre-test and post-scores for eight students. Note that Charles did not take the post-test, so cells C4 and D4 contain the NA/# error value (to indicate not available).

Cell D11 contains a formula that uses the AVERAGE function to calculate the average change. This formula returns an error:

```
=AVERAGE(D2:D9)
```

The formula in cell D12 uses the AGGREGATE function, with the option to ignore error values:

```
=AGGREGATE(1,6,D2:D9)
```

D12 =AGGREGATE(1,6,D2:D9)

	A	B	C	D	E	F
1	**Student**	**Pre-Test**	**Post-Test**	**Pct Change**		
2	Adam	86	91	5.81%		
3	Beth	79	83	5.06%		
4	Charles	90	#N/A	#N/A		
5	Diane	65	73	12.31%		
6	Elmer	82	81	-1.22%		
7	Francesca	90	93	3.33%		
8	George	87	91	4.60%		
9	Hank	00	81	1.25%		
10						
11		Average Change:		#N/A		
12		Average Change:		4.45%		
13						

Figure 45-2: Using the AGGREGATE function to calculate an average when the range contains an error value.

Remember that AGGREGATE works only with Excel 2010 and later. If a workbook that uses this function is opened in a previous version of Excel, the formula will display an error.

Making an Exact Copy of a Range of Formulas

When you copy a cell that contains a formula, Excel adjusts all the relative cell references. Assume that cell D1 contains this formula:

```
=A1*B1
```

When you copy this cell, the two cell references are changed relative to the destination. If you copy D1 to D12, for example, the copied formula is

```
=A12*B12
```

Sometimes, you may prefer to make an exact copy of a formula. One way is to convert all the cell references to absolute references (for example, change =A1*B1 to =$A$1*$B$1). Another way is to (temporarily) remove the equal sign from the formula, which converts the formula to text. Then you can copy the cell and manually insert the equal sign into the original formula and the copied formula.

What if you have a large range of formulas and you want to make an exact copy of those formulas? Editing each formula is tedious and error-prone. Here's a way to accomplish the task. It uses Windows Notepad, but any text editor (including Microsoft Word) will do.

For the following steps, assume that you want to copy the formulas in A1:D10 on Sheet1 and make an exact copy in A13:D22, also on Sheet1:

1. Put Excel in Formula view mode.

   To toggle Formula view mode, choose Formulas➜Formula Auditing➜Show Formulas.

2. Select the range to copy. In this case, A1:D10 on Sheet1.

3. Press Ctrl+C to copy the range.

4. Launch the Windows Notepad text editor.

5. Press Ctrl+V to paste the copied data into Notepad.

6. In Notepad, press Ctrl+A to select all of the text, followed by Ctrl+C to copy the text.

7. Activate Excel and activate the upper-left cell where you want to paste the formulas (in this example, A13 on Sheet2) and make sure that the sheet you're copying to is in Formula view mode.

8. Press Ctrl+V to paste.

9. Choose Formulas➜Formula Auditing➜Show Formulas to toggle out of Formula view mode.

The formulas will be pasted exactly as they appear in the source range.

Note

In some cases, the paste operation (in Step 8) won't work correctly and the formulas will be split across two or more cells. If that happens, chances are that you used Excel's Text-to-Columns feature recently, and Excel is trying to be helpful by remembering how you last parsed your data. You need to fire up the Text to Columns Wizard and change the options. Choose Data➜Data Tools➜Text to Columns. In the Convert Text to Columns Wizard dialog box, choose the Delimited option and click Next. Clear all of the Delimiter option check marks except Tab, and click Cancel. After making this change, pasting the formulas will work correctly.

Using the Background Error-Checking Features

If your worksheets use a lot of formulas, you may find it helpful to take advantage of the automatic error-checking feature. You enable this feature on the Formulas tab of the Excel Options dialog box (see Figure 47-1). To display this dialog box, choose File➔Options.

You turn error checking on or off by using the Enable Background Error Checking check box. In addition, you can specify which types of errors to check by selecting check boxes in the Error Checking Rules section.

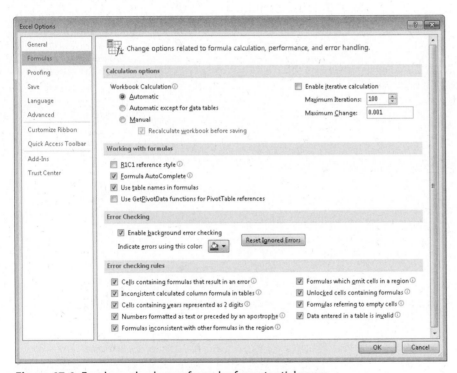

Figure 47-1: Excel can check your formulas for potential errors.

When error checking is turned on, Excel continually checks your formulas. If a potential error is identified, Excel places an error indicator (a small triangle) in the upper-left corner of the cell. When the cell is activated, an error-checking button appears. Clicking this buttons provides you with a list of options. Figure 47-2 shows the options that appear when you click the error-checking button for a cell that contains a #DIV/0! error. The options vary, depending on the type of error.

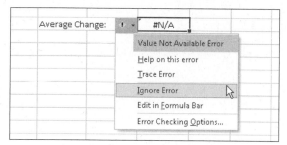

Figure 47-2: Clicking an error-checking button gives you a list of options.

In many cases, you choose to ignore an error by choosing the Ignore Error option, which eliminates the cell from subsequent error checks. You can select a range of formulas, and then choose Ignore Error to ignore them all. All previously ignored errors can be reset so that they appear again. (Click the Reset Ignored Errors button in the Excel Options dialog box.)

Even if you don't use the automatic error-checking option, you can choose the Formulas→Formula Auditing→Error Checking command to open a dialog box that displays each potential error cell in sequence, much like using a spell-checking feature. Figure 47-3 shows the Error Checking dialog box. Note that because it's a modeless dialog box, you can still access your worksheet when the Error Checking dialog box is open.

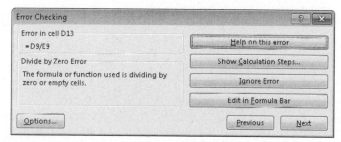

Figure 47-3: Using the Error Checking dialog box to cycle through potential errors identified by Excel.

Caution
Understand that the error-checking feature isn't perfect. In fact, it's not even close to perfect. In other words, you can't assume that you have an error-free worksheet simply because Excel doesn't identify any potential errors! Also, be aware that this error-checking feature doesn't catch a common type of error — overwriting a formula cell with a value.

Using the Inquire Add-In

Office 2013 Professional Plus includes a handy auditing add-in called Inquire. To install this add-in, follow these steps:

1. Choose File➜Options to display the Excel Options dialog box.

2. Click the Add-Ins tab.

3. Choose COM Add-Ins from the Manage drop-down list and click Go to display the COM Add-Ins dialog box.

4. In the COM Add-Ins dialog box, select the Inquire item and click OK.

If the Inquire item is not in the list, that means your version of Office doesn't include this add-in.

When the Inquire Add-In is installed, Excel displays a new tab: Inquire (see Figure 48-1).

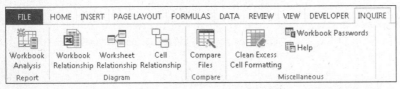

Figure 48-1: The Inquire tab appears when the Inquire add-in is installed.

Workbook analysis

To analyze the active workbook, choose Inquire➜Report➜Workbook Analysis to display the Workbook Analysis Report dialog box shown in Figure 48-2. Use the Items list on the left to select an analysis item, and the results (if any) appear in the Results section on the right. To create a report (in a new workbook), select the items to include in the report and choose Excel Export. The report is very detailed and is a good way to document an Excel workbook.

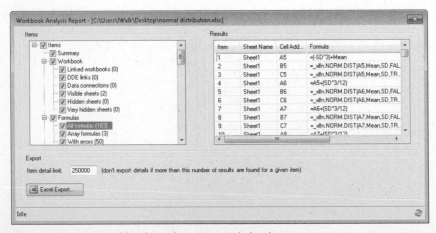

Figure 48-2: The Workbook Analysis Report dialog box.

Diagram tools

The items in the Inquire➔Diagram group each display a diagram:

➤ Workbook relationships

➤ Worksheet relationships

➤ Cell relationships

Figure 48-3 shows an example of worksheet relationships in a workbook that has four worksheets. It shows that Sheet3 contains formulas that refer to Sheet1 and Sheet2, and Sheet4 has formulas that refer to Sheet1.

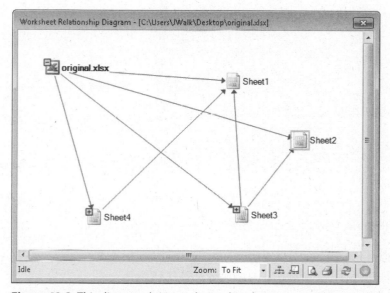

Figure 48-3: This diagram depicts relationships between worksheets.

Compare files

The Inquire➔Compare➔Compare Files command generates a detailed display that shows the differences between two workbooks. Both of the workbooks to be compared must be open.

Figure 48-4 shows an example of the output.

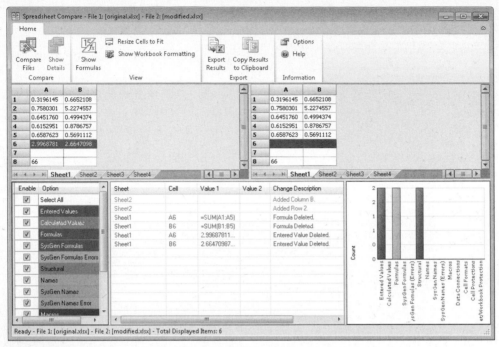

Figure 48-4: Output from the Compare Files command.

Other options

The Inquire add-in has some additional options in the Inquire➜Miscellaneous group:

➤ **Clean Excess Cell Formatting:** Removes unnecessary formatting from cells. For example, the command will remove formatting applied to entire rows or columns.

➤ **Workbook Passwords:** If you use Inquire to analyze or compare workbooks that are password-protected, you can avoid having to type the password each time those files are opened.

➤ **Help:** Displays help about the Inquire add-in features.

Hiding and Locking Your Formulas

If you distribute workbooks to other users, you may want to hide your formulas. This tip describes how to do so.

Every cell has two key properties: Locked and Hidden. A locked cell can't be changed, and the contents of a hidden cell don't appear in the Formula bar when the cell is selected. By default, every cell is locked and not hidden. But it's important to remember that these attributes have no effect unless the worksheet itself is protected.

A common scenario is to lock (and possibly hide) formula cells and unlock constant (nonformula cells).

Hiding and locking formula cells

Follow these steps to hide all of the formula cells on the active worksheet:

1. Select a single cell, and choose Home➜Editing➜Find & Select➜Go To Special. Excel displays the Go To Special dialog box.

2. In the Go To Special dialog box, choose the Formulas option and make sure all four check boxes are checked (see Figure 49-1).

3. Click OK, and Excel selects all of the formula cells.

4. Right-click any of the selected formula cells and choose Format Cells from the shortcut menu.

    The Format Cells dialog box appears.

5. Click the Protection tab to display the Locked and Hidden checkboxes.

6. Check both the Locked and the Hidden check boxes.

7. Click OK to close the Format Cells dialog box.

Figure 49-1: Using the Go To Special dialog box to select all formula cells.

Unlocking nonformula cells

Follow these steps to unlock all of the nonformula cells:

1. Select a single cell, and choose Home➜Editing➜Find & Select➜Go To Special. Excel displays the Go To Special dialog box.

2. In the Go To Special dialog box, choose the Constants option and make sure all four check boxes are checked.

3. Click OK, and Excel selects all of the constant (nonformula) cells.

4. Right-click any of the selected formula cells and choose Format Cells from the shortcut menu.

   The Format Cells dialog box appears.

5. Click the Protection tab to display the Locked and Hidden check boxes.

6. Uncheck both the Locked and the Hidden check boxes.

7. Click OK to close the Format Cells dialog box.

Protecting the worksheet

The steps in the two previous sections have no effect unless the worksheet is protected. Follow these steps to protect the worksheet:

1. Choose Review➜Changes➜Protect Sheet to access the Protect Sheet dialog box (see Figure 49-2).

Figure 49-2: The Protect Sheet dialog box.

2. In the Protect Sheet dialog box, specify a password (if desired). If you don't specify a password, anyone can unprotect the sheet and see (or modify) the formulas.

3. Click OK, and you will be prompted to reenter the password.

When you protect a worksheet, many common actions are disabled. For example, the user cannot insert rows or columns, change column width, or create embedded charts. Use the options in the Protect Sheet dialog box to specify the actions that are allowed when the sheet is protected.

After performing these steps, cells that contain a formula are not displayed in the Formula bar. If the user attempts to edit the cell, the alert box shown in Figure 49-3 appears. Nonformula cells can be edited, as usual.

Microsoft Excel

⚠ The cell or chart you're trying to change is on a protected sheet.

To make changes, click Unprotect Sheet in the Review tab (you might need a password).

OK

Figure 49-3: This alert box appears if the user attempts to edit a formula cell.

Note

Keep in mind that it is very easy to break the password for a protected sheet. If you're looking for absolute security, hiding and locking formula cells is not the solution.

Using the INDIRECT Function

To make a formula more flexible, you can use the Excel INDIRECT function to create a range reference. This rarely used function accepts a text argument that resembles a range reference and then
converts the argument to an actual range reference. When you understand how this function works,
you can use it to create more powerful interactive spreadsheets.

Specifying rows indirectly

Figure 50-1 shows an example that uses the INDIRECT function. The formula in cell E5 is

```
=SUM(INDIRECT("B"&E2&":B"&E3))
```

	A	B	C	D	E	F
1	**Month**	**Sales**				
2	January	67,932		First Row:	2	
3	February	72,345		Last Row:	4	
4	March	71,415				
5	April	74,393		SUM:	211,692	
6	May	71,795				
7	June	67,235				
8	July	69,575				
9	August	65,970				
10	September	66,521				
11	October	62,927				
12	November	64,299				
13	December	67,313				
14						

Figure 50-1: Using the INDIRECT function to sum user-specified rows.

The argument for the INDIRECT function uses the concatenation operator to build a range reference
by using the values in cells E2 and E3. So, if E2 contains 2 and E3 contains 4, the range reference evaluates to this string:

```
"B2:B4"
```

The INDIRECT function converts that string to an actual range reference, which is then passed to the SUM function. In effect, the formula returns

```
=SUM(B2:B4)
```

When you change the values in E2 or E3, the formula is updated to display the sum of the specified rows.

Specifying worksheet names indirectly

Figure 50-2 shows another example, this time using a worksheet reference.

Column A, on the Summary worksheet, contains text that corresponds to other worksheets in the workbook. Column B contains formulas that reference these text items. For example, the formula in cell B2 is

```
=SUM(INDIRECT(A2&"!F1:F10"))
```

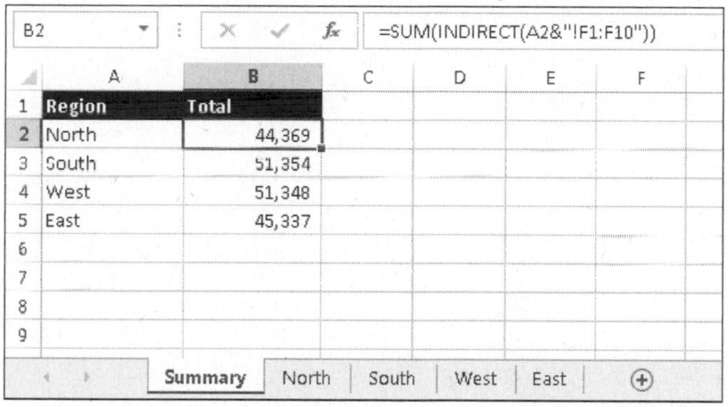

Figure 50-2: Using the INDIRECT function to create references.

This formula concatenates the text in A2 with a range reference. The INDIRECT function evaluates the result and converts it to an actual range reference. The result is equivalent to this formula:

```
=SUM(North!F1:F10)
```

This formula is copied down the column. Each formula returns the sum of range F1:F10 on the corresponding worksheet.

Making a cell reference unchangeable

Another use for the INDIRECT function is to create a reference to a cell that never changes. For example, consider this formula, which sums the values in the first 12 rows of column A:

```
=SUM(A1:A12)
```

If you insert a new row 1, Excel changes the formula to

```
=SUM(A2:A13)
```

In other words, the formula adjusts so that it continues to refer to the original data (and it no longer sums the first 12 rows of column A). To prevent Excel from changing the cell references, use the INDIRECT function:

```
=SUM(INDIRECT("A1:A12"))
```

This formula *always* returns the sum of the first 12 rows in column A.

Formula Editing in Dialog Boxes

This is a simple tip, but one that most users don't know about.

When Excel displays a dialog box that accepts a range reference, the field that contains the range reference is always in *point* mode. For example, consider the New Name dialog box, shown in Figure 51-1. This dialog box appears when you choose Formulas➜Defined Names➜Define Name.

If you activate the Refers to Field and use the arrow keys to edit the range reference, you'll find that you're actually pointing to a range in the worksheet — not editing the reference text. The solution: Press F2.

The F2 key toggles between point mode and edit mode. In edit mode, the arrow keys work the same as when you're editing a formula. Also notice that the current mode is displayed in the left corner of the status bar.

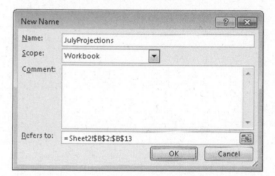

Figure 51-1: The Refers To field defaults to point mode. Press F2 to switch to edit mode.

This tip applies to all Excel dialog boxes that contain range selection fields.

Converting a Vertical Range to a Table

Often, tabular data is imported into Excel as a single column. Figure 52-1 shows an example. Column A contains employee information, and each "record" consists of three consecutive cells in a single column: Name, Department, and Location. The goal is to convert this data so that each record appears in a single row, with three columns.

	A	B	C
1	Lori Howard		
2	Accounting		
3	Main Office		
4	Jacqueline Espinoza		
5	Sales		
6	West Branch		
7	Jose Collins		
8	Accounting		
9	Main Office		
10	Bernice Ryan		
11	Sales		
12	East Branch		
13	Diana Brown		
14	Accounting		
15	West Branch		
16	Jay J. Davis		
17	Research		
18	Main Office		
19	Shandi Johnson		
20	Accounting		
21	Main Office		
22			
23			

Figure 52-1: Vertical data that needs to be converted to three columns.

You can convert this type of data several ways, but here's a method that's fairly easy. It uses a single formula, which is copied to a range.

Enter the following formula in cell C1, and then copy it down and across.

```
=INDIRECT("A" &COLUMN()-2 + (ROW()-1)*3)
```

Figure 52-2 shows the transformed data in C1:E7.

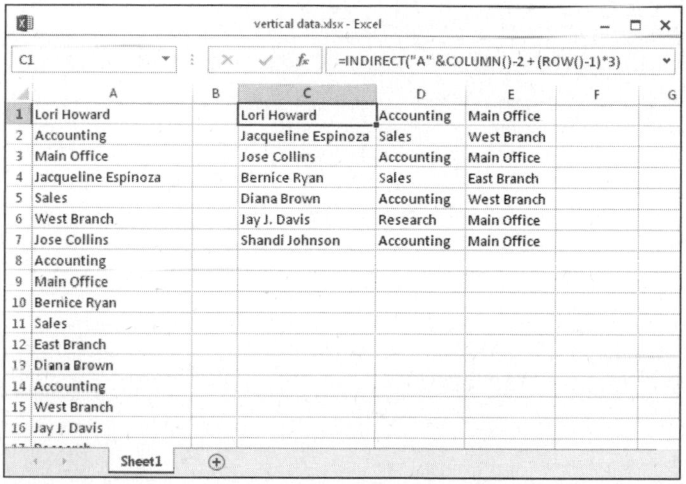

Figure 52-2: Vertical data transformed to a table.

The formula works for vertical data that uses three cells per record, but it can be modified to handle vertical data that uses any number of cells per record by changing the "3" in the formula. For example, if the vertical data has five fields, use this formula:

```
=INDIRECT("A" &COLUMN()-2 + (ROW()-1)*5)
```

PART IV

Working with Data

In this part, you'll find tips related to working with data of all types. There's an excellent chance that the tips here will improve your overall efficiency.

Tips and Where to Find Them

Selecting Cells Efficiently

Many Excel users think that the only way to select a range of cells is to drag over the cells with the mouse. Although selecting cells with a mouse works, it's rarely the most *efficient* way to accomplish the task. A better way is to use your keyboard to select ranges.

Selecting a range by using the Shift and arrow keys

The simplest way to select a range is to press (and hold) Shift and then use the arrow keys to highlight the cells. For larger selections, you can use PgDn or PgUp while pressing Shift to move in larger increments.

You can also use the End key to quickly extend a selection to the last non-empty cell in a row or column. To select the range B3:B8 (see Figure 53-1) by using the keyboard, move the cell pointer to B3 and then press the Shift key while you press End followed by the down-arrow key. Similarly, to select B3:D3, press the Shift key while you press End, followed by the right-arrow key.

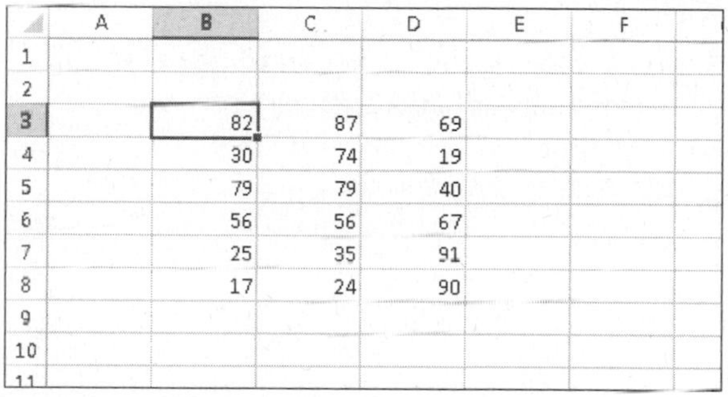

▲	A	B	C	D	E	F	
1							
2							
3		82	87	69			
4		30	74	19			
5		79	79	40			
6		56	56	67			
7		25	35	91			
8		17	24	90			
9							
10							
11							

Figure 53-1: A range of cells.

Selecting the current region

Often, you need to select a large rectangular selection of cells — the *current region*. To select the entire block of cells, move the cell pointer anywhere within the range and press Ctrl+A.

Note

If the cell pointer is within a table (created by using Insert→Tables→Table), pressing Ctrl+A selects only the data. Press Ctrl+A a second time to select the table's Header row and Total row.

Selecting a range by Shift+clicking

When you're selecting a very large range, using the mouse may be the most efficient method — but dragging is not required. Select the upper-left cell in the range. Then scroll to the lower-right corner of the range, press Shift, and click the lower-right cell.

Selecting noncontiguous ranges

Most of the time, your range selections are probably simple rectangular ranges. In some cases, you may need to make a *multiple selection* — a selection that includes nonadjacent cells or ranges. For example, you may want to apply formatting to cells in different areas of your worksheet. If you make a multiple selection, you can apply the formatting in one step to all selected ranges. Figure 53-2 shows an example of a multiple selection.

◢	A	B	C	D	E	F	
1							
2							
3		82	87	69			
4		30	74	19			
5		79	79	40			
6		56	56	67			
7		25	35	91			
8		17	24	90			
9							
10							
11							

Figure 53-2: A multiple selection that consists of noncontiguous ranges.

You can select a noncontiguous range by using either the mouse or the keyboard.

Press Ctrl as you click and drag the mouse to highlight individual cells or ranges.

From the keyboard, select a range as described previously (by using the Shift key). Then press Shift+F8 to select another range without canceling the previous range selection. Repeat this action as many times as needed. When you're finished, press Shift+F8 again to return to normal selecting mode.

Selecting entire rows

To select a single row, click a row number along the left of the worksheet. Or select any cell in the row and press Shift+spacebar.

To select multiple adjacent rows, click and drag in the row number area. Or select any cell in the first (or last) row and press Shift+spacebar to select the row. Then press Shift and use the arrow keys to extend the row selection down (or up).

To select multiple nonadjacent rows, press Ctrl while you click the row numbers for the rows you want to include.

Selecting entire columns

To select a single column, click a column letter along the top of the worksheet. Or select any cell in the column and press Ctrl+spacebar.

To select multiple adjacent columns, click and drag in the column letter section. Or select any cell in the first (or last) column and press Ctrl+spacebar to select the column. Then press Shift and use the arrow keys to extend the selection to the right (or left).

To select multiple nonadjacent columns, press Ctrl while you click the column letters for the columns you want to include.

Selecting multisheet ranges

In addition to two-dimensional ranges on a single worksheet, ranges can extend across multiple worksheets to be three-dimensional ranges.

Figure 53-3 shows a simple example of a multisheet workbook. The workbook has four sheets, named Totals, Operations, Marketing, and Manufacturing. The sheets are laid out identically.

	A	B	C	D	E	F	G	H
1	Budget Summary							
2								
3		Q1	Q2	Q3	Q4	Year Total		
4	Salaries	286,500	286,500	286,500	290,500	1,150,000		
5	Travel	40,500	42,525	44,651	46,884	174,560		
6	Supplies	55,500	62,475	65,599	68,879	256,452		
7	Facility	144,000	144,000	144,000	144,000	576,000		
8	Total	530,500	535,500	540,750	550,263	2,157,013		
9								
10								
11								
12								
13								
14								

Totals | Operations | Marketing | Manufacturing | ...

Figure 53-3: Each worksheet in this workbook is laid out identically.

Assume that you want to apply the same formatting to all sheets — for example, you want to make the column headings bold with background shading. Selecting a multisheet range is the best approach. When the ranges are selected, the formatting is applied to all sheets.

In general, selecting a multisheet range is a simple two-step process:

1. Select the range in one sheet.

2. Select the worksheets to include in the range.

Note

To select a group of contiguous worksheets, press Shift and click the sheet tab of the last worksheet that you want to include in the selection. To select individual worksheets, press Ctrl and click the sheet tab of each worksheet that you want to select. When you make the selection, the sheet tabs of the selected sheets appear with a white background, and Excel displays [Group] on the title bar. When you finish working with the multisheet range, click any sheet tab to leave Group mode.

Automatically Filling a Range with a Series

If you need to fill a range with a series of values, one approach is to enter the first value, write a formula to calculate the next value, and copy the formula. For example, Figure 54-1 shows a series of consecutive numbers in column A. Cell A1 contains the value 1, and cell A2 contains this formula, which was copied down the column:

```
=A1+1
```

	A	B	C	D
1	1			
2	2			
3	3			
4	4			
5	5			
6	6			
7	7			
8	8			
9	9			
10	10			
11	11			
12				
13				

Figure 54-1: Excel offers an easy way to generate a series of values like these.

Another approach is to let Excel do the work by using the handy AutoFill feature:

1. Enter 1 into cell A1.

2. Enter **2** into cell A2.

3. Select A1:A2.

4. Move the mouse cursor to the lower-right corner of cell A2 (the cell's *fill handle*), and when the mouse pointer turns into a black plus sign, drag down the column to fill in the cells.

Note You can turn this behavior on and off. If cells don't have a fill handle, choose File➜ Options and click the Advanced tab in the Excel Options dialog box. Select the check box labeled Enable Fill Handle and Cell Drag-And-Drop.

The data entered in Steps 1 and 2 provide Excel with the information it needs to determine which type of series to use. If you entered 3 in cell A2, the series will consist of odd integers: 1, 3, 5, 7, and so on.

When you release the mouse button after dragging, Excel displays an Auto Fill Options drop-down list. Click to select other options. The list of options is particular helpful with dates. Figure 54-2 shows the Auto Fill Options when working with a date series. You can quickly create a series of weekdays, months, or years.

◢	A	B	C	D	E	F
1	January 1, 2013					
2	January 2, 2013					
3	January 3, 2013					
4	January 4, 2013					
5	January 5, 2013					
6	January 6, 2013					
7	January 7, 2013					
8	January 8, 2013					
9	January 9, 2013					
10	January 10, 2013					
11	January 11, 2013					
12	January 12, 2013					
13						
14	○ Copy Cells					
15	◉ Fill Series					
16	○ Fill Formatting Only					
17						
18	○ Fill Without Formatting					
19	○ Fill Days					
20	○ Fill Weekdays					
21	○ Fill Months					
22	○ Fill Years					
23						
24	○ Flash Fill					

Figure 54-2: Use the Auto Fill Options drop-down list to change the type of fill.

Here's another AutoFill trick: If the data you start with is irregular, Excel completes the AutoFill action by doing a linear regression and fills in the predicted values. Figure 54-3 shows a worksheet with monthly sales values for January through July. If you use AutoFill after selecting C2:C8, Excel extends the best-fit linear sales trend and fills in the missing values. Figure 54-4 shows the predicted values, along with a chart.

◢	A	B	C	D	E
1		Month	Sales		
2		Jan	15,932		
3		Feb	18,933		
4		Mar	16,930		
5		Apr	19,387		
6		May	16,981		
7		Jun	22,553		
8		Jul	24,902		
9		Aug			
10		Sep			
11		Oct			
12		Nov			
13		Dec			
14					

Figure 54-3: Use AutoFill to perform a linear regression and predict sales values for August through December.

Figure 54-4: The sales figures, after using AutoFill to predict the next five months.

AutoFill also works with dates and even a few text items — day names and month names. The following table lists a few examples of the types of data that can be autofilled.

First Value	Autofilled Values
Sunday	Monday, Tuesday, Wednesday, and so on
Quarter-1	Quarter-2, Quarter-3, Quarter-4, Quarter-1, and so on
Jan	Feb, Mar, Apr, and so on
January	February, March, April, and so on
Month 1	Month 2, Month 3, Month 4, and so on

You can also create your own lists of items to be autofilled. To do so, open the Excel Options dialog box and click the Advanced tab. Then scroll down and click the Edit Custom Lists button to display the Custom Lists dialog box. Enter your items in the List Entries box (each on a new line). Then click the Add button to create the list. Figure 54-5 shows a custom list of region names that use Roman numerals.

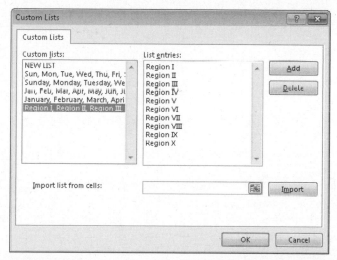

Figure 54-5: These region names work with the Excel AutoFill feature.

Fixing Trailing Minus Signs

Imported data sometimes displays negative values with a trailing minus sign. For example, a negative value may appear as **3,498-** rather than the more common **-3,498**. Excel doesn't convert these values. In fact, it considers them to be non-numeric text.

The solution is so simple it may surprise you:

1. Select the data that has the trailing minus signs. The selection can also include positive values.

2. Choose Data➜Data Tools➜Text to Columns.

3. When the Text to Columns dialog box appears, click Finish.

This procedure works because of a default setting in the Advanced Text Import Settings dialog box (which you don't even see, normally). To display this dialog box, shown in Figure 55-1, go to Step 3 in the Text to Columns Wizard dialog box and click Advanced.

Or you can use Flash Fill to fix the trailing minus signs. If the range contains any positive values, you may need to provide several examples. See Tip 64 for information about the Flash Fill feature.

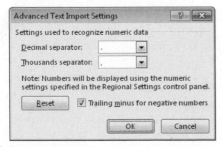

Figure 55-1: The Trailing Minus for Negative Numbers option makes it very easy to fix trailing minus signs in a range of data.

Restricting Cursor Movement to Input Cells

A common type of worksheet uses two types of cells: input cells and formula cells. The user enters data into the input cells, and the formulas calculate and display the results.

Figure 56-1 shows a simple example. The input cells are in the range C4:C7. These cells are used by the formulas in C10:C13. To prevent the user from accidentally typing over formula cells, it's useful to limit the cursor movement so that the formula cells can't even be selected.

	A	B	C	D
1		Mortgage Loan Worksheet		
2				
3		Input Cells		
4		Purchase Price:	$385,500	
5		Down Payment:	10%	
6		Loan Term (Months):	360	
7		Interest Rate (APR):	5.25%	
8				
9		Result Cells		
10		Loan Amount:	$346,950	
11		Monthly Payment:	$1,916	
12		Total Payments:	$689,713	
13		Total Interest:	$342,763	
14				
15				

Figure 56-1: This worksheet has input cells at the top and formula cells below.

Setting up this sort of arrangement is a two-step process: Unlock the input cells and then protect the sheet. The following specific instructions are for the example shown in Figure 56-1:

1. Select C4:C7.

2. Press Ctrl+1 to display the Format Cells dialog box.

3. In the Format Cells dialog box, click the Protection tab, deselect the Locked check box, and click OK.

   By default, all cells are locked.

4. Choose Review➜Changes➜Protect Sheet.

   The Protect Sheet dialog box appears.

5. Deselect the Select Locked Cells check box and make sure that the Select Unlocked Cells check box is selected.

6. (Optional) Specify a password that will be required to unprotect the sheet.

7. Click OK.

After you perform these steps, only the unlocked cells can be selected. If you need to make any changes to your worksheet, you need to unprotect the sheet first, by choosing Review➔Changes➔ Unprotect Sheet.

Although this example used a contiguous range of cells for the input, that isn't necessary for the steps to work. The input cells can be scattered throughout your worksheet.

Note

Protecting a worksheet with a password isn't a security feature. This type of password is easily cracked.

Transforming Data with and Without Using Formulas

Often, you have a range of cells containing data that must be transformed in some way. For example, you might want to increase all values by five percent. Or you might need to divide each value by two. This tip describes two ways to perform these types of transformations.

Transforming data without formulas

The following steps assume that you have values in a range and you want to increase all values by five percent. For example, the range can contain a price list and you're raising all prices by five percent:

1. Activate any empty cell and enter **1.05**.

   You will multiply the values by this number, which results in an increase of five percent.

2. Press Ctrl+C to copy that cell.

3. Select the range to be transformed.

   The range can include values, formulas, or text.

4. Choose Home→Clipboard→Paste→Paste Special to display the Paste Special dialog box (see Figure 57-1).

5. In the Paste Special dialog box, click the Multiply option.

6. Click OK.

7. Press Esc to cancel Copy mode.

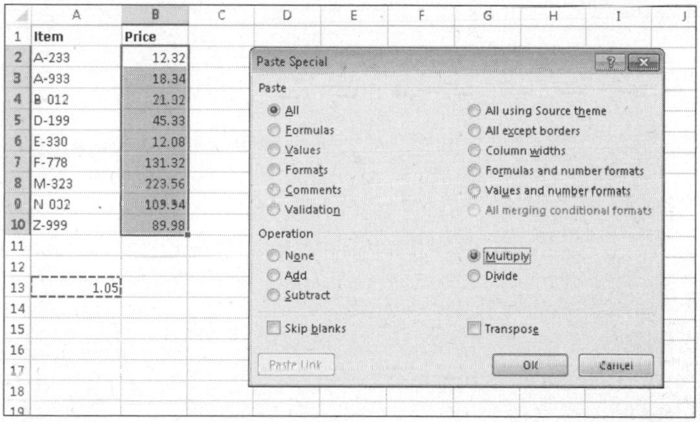

Figure 57-1: Using the Paste Special dialog box to multiply a range by a value.

The values in the range are multiplied by the copied value (1.05), and cells that contain text are ignored. Formulas in the range are modified accordingly. Assume that the range originally contained this formula:

```
=SUM(B18:B22)
```

After you perform the Paste Special operation, the formula is converted to

```
=(SUM(B18:B22))*1.05
```

This technique is limited to the four basic math operations: add, subtract, multiply, and divide.

For more versatility, keep reading to learn how to use formulas to transform values.

Transforming data by using temporary formulas

The previous section describes how to perform simple mathematical transformations on a range of numeric data. This tip describes the much more versatile method of transforming data (numerical or text) by using temporary formulas.

Figure 57-2 shows a worksheet with names in column A. These names are in all uppercase letters, and the goal is to convert them to proper case (only the first letter of each name is uppercase).

	A	B	C
1	**Name**	**Balance**	
2	SHIRLEY THOMAS	630.53	
3	ROBERT HARRIS	998.25	
4	ERIC HERNANDEZ	940.71	
5	MARTIN JACKSON	954.26	
6	WILLIAM CHAVEZ	928.43	
7	JERRY RUSSELL	308.75	
8	STANLEY WARD	714.30	
9	JANICE DAVIS	830.20	
10	TOD FISHER	655.37	
11	PHILLIP CARTER	896.46	
12	ANDREA PARKER	973.46	
13	ERIC HOBBS	909.49	
14	ELIZABETH MORALES	359.33	
15	MARY POWERS	262.92	
16	EDWARD SMITH	76.45	
17	NETA JONES	939.58	
18	JUSTIN ROSE	339.23	
19			

Figure 57-2: The goal is to transform the names in column A to proper case.

Follow these steps to transform the data in column A:

1. Create a temporary formula in an unused column.

   For this example, enter this formula in cell C2:

   ```
   =PROPER(A2)
   ```

2. Copy the formula down the column to accommodate all cells to be transformed.

3. Select the formula cells (in column C).

4. Press Ctrl+C.

5. Select the original data cells (in column A).

6. Choose Home→Clipboard→Paste→Paste Values (V).

   The original data is replaced with the transformed data (see Figure 57-3).

7. Press Esc to cancel Copy mode.

8. When you're satisfied that the transformation happened as you intended, you can delete the temporary formulas in column C.

	A	B	C	D
1	Name	Balance		
2	Shirley Thomas	630.53	Shirley Thomas	
3	Robert Harris	998.25	Robert Harris	
4	Eric Hernandez	940.71	Eric Hernandez	
5	Martin Jackson	954.26	Martin Jackson	
6	William Chavez	928.43	William Chavez	
7	Jerry Russell	308.75	Jerry Russell	
8	Stanley Ward	714.30	Stanley Ward	
9	Janice Davis	830.20	Janice Davis	
10	Tod Fisher	655.37	Tod Fisher	
11	Phillip Carter	896.46	Phillip Carter	
12	Andrea Parker	973.46	Andrea Parker	
13	Eric Hobbs	909.49	Eric Hobbs	
14	Elizabeth Morales	359.33	Elizabeth Morales	
15	Mary Powers	262.92	Mary Powers	
16	Edward Smith	76.45	Edward Smith	
17	Neta Jones	939.58	Neta Jones	
18	Justin Rose	339.23	Justin Rose	
19		(Ctrl) ▾		
20				
21				

Figure 57-3: The formula results from column C replace the original data in column A.

You can adapt this technique for just about any type of data transformation you need. The key, of course, is constructing the proper transformation formula in Step 1.

Creating a Drop-Down List in a Cell

Most Excel users probably assume that some advanced feature (such as a VBA macro) is required to display a drop-down list in a cell. But it's not. You can easily display a drop-down list in a cell — no macros required.

Figure 58-1 shows an example. Cell B2, when selected, displays a down arrow. Click the arrow, and you get a list of items (in this case, month names). Click an item, and it appears in the cell. The drop-down list can contain text, numeric values, or dates. Your formulas, of course, can refer to cells that contain a drop-down list. The formulas always use the value that's currently displayed.

◢	A	B	C	D	E	F	G
1						January	
2	Month:	March	▾			February	
3		January ▲				March	
4		February				April	
5		March ≡				May	
6		April				June	
7		May				July	
8		June				August	
9		July				September	
10		August ▾				October	
11						November	
12						December	
13							
14							

Figure 58-1: Creating a drop-down list in a cell is easy and doesn't require macros.

The trick to setting up a drop-down list is to use the data validation feature. The following steps describe how to create a drop-down list of items in a cell:

1. Enter the list of items in a range.

   In this example, the month names are in the range F1:F12.

2. Select the cell that will contain the drop-down list (cell B2, in this example).

3. Choose Data➜Data Tools➜Data Validation.

4. In the Data Validation dialog box, click the Settings tab.

5. In the Allow drop-down list, select List.

6. In the Source box, specify the range that contains the items.

   In this example, the range is E1:E12.

7. Make sure that the In-Cell Dropdown option is checked (see Figure 58-2) and click OK.

If your list is short, you can avoid Step 1. Rather, just type your list items (separated by commas) in the Source box in the Data Validation dialog box.

If you plan to share your workbook with others who use Excel 2007 or earlier, make sure that the list is on the same sheet as the drop-down list. Alternatively, you can put the list on any sheet, as long as it's a named range. For example, you can choose Formulas➜Defined Names➜Define Name to define the name *MonthNames* for E1:E12. Then, in the Data Validation dialog box, enter **=MonthNames** in the Source box.

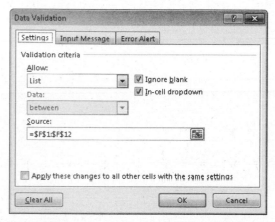

Figure 58-2: Using the Data Validation dialog box to create a drop-down list.

Comparing Two Ranges by Using Conditional Formatting

A common task is comparing two lists of items to identify differences between the two lists. Doing it manually is far too tedious and error-prone, but Excel can make it easy. This tip describes a method that uses conditional formatting.

Figure 59-1 shows an example of two multicolumn lists of names. Applying conditional formatting can make the differences in the lists become immediately apparent. These list examples contain text, but this technique also works with numeric data.

	A	B	C
1	**Old List**		**New List**
2	Jamaal O. Davis		Beatrice Jones
3	Marcy Brown		Beverlee Lewis
4	Warren Lee		Carola Rogers
5	Dana E. Turner		Cody Hendrix
6	Steven Y. Webb		Daniel A. Williams
7	Nichole Anderson		Eunice Coleman
8	John Aguilar		Jamaal O. Davis
9	John Stevens		Jessica Ford
10	Tracy S. Brooks		John Aguilar
11	Jessica Ford		John Coleman
12	Daniel A. Williams		John Stevens
13	Beverlee Lewis		Linda Logan
14	Cody Hendrix		Marvin Williams
15	Marvin Williams		Nichole Anderson
16	John Coleman		Stephen Harris
17	Etta Andrews		Stephen M. Rich
18	Stephen Harris		Steven Y. Webb
19	Tina Golden		Tracy S. Brooks
20	Beatrice Jones		Warren Lee
21			

Figure 59-1: You can use conditional formatting to highlight the differences in these two ranges.

The first list is in A2:A20, and this range is named *OldList*. The second list is in C2:C20, and the range is named *NewList*. The ranges were named by using the Formulas➜Defined Names➜Define Name command. Naming the ranges isn't necessary, but it makes them easier to work with.

Start by adding conditional formatting to the old list:

1. Select the cells in the *OldList* range.

2. Choose Home➜Conditional Formatting➜New Rule to display the New Formatting Rule dialog box.

3. In the New Formatting Rule dialog box, click the option labeled Use a Formula to Determine Which Cells to Format.

4. Enter this formula in the dialog box (see Figure 59-2):

```
=COUNTIF(NewList,A2)=0
```

When using this technique with your own data, substitute the actual range address (or name) for NewList, and substitute the address of the top left selected cell for A2.

5. Click the Format button and specify the formatting to apply when the condition is true.

A different fill color is a good choice.

6. Click OK.

Figure 59-2: Applying conditional formatting.

The cells in the *NewList* range use a similar conditional formatting formula.

1. Select the cells in the *NewList* range.
2. Choose Home→Conditional Formatting→New Rule to display the New Formatting Rule dialog box.
3. In the New Formatting Rule dialog box, click the option labeled Use a Formula to Determine Which Cells to Format.
4. Enter this formula in the dialog box:

```
=COUNTIF(OldList,C2)=0
```

When using this technique with your own data, substitute the actual range address (or name) for OldList, and substitute the address of the top left selected cell for C2.

5. Click the Format button and specify the formatting to apply when the condition is true (a different fill color).

6. Click OK.

Figure 59-3 shows the result. Names that are in the old list but not in the new list are highlighted. In addition, names in the new list that aren't in the old list are highlighted in a different color. Names that aren't highlighted appear in both lists.

	A	B	C	D
1	**Old List**		**New List**	
2	Jamaal O. Davis		Beatrice Jones	
3	Marcy Brown		Beverlee Lewis	
4	Warren Lee		Carola Rogers	
5	Dana E. Turner		Cody Hendrix	
6	Steven Y. Webb		Daniel A. Williams	
7	Nichole Anderson		Eunice Coleman	
8	John Aguilar		Jamaal O. Davis	
9	John Stevens		Jessica Ford	
10	Tracy S. Brooks		John Aguilar	
11	Jessica Ford		John Coleman	
12	Daniel A. Williams		John Stevens	
13	Beverlee Lewis		Linda Logan	
14	Cody Hendrix		Marvin Williams	
15	Marvin Williams		Nichole Anderson	
16	John Coleman		Stephen Harris	
17	Etta Andrews		Stephen M. Rich	
18	Stephen Harris		Steven Y. Webb	
19	Tina Golden		Tracy S. Brooks	
20	Beatrice Jones		Warren Lee	
21				

Figure 59-3: Conditional formatting causes differences in the two lists to be highlighted.

Both of these conditional-formatting formulas use the COUNTIF function. This function counts the number of times a particular value appears in a range. If the formula returns 0, it means that the item doesn't appear in the range. Therefore, the conditional formatting kicks in and the cell's background color is changed.

Finding Duplicates by Using Conditional Formatting

You might find it helpful to identify duplicate values within a range of cells. For example, take a look at Figure 60-1. Are any of the values duplicated?

One approach to identifying duplicate values is to use conditional formatting. After applying a conditional formatting rule, you can quickly spot duplicated cell values.

	A	B	C	D	E	F	G	H
1	1518	135	131	1244	348	1557	893	
2	430	558	154	1980	1254	874	313	
3	1845	1426	1830	1099	113	292	1780	
4	1503	1964	1929	577	1837	199	1825	
5	1988	1172	1130	1332	1113	1471	432	
6	284	180	1104	653	389	501	834	
7	1147	1042	1445	616	249	975	1452	
8	1657	852	1491	1539	1936	908	523	
9	1248	873	1541	1263	921	1722	128	
10	101	1697	717	1891	1180	434	602	
11	1697	1542	1793	521	1428	187	1708	
12	787	1669	1748	105	1422	167	594	
13	1083	229	1553	829	1304	1207	1610	
14	1472	1828	320	409	1865	1518	209	
15	698	629	489	1103	1704	1336	1016	
16	1754	1385	340	1439	509	1323	795	
17	944	1838	277	140	286	1927	1978	
18	1830	853	1830	876	1783	1135	132	
19	155	844	1740	1969	498	933	477	
20	1362	800	790	1218	723	612	1829	
21	413	230	175	215	824	746	1170	
22	1926	265	1590	111	677	1856	212	
23								

Figure 60-1: You can use conditional formatting to quickly identify duplicate values in a range.

Here's how to set up the conditional formatting:

1. Select the cells in the range (in this example, A1:G22).

2. Choose Home→Conditional Formatting→New Rule to display the Conditional Formatting dialog box.

3. In the Conditional Formatting dialog box, select the option labeled Use a Formula to Determine Which Cells to Format.

4. For this example, enter this formula (change the range references to correspond to your own data):

```
=COUNTIF($A$1:$G$22,A1)>1
```

5. Click the Format button and specify the formatting to apply when the condition is true. Changing the fill color is a good choice.

6. Click OK.

Figure 60-2 shows the result. The seven highlighted cells are the duplicated values in the range.

	A	B	C	D	E	F	G	H
1	1518	135	131	1244	348	1557	893	
2	430	558	154	1980	1254	874	313	
3	1845	1426	1830	1099	113	292	1780	
4	1503	1964	1929	577	1837	199	1825	
5	1988	1172	1130	1332	1113	1471	432	
6	284	180	1104	653	389	501	834	
7	1147	1042	1445	616	249	975	1452	
8	1657	852	1491	1539	1936	908	523	
9	1248	873	1541	1263	921	1722	128	
10	101	1697	717	1891	1180	434	602	
11	1697	1542	1793	521	1428	187	1708	
12	787	1669	1748	105	1422	167	594	
13	1083	229	1553	829	1304	1207	1610	
14	1472	1828	320	409	1865	1518	209	
15	698	629	489	1103	1704	1336	1016	
16	1754	1385	340	1439	509	1323	795	
17	944	1838	277	148	286	1927	1978	
18	1830	853	1830	876	1783	1135	132	
19	155	844	1740	1969	498	933	477	
20	1362	888	790	1218	723	612	1829	
21	413	230	175	215	824	746	1170	
22	1926	265	1590	111	677	1856	212	
23								

Figure 60-2: Conditional formatting causes the duplicated cells to be highlighted.

You can extend this technique to identify entire rows within a list that are identical. The trick is to add a new column and use a formula that concatenates the data in each row. For example, if your list is in A2:G500, enter this formula in cell H2:

```
=A2&B2&C2&D2&E2&F2&G2
```

Copy the formula down the column and then apply the conditional formatting to the formulas in column H. In this case, the conditional formatting formula is

```
=COUNTIF($H$2:$H$500,H2)>1
```

Highlighted cells in column H indicate duplicated rows.

Note You can use Data→Data Tools→Remove Duplicates to remove duplicate rows. That command, however, doesn't identify the duplicates before deleting them.

Working with Credit Card Numbers

If you've ever tried to enter a 16-digit credit card number into a cell, you may have discovered that Excel always changes the last digit to a zero. Even worse, maybe you *didn't* discover the changed credit card number until it was too late.

Why does Excel change your numbers? The reason is that Excel can handle only 15 digits of numerical accuracy.

Entering credit card numbers manually

If you need to store credit card numbers in a worksheet, you have three options:

➤ **Precede the credit card number with an apostrophe.** Excel then interprets the data as a text string rather than as a number.

➤ **Preformat the cell or range by using the Text number format.** Select the range, choose Home➜Number and then select Text from the Number Format drop-down control.

➤ **Enter the card number with dashes or spaces.** Embedding a dash character (or any other non-numeric character) forces Excel to interpret the entry as text.

This tip, of course, also applies to other long numbers (such as part numbers) that aren't used in numeric calculations.

Importing credit card numbers

If you're importing credit card numbers from a CSV text file, Excel will import the credit card numbers as values — and erroneously change the last digit to zero. To avoid this, don't use File➜Open to import the text. Rather, use Data➜Connections➜Get External Data➜From Text. When you use this command, Excel displays the TextImport Wizard. In Step 3 of the wizard, make sure that you specify Text as the column data format for the credit card numbers. See Figure 61-1.

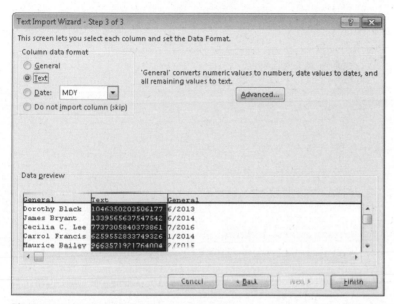

Figure 61-1: Using the TextImport Wizard to ensure that credit card numbers are imported as text.

Identifying Excess Spaces

A common type of spreadsheet error involves something that you can't even see: a space character. Consider the example shown in Figure 62-1. Cell B2 contains a formula that looks up the color name in cell B1 and returns the corresponding code from a table. The formula is

```
=VLOOKUP(B1,D2:E9,2,FALSE)
```

	A	B	C	D	E	F
1	Enter a color name:	Green		Color	Code	
2	The code:	65280		Black	0	
3				Blue	16711680	
4				Cyan	16776960	
5				Green	65280	
6				Magenta	16711935	
7				Red	255	
8				White	16777215	
9				Yellow	65535	
10						

Figure 62-1: A simple lookup formula returns the code for a color entered in cell B1.

In Figure 62-2, the formula in cell B2 returns an error — indicating that *Red* wasn't found in the table. Hundreds of thousands of Excel users have spent far too much time trying to figure out why this sort of thing doesn't work. In this case, the answer is simple: Cell D7 doesn't contain the word *Red*. Rather, it contains the word *Red* followed by a space. To Excel, these text strings are completely different.

	A	B	C	D	E	F
1	Enter a color name:	Red		Color	Code	
2	The code:	#N/A		Black	0	
3				Blue	16711680	
4				Cyan	16776960	
5				Green	65280	
6				Magenta	16711935	
7				Red	255	
8				White	16777215	
9				Yellow	65535	
10						

Figure 62-2: The lookup formula can't find the word *Red* in the table.

If your worksheet contains thousands of text entries — and you need to perform comparisons using that text — you may want to identify the cells that contain excess spaces and then fix those cells. The term *excess spaces* means a text entry that contains any of the following:

➤ One or more leading spaces

➤ One or more trailing spaces

➤ Two or more consecutive spaces within the text

One way to identify this type of cell is to use conditional formatting. To set up conditional formatting to identify excess spaces, follow these steps:

1. Select all text cells to which you want to apply conditional formatting.

2. Choose Home➜Conditional Formatting➜New Rule to display the New Formatting Rule dialog box.

3. In the top part of the dialog box, select the option labeled Use a Formula to Determine Which Cells to Format.

4. Enter a formula like the following in the bottom part of the dialog box (see Figure 62-3):

    ```
    =A1<>TRIM(A1)
    ```

    Note: This formula assumes that cell A1 is the upper-left cell in the selection. If that's not the case, substitute the address of the upper-left cell in the selection you made in Step 1.

5. Click the Format button to display the Format Cells dialog box and select the type of formatting you want for the cells that contain excess spaces — for example, a yellow fill color.

6. Click OK to close the Format Cells dialog box, and click OK again to close the New Formatting Rule dialog box.

After you complete these steps, each cell that contains excess spaces and is within the range you selected in Step 1 is highlighted with the formatting of your choice. You can then easily spot these cells and remove the spaces.

Figure 62-3: Using conditional formatting to identify cells that contain excess spaces.

Note

Because of the way the TRIM function works, the formula in Step 4 also applies the conditional formatting to all numeric cells. A slightly more complex formula that doesn't apply the formatting to numeric cells is

```
=IF(NOT(ISNONTEXT(A1)),A1<>TRIM(A1))
```

Transposing a Range

You may have a range of data that should be transposed. Transposing a range is essentially making the rows columns, and the columns rows. Figure 63-1 shows an example. The original data is in A1:H9, and the transposed data is in A12:I19.

This tip describes two methods to transpose a range of data.

	A	B	C	D	E	F	G	H	I	J
1	Account	January	February	March	April	May	June	Average		
2	A-329	789	823	851	875	864	868	845		
3	D-024	633	653	646	681	714	701	671		
4	C-732	15	16	17	13	15	15	15		
5	L-329	331	329	412	415	419	444	392		
6	J-332	97	101	77	73	58	66	79		
7	M-772	105	119	100	108	127	98	110		
8	D-666	335	320	313	292	321	314	316		
9	Total	2,305	2,361	2,416	2,457	2,518	2,506	2,427		
10										
11										
12	Account	A-329	D-024	C-732	L-329	J-332	M-772	D-666	Total	
13	January	789	633	15	331	97	105	335	2,305	
14	February	823	653	16	329	101	119	320	2,361	
15	March	851	646	17	412	77	100	313	2,416	
16	April	875	681	13	415	73	108	292	2,457	
17	May	864	714	15	419	58	127	321	2,518	
18	June	868	701	15	444	66	98	314	2,506	
19	Average	845	671	15	392	79	110	316	2,427	
20										

Figure 63-1: Data before and after being transposed.

Using Paste Special

To transpose a range of data by copying and pasting, follow these steps:

1. Select the range to be transposed.

2. Press Ctrl+C to copy the range.

3. Select the cell that will be the upper-left cell for the transposed range.

4. Choose Home→Clipboard→Paste→Paste Special to display the Paste Special dialog box.

5. Choose the Transpose option.

6. Click OK.

Excel pastes the copied data, but reoriented.

If the original range contains formulas, the formulas will be adjusted so they continue to refer to the correct cells.

Note

If the original range is in a table (created with Insert➔Tables➔Table), this technique has a few caveats. The original selection cannot include the Total Row or columns that contain a formula. You can still paste the transposed data, but you must choose the Values option in the Paste Special dialog box. The transposed range will include the values (but not the formulas).

Using the TRANSPOSE function

In some cases, you may want the transposed range to be linked to the original range. In such a situation, changes made to the original range also appear in the transposed range. Here's how to set up a transposed range that's linked to the original source. Refer to Figure 63-2.

| A13 | ▼ | ⋮ | ✕ ✓ | fx | {=TRANSPOSE(A1:E10)} |

	A	B	C	D	E	F	G	H	I	J	K
1	Student	Test-1	Test-2	Test-3	Test-4						
2	Allen	84	83	78	81						
3	Bob	83	96	76	87						
4	Carl	78	95	82	88						
5	Dana	95	80	78	73						
6	Elenore	92	91	90	97						
7	Frank	88	77	78	75						
8	George	94	79	76	95						
9	Homer	75	78	80	97						
10	Isaac	82	76	88	85						
11											
12											
13	Student	Allen	Bob	Carl	Dana	Elenore	Frank	George	Homer	Isaac	
14	Test-1	84	83	78	95	92	88	94	75	82	
15	Test-2	83	96	95	80	91	77	79	78	76	
16	Test-3	78	76	82	78	90	78	76	80	88	
17	Test-4	81	87	88	73	97	75	95	97	85	
18											
19											

Figure 63-2: A13:J17 contains a multicell array formula, linked to the source range.

1. Make a note of the number of rows and columns in the source range.

   In this example, the source range (A1:E10) has 10 rows and 5 columns.

2. Select a range of blank cells that has the same number of rows as source range columns, and the same number of column as source range rows.

   In this example, the selection should be 5 rows and 10 columns. For example, you can put the transposed range in A13:J17.

3. Type a formula that uses the TRANSPOSE function, with the source range address as its argument.

   In this example, the formula is

   ```
   =TRANSPOSE(A1:E10)
   ```

4. Press Ctrl+Shift+Enter (not just Enter) to create a multicell array formula in all of the selected cells.

Any changes made in the source range also appear in the transposed range.

Using Flash Fill to Extract Data

When you import data, it's often necessary to clean up some of the text. For example, names may appear in uppercase that they should be in proper case. One approach is to use formulas to modify the text (see Tip 57). Another approach uses a feature introduced in Excel 2013: Flash Fill.

Flash Fill uses pattern recognition to extract data (and also concatenate data) from adjoining columns. Just enter a few examples in a column that's adjacent to the data, and then choose Data→Data Tools→Flash Fill (or press Ctrl+E). Excel analyzes the examples you typed and attempts to fill in the remaining cells. If Excel didn't recognize the pattern you had in mind, press Ctrl+Z, add another example or two, and try again.

Changing the case of text

Figure 64-1 shows a list of U.S. presidents in column A. Column B shows the result of using Flash Fill to convert the text to proper case.

Start by providing a few examples: Type **George Washington** in cell B1 and **John Adams** in cell B2. You'll notice that Excel kicks in as soon as you start typing John Adams. It recognizes your pattern (which is "make all text proper case") and fills the column with the transformed text (in a light gray color). You can press Enter to keep Excel's suggestion, or continue typing more examples. At any time, you can press Ctrl+E to have Excel fill the column.

	A	B
1	GEORGE WASHINGTON	George Washington
2	JOHN ADAMS	John Adams
3	THOMAS JEFFERSON	Thomas Jefferson
4	JAMES MADISON	James Madison
5	JAMES MONROE	James Monroe
6	JOHN QUINCY ADAMS	John Quincy Adams
7	ANDREW JACKSON	Andrew Jackson
8	MARTIN VAN BUREN	Martin Van Buren
9	WILLIAM HENRY HARRISON	William Henry Harrison
10	JOHN TYLER	John Tyler
11	JAMES KNOX POLK	James Knox Polk
12	ZACHARY TAYLOR	Zachary Taylor
13	MILLARD FILLMORE	Millard Fillmore
14	FRANKLIN PIERCE	Franklin Pierce
15	JAMES BUCHANAN	James Buchanan
16	ABRAHAM LINCOLN	Abraham Lincoln
17	ANDREW JOHNSON	Andrew Johnson

Figure 64-1: Flash Fill quickly converted the names in Column A to proper case.

Extracting last names

In this example, we want to extract the last name of each president, so the list can be sorted by last name. This is a simple job for Flash Fill. It takes only two examples, and the pattern is recognized.

Figure 64-2 shows the worksheet after Excel extracted the last names. Now, you can sort the list by column C, so the name will be in alphabetical order, by last name.

	B	C
1	George Washington	Washington
2	John Adams	Adams
3	Thomas Jefferson	Jefferson
4	James Madison	Madison
5	James Monroe	Monroe
6	John Quincy Adams	Adams
7	Andrew Jackson	Jackson
8	Martin Van Buren	Buren
9	William Henry Harrison	Harrison
10	John Tyler	Tyler
11	James Knox Polk	Polk
12	Zachary Taylor	Taylor
13	Millard Fillmore	Fillmore
14	Franklin Pierce	Pierce
15	James Buchanan	Buchanan

Figure 64-2: Flash Fill extracted the last names.

Extracting first names

You'll find that Flash Fill is equally adept at extracting first names. Figure 64-3 shows the list of presidents after using Flash Fill to extract the first names in Column D. Again, it took only two examples before Excel identified the pattern.

	B	C	D
1	George Washington	Washington	George
2	John Adams	Adams	John
3	Thomas Jefferson	Jefferson	Thomas
4	James Madison	Madison	James
5	James Monroe	Monroe	James
6	John Quincy Adams	Adams	John
7	Andrew Jackson	Jackson	Andrew
8	Martin Van Buren	Buren	Martin
9	William Henry Harrison	Harrison	William
10	John Tyler	Tyler	John
11	James Knox Polk	Polk	James
12	Zachary Taylor	Taylor	Zachary

Figure 64-3: Flash Fill extracted the first names.

Extracting middle names

Some (but not all) of the presidents on the list have a middle name. Can Flash Fill extract the middle names?

The answer: Sort of. I provided several examples of middle names, and Flash Fill successfully extracted the other middle names. But for names without a middle name, it extracted the first name. No matter what I tried, I could not get Flash Fill to ignore names that had no middle name.

Extracting domain names from URLs

Here's another example of using Flash Fill. Say you have a list of URLs and need to extract the filename (the text that follows the last slash character).

Figure 64-4 shows a list of URLs. Flash Fill required just one example of a filename entered in column B. I pressed Ctrl+E, and Excel filled in the remaining rows. Flash fill worked equally well removing the filename from the URL, in column C.

	A	B	C
1	http://example.com/assets/images/horse.jpg	horse.jpg	http://example.com/assets/images/
2	http://spreadsheetpage.com/graphics/old/screenshot.jpg	screenshot.jpg	http://spreadsheetpage.com/graphics/old/
3	http://spreadsheetpage.com/graphics/jw.jpg	jw.jpg	http://spreadsheetpage.com/graphics/
4	http://j-walk.com/excel/examples/game.xls	game.xls	http://j-walk.com/excel/examples/
5	www.brr98.edu/index.htm	index.htm	www.brr98.edu/
6	http://pets4898.net/uploads/pets/dogs/puppies/spot332.jpg	spot332.jpg	http://pets4898.net/uploads/pets/dogs/puppies/
7	http://adsfkj9ki89.com/sjd48utt/adp/fopf/99/32/12/index.jpg	index.jpg	http://adsfkj9ki89.com/sjd48utt/adp/fopf/99/32/12/
8			

Figure 64-4: Flash Fill extracted the filenames from URLs.

Potential problems

Flash Fill is a great feature, but if you use it for important data, you should be aware of some potential problems:

> **Sometimes it just doesn't work.** Extracting middle names seems like a simple pattern, but Flash Fill was not capable of recognizing the pattern.

> **It's not always accurate.** With a small set of data, it's usually easy to check to ensure that Flash Fill worked as you intended it to work. But if you use Flash Fill on thousands of rows of data, you can't be assured that it worked perfectly unless you examine every row. Flash Fill works best with data that is very consistent.

> **It's not dynamic.** If you change any of the information that Flash Fill used, the changes are not reflected in the filled column.

> **There is no "audit trail."** If you use formulas to extract data, the formulas provide documentation so anyone can figure out how the data was extracted. Using Flash Fill, on the other hand, provides no such audit trail. There is no way to see which rules Excel used to extract the data.

Using Flash Fill to Combine Data

Tip 64 described how to extract data using the Excel 2013 Flash Fill feature. This tip looks at the other side of Flash Fill: combing data.

If you need to combine the data in two or more columns, you can write a formula that uses the concatenation operator (&). For example, this formula combines the contents of cells A1, B1, and C1:

```
=A1&B1&C1
```

For more complicated types of combinations, Flash Fill might be able to do the job and save you the trouble of creating (and debugging) a formula.

Figure 65-1 shows a worksheet with first names in column A and last names in column B. I used Flash Fill to create e-mail addresses (in Column C) for the domain example.com. The e-mail addresses consist of the first initial, an underscore, and the last name — all lowercase.

	A	B	C
1	Kenneth	Smith	k_smith@example.com
2	Lara	Hamilton	l_hamilton@example.com
3	Frances	Hawkins	f_hawkins@example.com
4	Leonard	Peterson	l_peterson@example.com
5	Beverly	Gonzalez	b_gonzalez@example.com
6	Richard	Wagner	r_wagner@example.com
7	Blanche	Davis	b_davis@example.com
8	James	Collins	j_collins@example.com
9	Mary	Garcia	m_garcia@example.com
10	Martha	Stewart	m_stewart@example.com
11	Andrew	Walker	a_walker@example.com
12	Maurice	Pena	m_pena@example.com
13	Marion	Curtis	m_curtis@example.com
14	Ryan	Torres	r_torres@example.com
15	Austin	Nelson	a_nelson@example.com
16	Steven	Pierce	s_pierce@example.com
17	Steven	Watkins	s_watkins@example.com
18	James	Burns	j_burns@example.com
19	James	Johnson	j_johnson@example.com
20	Claude	Watkins	c_watkins@example.com

Figure 65-1: Flash Fill can quickly convert these names into e-mail addresses.

It took only two examples before Flash Fill recognized the pattern and filled in the rest of the column.

Flash Fill is simpler than composing this equivalent formula:

```
=LOWER(LEFT(A1,1)&"_"&B1&"@example.com")
```

Figure 65-2 shows another example. Column A:D hold the original data, and the text in column E was filled in using Flash Fill, after providing two examples. The equivalent formula to generate the text in column E is

```
=A4&" "&B4&": "&TEXT(D4,"$0")&" due on 10/"&C4&"/2013"
```

	A	B	C	D	E
3	First	Last	Day	Amount	
4	Vicki	Wright	3	$475	Vicki Wright: $475 due on 10/3/2013
5	Michael	Adams	5	$574	Michael Adams: $574 due on 10/5/2013
6	Floyd	Mitchell	5	$93	Floyd Mitchell: $93 due on 10/5/2013
7	Amy	Kim	7	$575	Amy Kim: $575 due on 10/7/2013
8	Dennis	Young	8	$491	Dennis Young: $491 due on 10/8/2013
9	Rebekah	Wilson	11	$509	Rebekah Wilson: $509 due on 10/11/2013
10	Barbara	Flores	12	$133	Barbara Flores: $133 due on 10/12/2013
11	Carol	Jackson	14	$311	Carol Jackson: $311 due on 10/14/2013
12	Edward	Dawson	14	$554	Edward Dawson: $554 due on 10/14/2013
13	Rachelle	Wright	14	$33	Rachelle Wright: $33 due on 10/14/2013
14	John	Davis	15	$514	John Davis: $514 due on 10/15/2013
15	Lillian	Browning	17	$374	Lillian Browning: $374 due on 10/17/2013
16	Kurtis	Evans	18	$315	Kurtis Evans: $315 due on 10/18/2013
17	Janet	Adams	20	$405	Janet Adams: $405 due on 10/20/2013
18	Regina	Willis	20	$30	Regina Willis: $30 due on 10/20/2013
19	Susan	Caldwell	22	$332	Susan Caldwell: $332 due on 10/22/2013
20	Paul	Miller	23	$558	Paul Miller: $558 due on 10/23/2013
21	Stefani	Young	24	$432	Stefani Young: $432 due on 10/24/2013

Figure 65-2: Flash Fill generated the text in column E.

Inserting Stock Information

This tip describes how to insert refreshable stock data into a worksheet. For some reason, Microsoft makes this feature rather difficult to find.

Here's how to do it:

1. Make sure that you're connected to the Internet.

2. Type a stock symbol into a cell — for example, **MSFT** for Microsoft. Make sure the characters are all uppercase.

3. Right-click the cell and choose Addition Cell Actions➜Insert Refreshable Stock Price from the shortcut menu.

    The Insert Stock Price dialog box appears.

4. Specify the location for the information (on a new sheet, or starting at a particular cell).

5. Click OK.

Excel retrieves current information about the stock and inserts data that occupies 18 rows and 16 columns (see Figure 66-1).

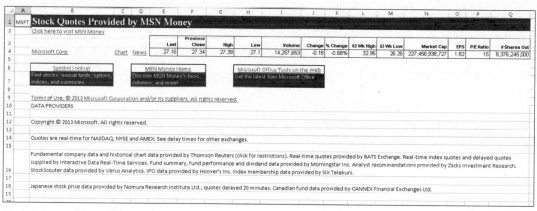

Figure 66-1: Refreshable stock information inserted into a worksheet.

You can refresh the information at any time. Select any cell in the table, right-click, and choose Refresh from the shortcut menu. If your worksheet has information for multiple stocks, you can refresh them all by choosing Data➜Connections➜Refresh All.

Hiding irrelevant rows and columns

Notice that, of the 18 rows, only one of them contains actual data. The other rows are links and disclaimers. Unfortunately, there is no direct way to retrieve the information without all of the extraneous information. But you can hide the irrelevant rows and columns — and the hidden rows and columns remain hidden when you refresh the information.

Figure 66-2 shows a worksheet that has information for four stocks. I hid the irrelevant rows and columns, for a concise display.

	A	D	E	F	G	H	I	J	K	L
3										
4		Last	Previous Close	High	Low	Volume	Change	% Change	52 Wk High	52 Wk Low
5	Google Inc	766.8	770.17	778.81	765.87	1,378,846	-3.37	-0.44%	776.6	556.52
25	Microsoft Corp	27.16	27.34	27.39	27.1	14,375,007	-0.18	-0.66%	32.95	26.26
44	Apple Inc	457.33	454.7	463.76	454.12	8,368,622	2.63	0.58%	705.07	435
63	Starbucks Corp	55.38	56.05	56.06	55.15	1,855,127	-0.67	-1.19%	62	43.04

Figure 66-2: Information for four stocks, after hiding irrelevant rows and columns.

Behind the scenes

Using the Addition Cell Actions➜Insert Refreshable Stock Price shortcut menu item is just a quick way of performing a web query and retrieving data from Microsoft's MSN Money site. You can retrieve the same information by performing a web query. Choose Data➜Get External Data➜From Web and use this URL:

```
http://moneycentral.msn.com/investor/external/excel/quotes.asp?symbol=MSFT
```

The URL retrieves information for Microsoft. You can replace MSFT with a different stock symbol. Figure 66-3 shows the New Web Query dialog box before the information is inserted into a worksheet.

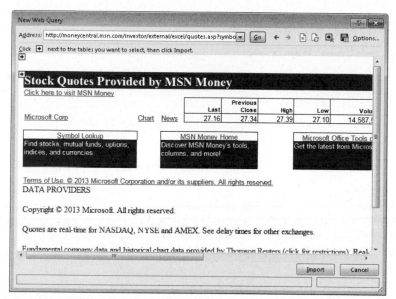

Figure 66-3: Using the New Web Query dialog box to retrieve stock information.

Cross-Ref

See Tip 67 for more information about web queries.

Getting Data from a Web Page

This tip describes three ways to capture data contained on a web page:

➤ Paste a static copy of the information.

➤ Create a refreshable link to the site.

➤ Open the page directly in Excel.

Pasting static information

One way to get data from a web page into a worksheet is to simply highlight the text in your browser, press Ctrl+C to copy it to the Clipboard, and then paste it into a worksheet. The results will vary, depending on what browser you use and how the web page is coded.

If pasting doesn't yield the results you want, choose Home→Clipboard→Paste→Paste Special and then try various paste options.

Figure 67-1 shows some currency exchange rates, pasted from a web page at msn.com. As you can see, even the hyperlinks are pasted.

	A	B	C	D
1	Currency	In US dollars	Per US Dollar	
2	Argentine Peso	0.2006	4.985	
3	Australian Dollar	1.02923	0.9716	
4	Brazilian Real	0.50841	1.9669	
5	British Pound	1.56961	0.6371	
6	Canadian Dollar	1.00166	0.99834	
7	Chinese Yuan	0.16046	6.2322	
8	Euro	1.33941	0.7466	
9	Hong Kong Dollar	0.12895	7.75473	
10	Indian Rupee	0.01879	53.23	
11	Japanese Yen	0.01072	93.29002	
12	Korean Won	0.00092	1,092.02	
13	Mexican Peso	0.07848	12.742	
14	Russian Ruble	0.0331	30.2117	
15	Swedish Krona	0.15562	6.42603	
16	Swiss Franc	1.09012	0.91733	
17	US Dollar	1	1	
18				

Figure 67-1: A table of exchange rates copied from a website and pasted to a worksheet.

Pasting refreshable information

If you need to regularly access updated data from a web page, create a web query. Figure 67-1 shows a website that contains currency exchange rates in a three-column table.

Note

The term web query is a bit misleading because this operation is not limited to the web. You can perform a web query on a local HTML file, a file stored on a network server, or a file stored on a web server on the Internet. To retrieve information from a web server, you must be connected to the Internet. After the information is retrieved, an Internet connection is not required to work with the information (unless you need to refresh the query).

These steps create a web query that allows this information to be retrieved and then refreshed at any time with a single mouse click:

1. Choose Data➜Get External Data➜From Web to display the New Web Query dialog box.

2. In the Address field, enter the URL of the website and click Go.

   For this example, the URL for the web page shown in Figure 67-2 is

   ```
   http://investing.money.msn.com/investments/exchange-rates
   ```

   Notice that the New Web Query dialog box contains a web browser (Internet Explorer). You can click links and navigate the website until you locate the data you're interested in.

   When a web page is displayed in the New Web Query dialog box, you see one or more yellow boxes with an arrow, which correspond to tables defined in the web page — plus another yellow box that will retrieve the entire page.

3. Click a yellow box, and it turns into a green check box, which indicates that the data in that table will be imported.

   Unfortunately, the table in the example is not selectable, so the only choice is to retrieve the entire page.

4. Click the Import button to display the Import Data dialog box.

5. In the Import Data dialog box, specify the location for the imported data.

   It can be a cell in an existing worksheet or a new worksheet.

6. Click OK, and Excel imports the data.

Figure 67-2: Using the New Web Query dialog box to specify the data to be imported.

Part of the results is shown in Figure 67-3. Although I was interested only in the 17-row and 3-column currency table, this web query retrieved 145 rows of mostly irrelevant information.

By default, the imported data is a web query. To refresh the information, right-click any cell in the imported range and choose Refresh from the shortcut menu.

If you don't want to create a refreshable query, specify this choice in Step 5 of the preceding step list. In the Import Data dialog box, click the Properties button and deselect the Save Query Definition check box.

Note

Excel's Web query feature works by identifying tables (specified using the HTML <TABLE> tag) in the document. Increasingly, website designers use cascading style sheets (CSS) to display tabular information. As demonstrated in this example, Excel doesn't recognize these as tables and, therefore, doesn't display a yellow arrow so you can retrieve only the table. Therefore, you may have to retrieve the entire document and then delete (or hide) everything except the table that you want.

⋀	A	B	C	D	E	F	G	H	I	J	K
102											
103	To change the currencies in the first column, choose an option from the first drop-down. To change the rates that appear in the other columns, choose an option from the										
104	**CURRENCY RATES LIST**										
105	Currencies:										
106	**Currency**	**In US dollars**	**Per US Dollar**								
107	Argentine Peso	0.2006	4.985								
108	Australian Dollar	1.0287	0.9721								
109	Brazilian Real	0.50787	1.969								
110	British Pound	1.57159	0.6363								
111	Canadian Dollar	1.00122	0.99878								
112	Chinese Yuan	0.16046	6.2322								
113	Euro	1.33851	0.7471								
114	Hong Kong Dollar	0.12895	7.7549								
115	Indian Rupee	0.01879	53.23								
116	Japanese Yen	0.01073	93.24001								
117	Korean Won	0.00092	1,092.14								
118	Mexican Peso	0.0785	12.739								
119	Russian Ruble	0.03313	30.1847								
120	Swedish Krona	0.15554	6.42911								
121	Swiss Franc	1.08993	0.91749								
122	US Dollar	1	1								
123	DATA PROVIDERS										
124											
125	Copyright © 2013 Microsoft. All rights reserved.										
126											
127	Quotes are real-time for NASDAQ, NYSE and AMEX. See delay times for other exchanges.										
128											
129	Fundamental company data and historical chart data provided by Thomson Reuters (click for restrictions). Real-time quotes provided by BATS Exchange. Real-time index										
130											
131	Japanese stock price data provided by Nomura Research Institute Ltd ; quotes delayed 20 minutes. Canadian fund data provided by CANNEX Financial Exchanges Ltd.										
132											
133	Ad ChoiceFeedback										

Figure 67-3: Information retrieved from a web query.

Opening the web page directly

Another way to get web page data into a worksheet is to open the URL directly, by using Excel's File➔Open command. Just enter the complete URL into the File Name field and click Open.

The results will vary, depending on how the web page is laid out. Most of the time, you'll get satisfactory results. In some cases, you'll retrieve quite a bit of extraneous information. Also, note that the information is not refreshable. If the data on the web page changes, you'll need to close the workbook and use the File➔Open command again.

Importing a Text File into a Worksheet Range

If you need to insert a text file into a specific range in a worksheet, you may think that your only choice is to import the text into a new workbook (by choosing Office→Open) and then to copy the data and paste it to the range where you want it to appear. However, you can do it in a more direct way.

Figure 68-1 shows a small CSV (comma separated value) file. The following instructions describe how to import this file, named monthly.csv, beginning at cell C3.

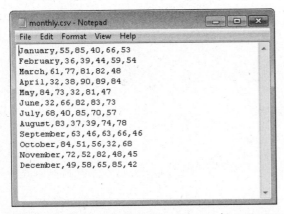

Figure 68-1: This CSV file will be imported into a range.

1. Choose Data→Get External Data→From Text to display the Import Text File dialog box.

2. Navigate to the folder that contains the text file.

3. Select the file from the list and then click the Import button to display the Text Import Wizard.

4. Use the Text Import Wizard to specify how the data will be imported.

   For a CSV file, specify Delimited, with a Comma Delimiter.

5. Click the Finish button.

   The Import Data dialog box appears.

6. Click the Properties button, and the External Data Range Properties dialog box appears.

7. Deselect the Save Query Definition check box and click OK to return to the Import Data dialog box.

8. Here, specify the location for the imported data.

   It can be a cell in an existing worksheet or a new worksheet.

9. Click OK, and Excel imports the data (see Figure 68-2).

Note

You can ignore Step 7 if the data you're importing will be changing. By saving the query definition, you can quickly update the imported data by right-clicking any cell in the range and choosing Refresh.

	A	B	C	D	E	F	G	H	I	J
1										
2										
3			January	55	85	40	66	53		
4			February	36	39	44	59	54		
5			March	61	77	81	82	48		
6			April	32	38	90	89	84		
7			May	84	73	32	81	47		
8			June	32	66	82	83	73		
9			July	68	40	85	70	57		
10			August	83	37	39	74	78		
11			September	63	46	63	66	46		
12			October	84	51	56	32	68		
13			November	72	52	82	48	45		
14			December	49	58	65	85	42		
15										

Figure 68-2: This range contains data imported directly from a CSV file.

Using the Quick Analysis Feature

One of the new features in Excel 2013 is Quick Analysis. When you select a range of data, Excel displays a Quick Analysis button in the lower-right corner of the range. Click the button to view some options, shown in Figure 69-1. You can also press Ctrl+Q on the keyboard to display the Quick Analysis options.

	A	B	C	D	E	F	G	H	I	J	K
1											
2											
3		January	55	85	40	66	53				
4		February	36	39	44	59	54				
5		March	61	77	81	82	48				
6		April	32	38	90	89	84				
7		May	84	73	32	81	47				
8		June	32	66	82	83	73				
9		July	68	40	85	70	57				
10		August	83	37	39	74	78				
11		September	63	46	63	66	46				
12		October	84	51	56	32	68				
13		November	72	52	82	48	45				
14		December	49	58	65	85	42				
15											
16											
17			FORMATTING	CHARTS	TOTALS	TABLES	SPARKLINES				
18											
19											
20			Data Bars	Color Scale	Icon Set	Greater Than	Top 10%	Clear Format			
21											
22											
23			Conditional Formatting uses rules to highlight interesting data.								
24											
25											

Figure 69-1: Quick Analysis options for the selected range.

The words along the top (Formatting, Charts, Totals, Tables, and Sparklines) are menu items. Click an item and a different set of icons appears. When you hover your mouse over an icon, Excel sometimes displays a preview of how the option will appear.

The options available depend on the type of data in the selected range. For example, if the range contains only text, the Sparklines option will not be available.

Figure 69-2 shows an example of a range of numbers in column C, with a preview of the Quick Analysis option to create running totals in column D.

⊿	A	B	C	D	E	F	G
1							
2							
3		January	55	**55**			
4		February	36	**91**			
5		March	61	**152**			
6		April	32	**184**			
7		May	84	**268**			
8		June	32	**300**			
9		July	68	**368**			
10		August	83	**451**			
11		September	63	**514**			
12		October	84	**598**			
13		November	72	**670**			
14		December	49	**719**			
15							
16							

FORMATTING　CHARTS　**TOTALS**　TABLES　SPARKLINES

Running Total　Sum　Average　Count　% Total　Running Total

Formulas automatically calculate totals for you.

Figure 69-2: A preview of Quick Analysis running totals.

Figure 69-3 shows another example. The range A2:G7 is selected, and Quick Analysis is previewing the Line Sparklines option in column H.

⊿	A	B	C	D	E	F	G	H	I	J	K
1											
2	**Fund Number**	**Jan**	**Feb**	**Mar**	**Apr**	**May**	**Jun**				
3	A-13	103.98	98.92	88.12	86.34	75.58	71.2				
4	C-09	212.74	218.7	202.18	198.56	190.12	181.74				
5	K-88	75.74	73.68	69.86	60.34	64.92	59.46				
6	W-91	91.78	95.44	98.1	99.46	98.68	105.86				
7	M-03	324.48	309.14	313.1	287.82	276.24	260.9				

FORMATTING　CHARTS　TOTALS　TABLES　**SPARKLINES**

Line　Column　Win/Loss

Sparklines are mini charts placed in single cells.

Figure 69-3: A preview of Quick Analysis Sparklines.

Note　The Quick Analysis options don't enable you to do anything that you can't do using Excel's normal commands. But sometimes it can you save a bit of time. If you find the Quick Analysis button annoying, turn if off in the General tab of the Excel Options dialog box. Deselect the check box labeled Show Quick Analysis Options on Selection.

Filling the Gaps in a Report

When you import data, you can sometimes end up with a worksheet that looks something like the one shown in Figure 70-1. This type of report formatting is common. As you can see, an entry in column A applies to several rows of data. If you sort this type of list, the missing data messes things up, and you can no longer tell who sold what when.

	A	B	C	D	E
1					
2	**Sales Rep**	**Month**	**Units Sold**	**Amount**	
3	Jane	Jan	182	$15,101	
4		Feb	3350	$34,230	
5		Mar	114	$9,033	
6	George	Jan	135	$8,054	
7		Feb	401	$9,322	
8		Mar	357	$32,143	
9	Beth	Jan	509	$29,239	
10		Feb	414	$38,993	
11		Mar	53	$309	
12	Dan	Jan	323	$9,092	
13		Feb	283	$12,332	
14		Mar	401	$32,933	
15					
16					

Figure 70-1: This report contains gaps in the Sales Rep column.

If your list is small, you can enter the missing cell values manually or by using a series of Home→Editing→Fill→Down commands (or its Ctrl+D shortcut). But if you have a large list that's in this format, you need a better way of filling in those cell values. Here's how:

1. Select the range that has the gaps (A3:A14, in this example).

2. Choose Home→Editing→Find & Select→Go To Special.

   The Go To Special dialog box appears.

3. Select the Blanks option and click OK.

   This action selects the blank cells in the original selection.

4. On the Formula bar, type an equal sign (=) followed by the address of the first cell with an entry in the column (**=A3,** in this example) and press Ctrl+Enter.

5. Reselect the original range and press Ctrl+C to copy the selection.

6. Choose Home→Clipboard→Paste→Paste Values to convert the formulas to values.

After you complete these steps, the gaps are filled in with the correct information, and your worksheet looks similar to the one shown in Figure 70-2. Now it's a normal list, and you can do whatever you like with it — including sorting.

	A	B	C	D	E
1					
2	**Sales Rep**	**Month**	**Units Sold**	**Amount**	
3	Jane	Jan	182	$15,101	
4	Jane	Feb	3350	$34,230	
5	Jane	Mar	114	$9,033	
6	George	Jan	135	$8,054	
7	George	Feb	401	$9,322	
8	George	Mar	357	$32,143	
9	Beth	Jan	509	$29,239	
10	Beth	Feb	414	$38,993	
11	Beth	Mar	53	$309	
12	Dan	Jan	323	$9,092	
13	Dan	Feb	283	$12,332	
14	Dan	Mar	401	$32,933	
15					

Figure 70-2: The gaps are gone, and this list can now be sorted.

Performing Inexact Searches

If you have a large worksheet with lots of data, locating what you're looking for can be difficult. The Excel Find and Replace dialog box is a useful tool for locating information, and it has a few features that many users overlook.

Access the Find and Replace dialog box by choosing Home→Editing→Find & Select→Find (or by pressing Ctrl+F). If you're replacing information, you can use Home→Editing→Find & Select→Replace (or Ctrl+H). The only difference is which of the two tabs is displayed in the dialog box. Figure 71-1 shows the Find and Replace dialog box after clicking the Options button, which expands the dialog box to show additional options.

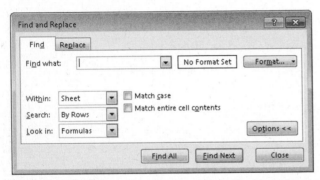

Figure 71-1: The Find and Replace dialog box with the Find tab selected.

In many cases, you want to locate "approximate" text. For example, you may be trying to find data for a customer named Stephen R. Rosencrantz. You can, of course, search for the exact text: *Stephen R. Rosencrantz*. However, there's a reasonably good chance that the search will fail. The name may have been entered differently, as Steve Rosencrantz or S.R. Rosencrantz, for example. It may have even been misspelled as Rosentcrantz.

The most efficient search for this name is to use a wildcard character and search for st*rosen* and then click the Find All button. In addition to reducing the amount of text that you enter, this search is practically guaranteed to locate the customer, if the record is in your worksheet. The search may also find some records that you aren't looking for, but that's better than not finding anything.

The Find and Replace dialog box supports two wildcard characters:

➤ ? matches any single character.

➤ * matches any number of characters.

Wildcard characters also work with values. For example, searching for 3* locates all cells that contain an entry that begins with 3. Searching for 1?9 locates all three-digit entries that begin with 1 and end with 9.

Note

To search for a question mark or an asterisk, precede the character with a tilde character (~). For example, the following search string finds the text *NONE*:

```
~*NONE~*
```

If you need to search for the tilde character, use two tildes.

If your searches don't seem to be working correctly, double-check these three options (which sometimes have a way of changing on their own):

➤ **Match Case:** If this check box is selected, the case of the text must match exactly. For example, searching for smith does not locate Smith.

➤ **Match Entire Cell Contents:** If this check box is selected, a match occurs if the cell contains only the search string (and nothing else). For example, searching for Excel doesn't locate a cell that contains Microsoft Excel.

➤ **Look In:** This drop-down list has three options: Values, Formulas, and Comments. If, for example, Values is selected, searching for 900 doesn't find a cell that contains 900 if that value is generated by a formula.

Remember that searching operates on the selected range of cells. If you want to search the entire worksheet, select only one cell before you begin your search.

Also, remember that searches do not include numeric formatting. For example, if you have a value that uses currency formatting so that it appears as $54.00, searching for $5* doesn't locate that value.

Working with dates can be a bit tricky because Excel offers many ways to format dates. If you search for a date by using the default date format, Excel locates the dates even if they're formatted differently. For example, if your system uses the m/d/y date format, the search string 10/*/2013 finds all dates in October 2013, regardless of how the dates are formatted.

You can also use an empty Replace With field. For example, to quickly delete all asterisks from your worksheet, enter ~* in the Find What field and leave the Replace With field blank. When you click the Replace All button, Excel finds all the asterisks and replaces them with nothing.

Proofing Your Data with Audio

Excel 2002 introduced a handy feature: text-to-speech. In other words, Excel is capable of speaking to you. You can have this feature read back a specific range of cells, or you can set it up so that it reads the data as you enter it.

For some reason, this feature appears to be missing in action, beginning with Excel 2007. You can search the Ribbon all day and not find a trace of the text-to-speech feature. But the feature is still available — you just need to spend a few minutes to make it accessible.

Adding speech commands to the Ribbon

Following are instructions to add these commands to a new group in the Review tab of the Ribbon:

1. Right-click the Ribbon and then choose Customize the Ribbon from the shortcut menu.

   The Customize Ribbon tab of the Excel Options dialog box appears.

2. In the list box on the right, select Review and click New Group.

3. Click Rename and overwrite the default name with a more descriptive name, such as Text To Speech.

4. Click the drop-down list on the left and choose Commands Not in the Ribbon.

5. Scroll down the list, and you find five items that begin with the word *Speak;* select each one and then click Add.

   They're added to the newly created group (see Figure 72-1).

6. Click OK to close the Excel Options dialog box.

After you perform these steps, the Review tab displays a new group with five new icons (see Figure 72-2).

Using the speech commands

To read a range of cells, select the range first and then click the Speak Cells button. You can also specify the orientation (By Rows or By Columns). To read the data as it's entered, click the Speak On Enter button.

Some people (myself included) find the voice in this "love it or hate it" feature much too annoying to use for any extended period. And, if you enter the data at a relatively rapid clip, the voice simply cannot keep up with you.

You have a small bit of control over the voice used in the Excel Text To Speech feature. To adjust the voice, open the Windows Control Panel and display the Text to Speech tab of the Speech Properties dialog box. You can adjust the speed and select a different voice (if other voices are installed). Click the Preview Voice button to help make your choices.

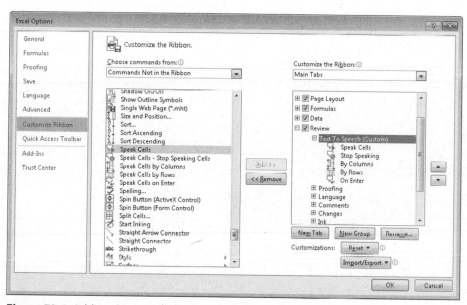

Figure 72-1: Adding the speech commands to the Ribbon.

Figure 72-2: Speech commands added to the Ribbon.

Getting Data from a PDF File

A PDF file is a document format that displays text or graphics in a way that's independent of the hardware and operating system used to create the document. PDF files are very common, and just about everyone has software that can read PDF files.

Excel can export a worksheet (or workbook) as a PDF file, but it cannot open PDF files. This tip describes two ways to get data from a PDF file into an Excel worksheet.

Using copy and paste

Figure 73-1 shows a PDF file displayed in Adobe Reader. I selected the table of data and pressed Ctrl+C to copy it to the Clipboard. Then I activated Excel and pressed Ctrl+V to copy the Clipboard contents. The result is shown in Figure 73-2.

county data.pdf - Adobe Reader

File Edit View Document Tools Window Help

Population Growth by State (1990 - 2000)

	Census 1990 Population	Census 2000 Population	Pop Change	Pct Pop Change	Pop Per Sq Mile
Region I	**13,206,943**	**13,922,517**	**715,574**	**5.4%**	**222**
Connecticut	3,287,116	3,405,565	118,449	3.6%	703
Maine	1,227,928	1,274,923	46,995	3.8%	41
Massachusetts	6,016,425	6,349,097	332,672	5.5%	810
New Hampshire	1,109,252	1,235,786	126,534	11.4%	138
Rhode Island	1,003,464	1,048,319	44,855	4.5%	1,003
Vermont	562,758	608,827	46,069	8.2%	66
Region II	**25,720,643**	**27,390,807**	**1,670,164**	**6.5%**	**501**
New Jersey	7,730,188	8,414,350	684,162	8.9%	1,134
New York	17,990,455	18,976,457	986,002	5.5%	402
Region III	**25,917,014**	**27,828,549**	**1,911,535**	**7.4%**	**231**
Delaware	666,168	783,600	117,432	17.6%	401
District of Columbia	606,900	572,059	(34,841)	-5.7%	9,316
Maryland	4,781,468	5,296,486	515,018	10.8%	542
Pennsylvania	11,881,643	12,281,054	399,411	3.4%	274
Virginia	6,187,358	7,087,006	899,648	14.5%	179
West Virginia	1,793,477	1,808,344	14,867	0.8%	75
Region IV	**46,643,644**	**55,506,328**	**8,862,684**	**19.0%**	**150**
Alabama	4,040,587	4,447,100	406,513	10.1%	88
Florida	14,873,804	18,235,740	3,361,936	22.6%	326
Georgia	6,478,216	8,186,453	1,708,237	26.4%	141
Kentucky	3,685,296	4,041,769	356,473	9.7%	102
Mississippi	2,573,216	2,844,658	271,442	10.5%	61
North Carolina	6,628,637	8,049,313	1,420,676	21.4%	165
South Carolina	3,486,703	4,012,012	525,309	15.1%	133
Tennessee	4,877,185	5,689,283	812,098	16.7%	138
Region V	**46,384,041**	**50,074,516**	**3,690,475**	**8.0%**	**155**
Illinois	11,430,602	12,419,293	988,691	8.6%	223
Indiana	5,544,159	6,080,485	536,326	9.7%	170

Figure 73-1: Data in a PDF file that needs to be transferred to a worksheet.

	A	B	C	D
1	Census 1990 Population			
2	Census 2000 Population			
3	Pop Change			
4	Pct Pop Change			
5	Pop Per Sq Mile			
6	Region I			
7	13,206,943			
8	13,922,517			
9	715,574			
10	5.40%			
11	222			
12	Connecticut			
13	3,287,116			
14	3,405,565			
15	118,449			
16	3.60%			
17	703			
18	Maine			
19	1,227,928			
20	1,274,923			
21	46,995			
22	3.80%			

Figure 73-2: Using copy and paste doesn't work very well.

The data is copied, but it's all in a single column. I could spend some time and rearrange the data, but there's a more efficient way to transfer the PDF file data to Excel.

Note When coping from a PDF file and pasting to a worksheet, the actual results will vary, depending on the layout of the PDF file. In some cases, the pasted text is usable. But in most cases, it's not.

Using Word 2013 as an intermediary

Excel can't open PDF files, but Word 2013 can. Figure 73-3 shows a Word document after importing the PDF file. The information can be copied and pasted to an Excel worksheet — and the result will require minimal reformatting (see Figure 73-4).

After making a few minor edits, the table looks perfect.

Population Growth by State (1990 - 2000)

	Census 1990	Census 2000	Pct Pop Pop Change	Pop Per Sq Population Change Mile	Population
Region I	13,206,943	13,922,517	715,574	5.4%	222
Connecticut	3,287,116	3,405,565	118,449	3.6%	703
Maine	1,227,928	1,274,923	46,995	3.8%	41
Massachusetts	6,016,425	6,349,097	332,672	5.5%	810
New Hampshire	1,109,252	1,235,786	126,534	11.4%	138
Rhode Island	1,003,464	1,048,319	44,855	4.5%	1,003
Vermont	562,758	608,827	46,069	8.2%	66
Region II	25,720,643	27,390,807	1,670,164	6.5%	501
New Jersey	7,730,188	8,414,350	684,162	8.9%	1,134
New York	17,990,455	18,976,457	986,002	5.5%	402
Region III	25,917,014	27,828,549	1,911,535	7.4%	231
Delaware	666,168	783,600	117,432	17.6%	401
District of Columbia	606,900	572,059	(34,841)	-5.7%	9,316
Maryland	4,781,468	5,296,486	515,018	10.8%	542
Pennsylvania	11,881,643	12,281,054	399,411	3.4%	274
Virginia	6,187,358	7,087,006	899,648	14.5%	179

Figure 73-3: A PDF file, imported into World 2013.

Population Growth by State (1990 - 2000)

	Census 1990	Census 2000	Pct Pop Pop Per Sq Population Population Pop Change Change Mile			
	A	B	C	D	E	F	G
Region I	13,206,943	13,922,517	715,574	5.40%	222	
Connecticut	3,287,116	3,405,565	118,449	3.60%	703	
Maine	1,227,928	1,274,923	46,995	3.80%	41	
Massachusetts	6,016,425	6,349,097	332,672	5.50%	810	
New Hampshire	1,109,252	1,235,786	126,534	11.40%	138	
Rhode Island	1,003,464	1,048,319	44,855	4.50%	1,003	
Vermont	562,758	608,827	46,069	8.20%	66	
Region II	25,720,643	27,390,807	1,670,164	6.50%	501	
New Jersey	7,730,188	8,414,350	684,162	8.90%	1,134	
New York	17,990,455	18,976,457	986,002	5.50%	402	
Region III	25,917,014	27,828,549	1,911,535	7.40%	231	
Delaware	666,168	783,600	117,432	17.60%	401	
District of Columbia	606,900	572,059	-34,841	-5.70%	9,316	
Maryland	4,781,468	5,296,486	515,018	10.80%	542	
Pennsylvania	11,881,643	12,281,054	399,411	3.40%	274	
Virginia	6,187,358	7,087,006	899,648	14.50%	179	

Figure 73-4: A Word 2013 document pasted into an Excel worksheet.

Note The ability to open PDF files is new to Word 2013, so this method won't work with other previous versions of Word.

PART V

Tables and Pivot Tables

This part contains tips that deal with two of Excel's most useful features: tables and pivot tables. If you work with large amounts of structured data, you owe it to yourself to understand these features.

Tips and Where to Find Them

Understanding Tables

An important but often underutilized feature in Excel is tables. This tip describes when to use a table and also lists the advantages and disadvantages.

Understanding what a table is

A *table* is a rectangular range of structured data. Each row in the table corresponds to a single entity. For example, a row can contain information about a customer, a bank transaction, an employee, or a product. Each column contains a specific piece of information. For example, if each row contains information about an employee, the columns can contain data, such as name, employee number, hire date, salary, or department. Tables have a header row at the top that describes the information contained in each column.

You've probably created ranges that meet this description. The magic happens when you tell Excel to convert a range of data into an "official" table. You do so by selecting any cell within the range and then choosing Insert➜Tables➜Table.

When you explicitly identify a range as a table, Excel can respond more intelligently to the actions you perform with that range. For example, if you create a chart from a table, the chart expands automatically as you add new rows to the table. If you create a pivot table from a table, refreshing the pivot table will include any new data that you added to the table.

Figure 74-1 shows a range before it was converted to a table, and Figure 74-2 shows the range after it was converted to a table.

	A	B	C	D	E	F	G	H	I	J
1	Agent	Date Listed	Area	List Price	Bedrooms	Baths	SqFt	Type	Pool	Sold
2	Jenkins	8/22/2012	N. County	$1,200,500	5	5	4,696	Single Family	TRUE	FALSE
3	Romero	3/28/2012	N. County	$799,000	6	5	4,800	Single Family	FALSE	FALSE
4	Shasta	4/30/2012	Central	$625,000	6	4	3,950	Single Family	TRUE	FALSE
5	Shasta	5/28/2012	S. County	$574,900	5	4	4,700	Single Family	FALSE	FALSE
6	Bennet	5/2/2012	Central	$549,000	4	3	1,940	Single Family	TRUE	FALSE
7	Hamilton	2/18/2012	N. County	$425,900	5	3	2,414	Single Family	TRUE	FALSE
8	Randolph	4/17/2012	N. County	$405,000	3	3	2,444	Single Family	TRUE	TRUE
9	Shasta	3/17/2012	N. County	$398,000	4	2.5	2,620	Single Family	FALSE	FALSE
10	Randolph	8/5/2012	Central	$389,900	4	2.5	2,284	Single Family	FALSE	TRUE
11	Kelly	6/2/2012	Central	$389,500	4	2	1,971	Single Family	FALSE	FALSE
12	Shasta	8/10/2012	N. County	$389,000	4	3	3,109	Single Family	FALSE	FALSE
13	Adams	5/30/2012	N. County	$379,900	3	2.5	2,468	Condo	FALSE	FALSE
14	Adams	8/1/2012	N. County	$379,000	3	3	2,354	Condo	FALSE	TRUE
15	Robinson	3/23/2012	N. County	$379,000	4	3	3,000	Single Family	FALSE	TRUE
16	Chung	4/14/2012	Central	$375,000	4	3	2,467	Single Family	TRUE	FALSE
17	Robinson	11/18/2012	Central	$375,000	4	3	2,368	Single Family	TRUE	TRUE
18	Shasta	7/8/2012	N. County	$374,900	4	3	3,927	Single Family	FALSE	FALSE
19	Lang	4/26/2012	N. County	$369,900	3	2.5	2,030	Condo	TRUE	FALSE
20	Romero	11/21/2012	N. County	$369,900	4	3	1,988	Condo	FALSE	FALSE
21	Shasta	7/16/2012	N. County	$369,900	5	3	2,477	Single Family	FALSE	FALSE

Sheet1

Figure 74-1: A range of data that's not an official table.

	A	B	C	D	E	F	G	H	I	J
1	Agent	Date Listed	Area	List Price	Bedrooms	Baths	SqFt	Type	Pool	Sold
2	Jenkins	8/22/2012	N. County	$1,200,500	5	5	4,696	Single Family	TRUE	FALSE
3	Romero	3/28/2012	N. County	$799,000	6	5	4,800	Single Family	FALSE	FALSE
4	Shasta	4/30/2012	Central	$625,000	6	4	3,950	Single Family	TRUE	FALSE
5	Shasta	5/28/2012	S. County	$574,900	5	4	4,700	Single Family	FALSE	FALSE
6	Bennet	5/2/2012	Central	$549,000	4	3	1,940	Single Family	TRUE	FALSE
7	Hamilton	2/18/2012	N. County	$425,900	5	3	2,414	Single Family	TRUE	FALSE
8	Randolph	4/17/2012	N. County	$405,000	3	3	2,444	Single Family	TRUE	TRUE
9	Shasta	3/17/2012	N. County	$398,000	4	2.5	2,620	Single Family	FALSE	FALSE
10	Randolph	8/5/2012	Central	$389,900	4	2.5	2,284	Single Family	FALSE	TRUE
11	Kelly	6/2/2012	Central	$389,500	4	2	1,971	Single Family	FALSE	FALSE
12	Shasta	8/10/2012	N. County	$389,000	4	3	3,109	Single Family	FALSE	FALSE
13	Adams	5/30/2012	N. County	$379,900	3	2.5	2,468	Condo	FALSE	FALSE
14	Adams	8/1/2012	N. County	$379,000	3	3	2,354	Condo	FALSE	TRUE
15	Robinson	3/23/2012	N. County	$379,000	4	3	3,000	Single Family	FALSE	TRUE
16	Chung	4/14/2012	Central	$375,000	4	3	2,467	Single Family	TRUE	FALSE
17	Robinson	11/18/2012	Central	$375,000	4	3	2,368	Single Family	TRUE	TRUE
18	Shasta	7/8/2012	N. County	$374,900	4	3	3,927	Single Family	FALSE	FALSE
19	Lang	4/26/2012	N. County	$369,900	3	2.5	2,030	Condo	TRUE	FALSE
20	Romero	11/21/2012	N. County	$369,900	4	3	1,988	Condo	FALSE	FALSE
21	Shasta	7/16/2012	N. County	$369,900	5	3	2,477	Single Family	FALSE	FALSE
22	Peterson	8/25/2012	S. County	$365,000	5	3	3,938	Single Family	FALSE	FALSE
23	Shasta	3/31/2012	Central	$365,000	3	2.5	1,871	Single Family	FALSE	FALSE
24	Peterson	3/7/2012	Central	$364,900	4	2.5	2,507	Single Family	FALSE	FALSE

Sheet1

Figure 74-2: A range of data that has been designated a table.

Range versus table

What's the difference between a standard range and a range that has been converted to a table?

➤ Activating any cell in the table gives you access to a new Table Tools context tab on the Ribbon.

➤ You can quickly apply background color and text color formatting by choosing from a gallery. This type of formatting is optional.

➤ Each column header contains a filter button that, when clicked, lets you easily sort the rows or filter the data by hiding rows that don't meet your criteria.

➤ A table can have "slicers," which makes it easy for novices to quickly apply filters to a table.

➤ If you scroll down the sheet so that the header row disappears, the table headers replace the column letters in the worksheet header. In other words, you don't need to freeze the top row to keep the column labels visible.

➤ If you create a chart from data in a table, the chart automatically expands if you add new rows to the end of the table.

➤ If you create a name for a column in a table, the "refers to" range for the name adjusts as you add new rows to the table.

➤ Tables support calculated columns. A single formula entered in a cell is automatically propagated to all cells in the column (see Tip 75).

➤ Tables support structured references in formulas outside of the table. Rather than use cell references, formulas can use table names and column headers.

➤ When you move your mouse pointer to the lower-right corner of the lower-right cell, you can click and drag to extend the table's size, either horizontally (add more columns) or vertically (add more rows).

➤ Selecting rows and columns within the table is simplified.

Limitations of using a table

If a workbook contains at least one table, a few Excel features are not available:

➤ For some reason, when a workbook contains at least one table, Excel doesn't allow you to use the Custom Views feature (choose View➜Workbook Views➜Custom Views).

➤ You cannot share a workbook (using Review➜Changes➜Share) if the workbook contains a table.

➤ You can't insert automatic subtotals within a table (by choosing Data➜Outline➜Subtotal).

➤ You cannot use array formulas within a table.

Using Formulas with a Table

This tip describes some ways to use formulas with a table. The example uses a simple sales summary table with three columns: Month, Projected, and Actual, as shown in Figure 75-1. I entered the data and then converted the range to a table by using the Insert→Tables→Table command. Note that I didn't define any names, but the data area of the table is named Table1 by default.

◢	A	B	C	D	E
1					
2	**Month**	**Projected**	**Actual**	
3		January	4,000	3,747	
4		February	4,000	4,448	
5		March	4,000	3,757	
6		April	5,000	5,090	
7		May	5,000	4,521	
8		June	5,000	4,931	
9		July	6,000	5,585	
10		August	6,000	6,297	
11		September	6,000	5,742	
12		October	7,000	7,465	
13		November	7,000	6,670	
14		December	7,000	7,330	
15					
16					

Figure 75-1: A simple table with three columns.

Working with the Total row

If you want to calculate the total projected and total actual sales, you don't even need to write a formula. Just click a button to add a row of summary formulas to the table:

1. Activate any cell in the table.

2. Select the Table Tools→Design→Table Style Options→Total Row command and check the Total Row check box.

3. Activate a cell in the Total row and select a summary formula from the drop-down list (see Figure 75-2).

   For example, to calculate the sum of the Actual column, select SUM from the drop-down list in cell D15. Excel creates this formula:

   ```
   =SUBTOTAL(109,[Actual])
   ```

For the SUBTOTAL function, 109 is an enumerated argument that represents SUM. The second argument for the SUBTOTAL function is the column name, in square brackets. Using the column name within brackets is a way to create structured references within a table.

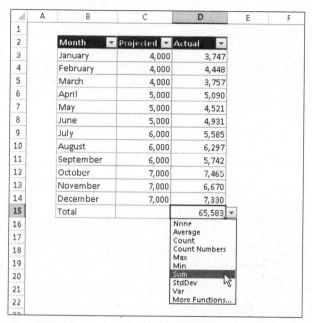

Figure 75-2: A drop-down list enables you to select a summary formula for a table column.

Note

You can toggle the Total row display on and off by choosing Table Tools➔Design➔ Table Style Options➔Total Row. If you turn it off, the summary options you selected are remembered when you turn it back on.

Using formulas within a table

In many cases, you want to use formulas within a table. For example, in the table shown in Figure 75-1, you may want a column that shows the difference between the actual and projected amounts for each month. As you can see, Excel makes this process very easy:

1. Activate cell E2 and type **Difference** for the column header.

   Excel automatically expands the table for you.

2. Move to cell E3 and type an equal sign (=) to signal the beginning of a formula.

3. Press the left-arrow key to point to the corresponding value in the Actual column.

4. Type a minus sign (–) and then press the left-arrow key twice to point to the corresponding value in the Projected column.

5. Press Enter to end the formula.

   The formula is entered into the other cells in the column, and the Formula bar displays this formula:

   ```
   =[@Actual]-[@Projected]
   ```

Figure 75-3 shows the table with the new column.

E3	▼	⋮	✕ ✓	*fx*	=[@Actual]-[@Projected]	

	A	B	C	D	E	F
1						
2		Month ▼	Projected ▼	Actual ▼	Difference ▼	
3		January	4,000	3,747	-253	
4		February	4,000	4,448	448	
5		March	4,000	3,757	-243	
6		April	5,000	5,090	90	
7		May	5,000	4,521	-479	
8		June	5,000	4,931	-69	
9		July	6,000	5,585	-415	
10		August	6,000	6,297	297	
11		September	6,000	5,742	-258	
12		October	7,000	7,465	465	
13		November	7,000	6,670	-330	
14		December	7,000	7,330	330	
15		Total		65,583		

Figure 75-3: The Difference column contains a formula.

Although the formula was entered into the first row of the table, that's not necessary. Anytime a formula is entered into an empty table column, it propagates to the other cells in the column. If you need to edit the formula, edit any formula in the column, and the change is applied to the other cells in the column.

Note

Propagating a formula to other cells in a table column is actually one of Excel's AutoCorrect options. To turn off this feature, click the icon that appears when you enter a formula and choose Stop Automatically Creating Calculated Columns.

The preceding set of steps uses the column names to create the formula. Alternatively, you can enter the formula by using standard cell references. For example, you can enter the following formula in cell E3:

```
=D3-C3
```

If you type the cell references, Excel still automatically copies the formula to other cells in the column.

Referencing data in a table

Formulas that are outside of a table can refer to data within a table by using the table name and column headers. You don't need to create names for these items. The table itself has a name (for example, Table1), and you can refer to data within the table by using column headers.

You can, of course, use standard cell references to refer to data in a table, but using table references has a distinct advantage: The names adjust automatically if the table size changes by adding or deleting rows.

Refer to the table shown earlier in Figure 75-1. This table was given the name Table1 when it was created. To calculate the sum of all data in the table, use this formula:

```
=SUM(Table1)
```

This formula always returns the sum of all the data, even if rows or columns are added or deleted. And, if you change the name of Table1, Excel automatically adjusts formulas that refer to that table. For example, if you rename Table1 as AnnualData (by using the Name Manager), the preceding formula changes to

```
=SUM(AnnualData)
```

Most of the time, you want to refer to a specific column in the table. The following formula returns the sum of the data in the Actual column (but ignores the total row):

```
=SUM(Table1[Actual])
```

Notice that the column name is enclosed in square brackets. Again, the formula adjusts automatically if you change the text in the column heading.

Even better, Excel provides some helpful assistance when you create a formula that refers to data within a table. Figure 75-4 shows the Formula AutoComplete feature helping to create a formula by showing a list of the elements in the table.

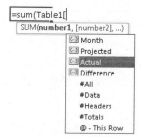

Figure 75-4: The Formula AutoComplete feature is useful when creating a formula that refers to data in a table.

Numbering Table Rows Automatically

In some situations, you may want a table to include sequential row numbers. This tip describes how to take advantage of the calculated column feature (explained in Tip 75) and create a formula that numbers table rows automatically.

Figure 76-1 shows a table (named *Table1*) with information about job applicants. The first column of the table, labeled *Num*, displays sequential numbers.

Num	First	Last	Title	Email	Date	Position	Interview
1	Oliver	Davis	Mr.	odavis@vrp99.org	3/19/2013	Supervisor	FALSE
2	Ken	Franklin	Mr.	kfranklin@prot09.com	3/12/2013	Accountant	TRUE
3	Rita	Gordon	Ms.	rita.gordon@dddx.org	3/17/2013	Clerk	FALSE
4	Patricia	Hensen	Dr.	phenson@w887t.org	3/13/2013	Sales	FALSE
5	Tim	Horwell	Mr.	thorwell@bp0klb6.com	3/16/2013	Clerk	FALSE
6	Paul	Jenson	Mr.	paulj@bbnr.edu	3/15/2013	Clerk	TRUE
7	Sam	Ralston	Mr.	sr@sr90.com	3/20/2013	Sales	TRUE
8	Jane	Smith	Ms.	jane@smith.org	3/12/2013	Supervisor	TRUE
9	Harvey	Thorenson	Mr.	ht@bmail3.com	3/12/2013	Clerk	FALSE

Formula bar: B7 = =ROW()-ROW(Table1)+1

Figure 76-1: The numbers in column B are generated with a formula.

The calculated column formula, which you can enter into any cell in the *Num* column, is

```
=ROW()-ROW(Table1)+1
```

When you enter the formula, it's automatically propagated to all other cells in the *Num* column.

The ROW function, when used without an argument, returns the row that contains the formula. When the ROW function has an argument that consists of a multirow range, it returns the first row of the range.

Note

A table's name does not include the header row of the table. So, in this example, the first row of Table1 is row 5.

The numbers are table row numbers, not numbers that correspond to a particular row of data. For example, if you sort the table, the numbers will remain consecutive — and they will no longer be associated with the same row of data.

If you filter the table, rows that don't meet the filter criteria will be hidden. In such a case, some table row numbers will not be visible. Figure 76-2 shows the table after filtering to display only the Clerk positions.

Num	First	Last	Title	Email	Date	Position	Interview
3	Rita	Gordon	Ms.	rita.gordon@dddx.org	3/17/2013	Clerk	FALSE
5	Tim	Horwell	Mr.	thorwell@bp0klb6.com	3/16/2013	Clerk	FALSE
6	Paul	Jenson	Mr.	paulj@bbnr.edu	3/15/2013	Clerk	TRUE
9	Harvey	Thorenson	Mr.	ht@bmail3.com	3/12/2013	Clerk	FALSE

Figure 76-2: When the table is filtered, the row numbers are no longer consecutive.

If you want the table row numbers to remain consecutive when the table is filtered, a different formula is required. Referring to the example in Figure 76-1, enter this formula in cell B5, and it will be propagated to the other rows:

```
=SUBTOTAL(3,C$5:C5)
```

This formula uses the SUBTOTAL function, with a first argument of 3 (which corresponds to COUNTA). The SUBTOTAL function ignores hidden rows, so only visible rows are counted. Notice that the formula refers to a different column — which is necessary to avoid a circular reference error.

Figure 76-3 shows the filtered table using the SUBTOTAL formula in column B.

Num	First	Last	Title	Email	Date	Position	Interview
1	Rita	Gordon	Ms.	rita.gordon@dddx.org	3/17/2013	Clerk	FALSE
2	Tim	Horwell	Mr.	thorwell@bp0klb6.com	3/16/2013	Clerk	FALSE
3	Paul	Jenson	Mr.	paulj@bbnr.edu	3/15/2013	Clerk	TRUE
4	Harvey	Thorenson	Mr.	ht@bmail3.com	3/12/2013	Clerk	FALSE

Figure 76-3: When the table is filtered, the row numbers remain consecutive.

Identifying Data Appropriate for a Pivot Table

A pivot table requires that your data is in the form of a rectangular database table. You can store the database in either a worksheet range (which can be a table or just a normal range) or an external database file. And although Excel can generate a pivot table from any database, not all databases benefit.

Figure 77-1 shows part of a simple database table that has five columns and 3,144 rows (one row for each county). This data is appropriate for a pivot table. For example, a pivot table can instantly calculate the total population by state or by region and display the values in a nicely formatted table.

	County	State	Region	1990 Population	2000 Population	
1	County	State	Region	1990 Population	2000 Population	
2	Abbeville	South Carolina	Region IV	23,862	26,167	
3	Acadia Parish	Louisiana	Region VI	55,882	58,861	
4	Accomack	Virginia	Region III	31,703	38,305	
5	Ada	Idaho	Region X	205,775	300,904	
6	Adair	Kentucky	Region IV	15,360	17,244	
7	Adair	Oklahoma	Region VI	18,421	21,038	
8	Adair	Missouri	Region VII	24,577	24,977	
9	Adair	Iowa	Region VII	8,409	8,243	
10	Adams	Pennsylvania	Region III	78,274	91,292	
11	Adams	Mississippi	Region IV	35,356	34,340	
12	Adams	Illinois	Region V	66,090	68,277	
13	Adams	Ohio	Region V	25,371	27,330	
14	Adams	Indiana	Region V	31,095	33,625	
15	Adams	Wisconsin	Region V	15,682	18,643	
16	Adams	Iowa	Region VII	4,866	4,482	
17	Adams	Nebraska	Region VII	29,625	31,151	
18	Adams	Colorado	Region VIII	265,038	363,857	
19	Adams	North Dakota	Region VIII	3,174	2,593	
20	Adams	Washington	Region X	13,603	16,428	
21	Adams	Idaho	Region X	3,254	3,476	
22	Addison	Vermont	Region I	32,953	35,974	
23	Aiken	South Carolina	Region IV	120,940	142,552	
24	Aitkin	Minnesota	Region V	12,425	15,301	
25	Alachua	Florida	Region IV	181,596	217,955	
26	Alamance	North Carolina	Region IV	108,213	130,800	

Figure 77-1: This data is appropriate for a pivot table.

Generally speaking, fields in a database table consist of two types of information:

➤ **Data:** Contains a value or data to be summarized. For this example, the 1990 Population and the 2000 Population fields are data fields.

➤ **Category:** Describes the data. For this example, the Country, State, and Region fields are category fields because they describe the two data fields.

The data versus category distinction can be blurry at times. Often a pivot table will display counts of items within a category. In such a case, a category is serving as a data field.

Note

A database table that's appropriate for a pivot table is said to be normalized. In other words, each row contains information that describes the data in the row.

A single database table can have any number of data fields and category fields. When you create a pivot table, you usually want to summarize one or more of the data fields. Conversely, the values in the category fields appear in the pivot table as rows, columns, or filters.

Figure 77-2 shows a pivot table created from the example. This pivot table displays the 2000 Population values, totaled by state.

	A	B	C
1			
2			
3	**Row Labels** ▼	**Sum of 2000 Population**	
4	Alabama	4,447,100	
5	Alaska	632,143	
6	Arizona	5,130,632	
7	Arkansas	2,673,400	
8	California	33,871,648	
9	Colorado	4,301,261	
10	Connecticut	3,405,565	
11	Delaware	783,600	
12	District of Columbia	572,059	
13	Florida	18,235,740	
14	Georgia	8,186,453	
15	Hawaii	1,211,537	
16	Idaho	1,293,953	
17	Illinois	12,419,293	
18	Indiana	6,080,485	
19	Iowa	2,926,324	
20	Kansas	2,688,418	
21	Kentucky	4,041,769	
22	Louisiana	4,468,976	
23	Maine	1,274,923	

Figure 77-2: A pivot table created from the data.

Figure 77-3 shows an example of an Excel range that is *not* appropriate for a pivot table. Although the range contains descriptive information about each value, it does *not* consist of normalized data, and you cannot create a useful pivot table from it. In fact, this range actually resembles a pivot table summary, but it's much less flexible.

	A	B	C	D	E	F	G	H
1	**State**	**Jan**	**Feb**	**Mar**	**Apr**	**May**	**Jun**	
2	California	1,118	1,960	1,252	1,271	1,557	1,679	
3	Washington	1,247	1,238	1,028	1,345	1,784	1,574	
4	Oregon	1,460	1,954	1,726	1,461	1,764	1,144	
5	Arizona	1,345	1,375	1,075	1,736	1,555	1,372	
6	New York	1,429	1,316	1,993	1,832	1,740	1,191	
7	New Jersey	1,735	1,406	1,224	1,706	1,320	1,290	
8	Massachusetts	1,099	1,233	1,110	1,637	1,512	1,006	
9	Florida	1,705	1,792	1,225	1,946	1,327	1,357	
10	Kentucky	1,109	1,078	1,155	1,993	1,082	1,551	
11	Oklahoma	1,309	1,045	1,641	1,924	1,499	1,941	
12	Missouri	1,511	1,744	1,414	1,243	1,493	1,820	
13	Illinois	1,539	1,493	1,211	1,165	1,013	1,445	
14	Kansas	1,973	1,560	1,243	1,495	1,125	1,387	
15								
16								

Figure 77-3: This range is not appropriate for a pivot table.

Figure 77-4 shows the same data, but normalized. This range contains 78 rows of data — one for each of the six monthly sales values for the 13 states. Notice that each row contains category information for the sales value. This table is an ideal candidate for a pivot table and contains all information necessary to summarize the information by region or quarter.

Figure 77-5 shows a pivot table created from the normalized data. As you can see, it's virtually identical to the non-normalized data shown in Figure 77-3. Working with normalized data provides ultimate flexibility in designing reports.

	A	B	C	D	E	F
1	State	Region	Month	Qtr	Sales	
2	California	West	Jan	Qtr-1	1,118	
3	California	West	Feb	Qtr-1	1,960	
4	California	West	Mar	Qtr-1	1,252	
5	California	West	Apr	Qtr-2	1,271	
6	California	West	May	Qtr-2	1,557	
7	California	West	Jun	Qtr-2	1,679	
8	Washington	West	Jan	Qtr-1	1,247	
9	Washington	West	Feb	Qtr-1	1,238	
10	Washington	West	Mar	Qtr-1	1,028	
11	Washington	West	Apr	Qtr-2	1,345	
12	Washington	West	May	Qtr-2	1,784	
13	Washington	West	Jun	Qtr-2	1,574	
14	Oregon	West	Jan	Qtr-1	1,460	
15	Oregon	West	Feb	Qtr-1	1,954	
16	Oregon	West	Mar	Qtr-1	1,726	
17	Oregon	West	Apr	Qtr-2	1,461	
18	Oregon	West	May	Qtr-2	1,764	
19	Oregon	West	Jun	Qtr-2	1,144	
20	Arizona	West	Jan	Qtr-1	1,345	
21	Arizona	West	Feb	Qtr-1	1,375	
22	Arizona	West	Mar	Qtr-1	1,075	
23	Arizona	West	Apr	Qtr-2	1,736	
24	Arizona	West	May	Qtr-2	1,555	
25	Arizona	West	Jun	Qtr-2	1,372	
26	New York	East	Jan	Qtr-1	1,429	
27	New York	East	Feb	Qtr-1	1,316	

Figure 77-4: This range contains normalized data and is appropriate for a pivot table.

	A	B	C	D	E	F	G	H	I
1									
2									
3	Sum of Sales	Column							
4	Row Labels	Jan	Feb	Mar	Apr	May	Jun	Grand Total	
5	Arizona	1,345	1,375	1,075	1,736	1,555	1,372	8,458	
6	California	1,118	1,960	1,252	1,271	1,557	1,679	8,837	
7	Florida	1,705	1,792	1,225	1,946	1,327	1,357	9,352	
8	Illinois	1,539	1,493	1,211	1,165	1,013	1,445	7,866	
9	Kansas	1,973	1,560	1,243	1,495	1,125	1,387	8,783	
10	Kentucky	1,109	1,078	1,155	1,993	1,082	1,551	7,968	
11	Massachusetts	1,099	1,233	1,110	1,637	1,512	1,006	7,597	
12	Missouri	1,511	1,744	1,414	1,243	1,493	1,020	9,225	
13	New Jersey	1,735	1,406	1,224	1,706	1,320	1,290	8,681	
14	New York	1,429	1,316	1,993	1,832	1,740	1,191	9,501	
15	Oklahoma	1,309	1,045	1,641	1,924	1,499	1,941	9,359	
16	Oregon	1,460	1,954	1,726	1,461	1,764	1,144	9,509	
17	Washington	1,247	1,238	1,028	1,345	1,784	1,574	8,216	
18	Grand Total	18,579	19,194	17,297	20,754	18,771	18,757	113,352	
19									
20									

Figure 77-5: A pivot table created from normalized data.

Using a Pivot Table Instead of Formulas

The Excel PivotTable feature is incredibly powerful, and you can often create pivot tables in lieu of creating formulas. This tip describes a specific problem and provides three different solutions.

Figure 78-1 shows a range of data that contains student test scores. The goal is to calculate the average score for all students plus the average score for each gender.

	A	B	C
1	**Student**	**Score**	**Gender**
2	Anne	90	Female
3	Billy	96	Male
4	Chuck	87	Male
5	Darlene	75	Female
6	Ella	84	Female
7	Frank	89	Male
8	George	85	Male
9	Hilda	97	Female
10	Ida	77	Female
11	John	93	Male
12	Keith	89	Male
13	Larry	77	Male
14	Mary	85	Female
15	Nora	100	Female
16	Opie	71	Male
17	Peter	89	Male
18	Quincy	83	Male
19	Rhoda	91	Female
20	Sally	87	Female
21	Tim	97	Male
22	Ubella	83	Female
23	Vince	86	Male
24	Walter	83	Male
25	Xavier	78	Male
26	Yolanda	100	Female
27	Zola	84	Female
28			

Figure 78-1: What's the best way to calculate the average test score for males versus females?

Inserting subtotals

The first solution involves automatically inserting subtotals. To use this method, the data must be sorted by the column that will trigger the subtotaling. In this case, you need to sort by the Gender column. Follow these steps:

1. Select any cell in column C.

2. Right-click and choose Sort➡Sort A to Z from the shortcut menu.

3. Choose Data➡Outline➡Subtotal.

   The Subtotal dialog box appears.

4. Specify At Each Change in Gender, Use Function Average, and Add Subtotal to Score.

The result of adding subtotals is shown in Figure 78-2. Notice that Excel also creates an outline, so you can hide the details and view just the summary.

The formulas inserted by Excel use the SUBTOTAL function, with 1 as the first argument (1 represents average). Here are the formulas:

```
=SUBTOTAL(1,B2:B13)
=SUBTOTAL(1,B15:B28)
=SUBTOTAL(1,B2:B28)
```

The formula in cell B30 calculates the Grand Average and uses a range that includes the other two SUBTOTAL formulas in cells B14 and B29. The SUBTOTAL function ignores cells that contain other SUBTOTAL formulas.

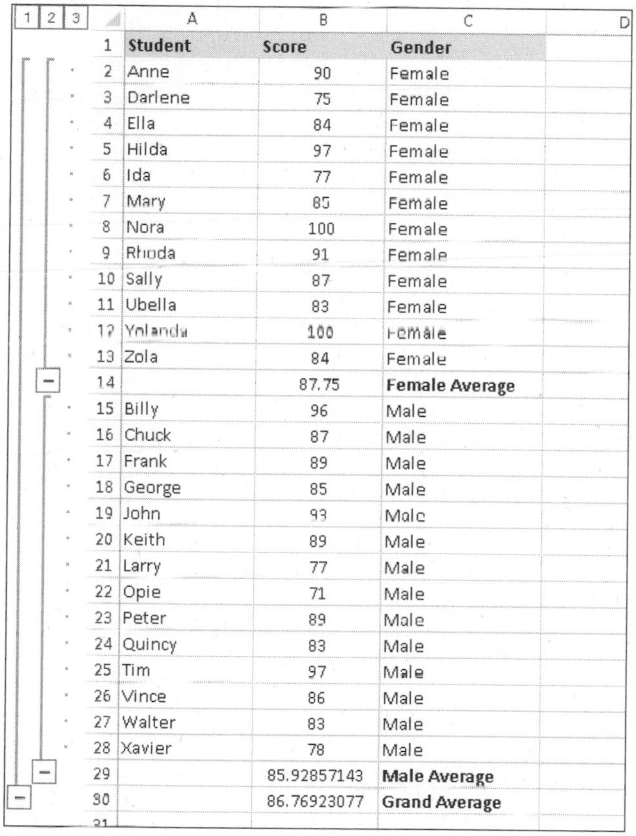

	A	B	C	D
1	Student	Score	Gender	
2	Anne	90	Female	
3	Darlene	75	Female	
4	Ella	84	Female	
5	Hilda	97	Female	
6	Ida	77	Female	
7	Mary	85	Female	
8	Nora	100	Female	
9	Rhoda	91	Female	
10	Sally	87	Female	
11	Ubella	83	Female	
12	Yolanda	100	Female	
13	Zola	84	Female	
14		87.75	**Female Average**	
15	Billy	96	Male	
16	Chuck	87	Male	
17	Frank	89	Male	
18	George	85	Male	
19	John	93	Male	
20	Keith	89	Male	
21	Larry	77	Male	
22	Opie	71	Male	
23	Peter	89	Male	
24	Quincy	83	Male	
25	Tim	97	Male	
26	Vince	86	Male	
27	Walter	83	Male	
28	Xavier	78	Male	
29		85.92857143	**Male Average**	
30		86.76923077	**Grand Average**	
31				

Figure 78-2: Excel adds subtotals automatically.

Using formulas

Another method of creating averages is to use formulas. The formula to calculate the average of all students is simple:

```
=AVERAGE(B2:B27)
```

To calculate the average of the genders, you can use the AVERAGEIF function and create these formulas:

```
=AVERAGEIF(C2:C27,"Female",B2:B27)
=AVERAGEIF(C2:C27,"Male",B2:B27)
```

Using Excel's PivotTable feature

A third method of averaging the scores is to create a pivot table. Many users avoid creating pivot tables because they consider this feature too complicated. As you can see, it's simple to use:

1. Select any cell in the data range and choose Insert➜Tables➜PivotTable.

   The Create PivotTable dialog box appears.

2. Verify that Excel selected the correct data range and specify a cell on the existing worksheet as the location.

   Cell E1 is a good choice.

3. Click OK.

   Excel displays the PivotTable Fields task pane.

4. Drag the Gender item to the Rows section, at the bottom.

5. Drag the Score item to the Values section.

   Excel creates the pivot table but calculates the sum of the scores rather than the average.

6. To change the summary function that's used, right-click any of the values in the pivot table and choose Summarize Data By➜Average from the shortcut menu.

Figure 78-3 shows the pivot table and the PivotTable Fields task pane.

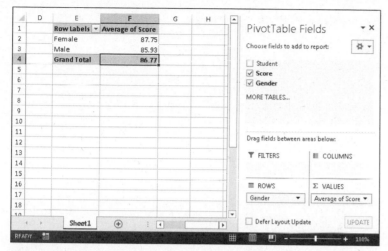

Figure 78-3: This pivot table calculates the averages without using formulas.

Note Unlike a formula-based solution, a pivot table doesn't update itself automatically if the data changes. If the data changes, you must refresh the pivot table. Just right-click any cell in the pivot table and choose Refresh from the shortcut menu.

The pivot table in this example is extremely simple, but it's also very easy to create. Pivot tables can be much more complex, and they can summarize massive amounts of data in just about any way you can think of — without using any formulas.

Controlling References to Cells Within a Pivot Table

In some cases, you may want to create a formula that references one or more cells within a pivot table. Figure 79–1 shows a simple pivot table that displays income and expense information for three years. In this pivot table, the Month field is hidden, so the pivot table shows the year totals.

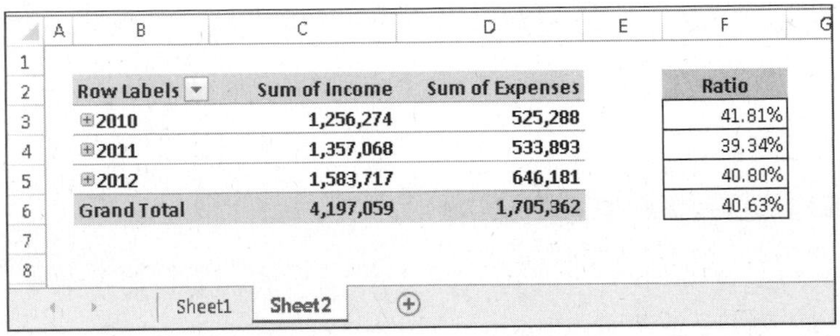

Figure 79-1: The formulas in column F reference cells in the pivot table.

Column F contains formulas, and this column is not part of the pivot table. These formulas calculate the expense-to-income ratio for each year. I created these formulas by pointing to the cells. You may expect to see this formula in cell F3:

```
=D3/C3
```

In fact, the formula in cell F3 is

```
=GETPIVOTDATA("Sum of Expenses",$B$2,"Year",2010)
/GETPIVOTDATA("Sum of Income",$B$2,"Year",2010)
```

When you use the pointing technique to create a formula that references a cell in a pivot table, Excel replaces those simple cell references with a much more complicated GETPIVOTDATA function. If you type the cell references manually (rather than pointing to them), Excel does not use the GETPIVOTDATA function.

The reason? Using the GETPIVOTDATA function helps ensure that the formula will continue to reference the intended cells if the pivot table layout is changed.

Figure 79-2 shows the pivot table after expanding the years to show the month detail. As you can see, the formulas in column F still show the correct result even though the referenced cells are in a different location. For example, the summary row for 2011 was originally row 4. After expanding the years, the summary row for 2011 is row 16. Had I used simple cell references, the formula would have returned incorrect results after expanding the years.

	A	B	C	D	E	F	
1							
2		Row Labels ▼	Sum of Income	Sum of Expenses		Ratio	
3		⊟2010	1,256,274	525,288		41.81%	
4		Jan	98,085	42,874		39.34%	
5		Feb	98,698	44,167		40.80%	
6		Mar	102,403	43,349		40.63%	
7		Apr	106,044	43,102			
8		May	105,361	45,005			
9		Jun	105,729	44,216			
10		Jul	105,557	43,835			
11		Aug	109,669	41,952			
12		Sep	107,233	44,071			
13		Oct	105,048	43,185			
14		Nov	107,446	44,403			
15		Dec	105,001	45,129			
16		⊟2011	1,357,068	533,893			
17		Jan	109,699	46,245			
18		Feb	109,146	45,672			
19		Mar	106,576	44,143			
20		Apr	108,911	43,835			
21		May	108,011	44,114			
22		Jun	111,361	44,648			

Sheet1   Sheet2   ⊕

Figure 79-2: After expanding the pivot table, formulas that used the GETPIVOTDATA function continue to display the correct result.

Using the GETPIVOTDATA function has one caveat: The data that it retrieves must be visible in the pivot table. If you modify the pivot table so that the value used by GETPIVOTDATA is no longer visible, the formula returns an error.

Note   You may want to prevent Excel from using the GETPIVOTDATA function when you point to pivot table cells when creating a formula. If so, choose PivotTable Tools➔Analyze➔ PivotTable➔Options➔Generate GetPivot Data (this command is a toggle).

Creating a Quick Frequency Tabulation

This tip describes a quick method for creating a frequency tabulation for a single column of data. Figure 80-1 shows a small part of a range that contains more than 20,000 rows of city and state data. The goal is to tally the number of times each state appears in the list.

Although you can tally the states in a number of ways, a pivot table is the easiest choice for this task.

	A	B	C
1	City	State	
2	Bellevue	WA	
3	Simsbury	CT	
4	Washington	DC	
5	Campbell	CA	
6	Los Angelese	CA	
7	Sterling	IL	
8	Bloomington	IN	
9	Gastonia	NC	
10	Chicago	IL	
11	Wilmington	DE	
12	New York	NY	
13	San Jose	CA	
14	Toledo	OH	
15	New York	NY	
16	Norman	OK	
17	Longmeadow	MA	
18	Boulder	CO	
19	San Jose	CA	
20	Winter Haven	FL	
21	Gainesville	FL	
22	Ankeny	IA	
23	Tacoma	WA	
24	West Windsor	NJ	

Figure 80-1: You can use a pivot table to generate a frequency tabulation for these state abbreviations.

Before you get started on this task, make sure that your data column has a heading. In this example, it's in cell B1.

Activate any cell in the column A or B and then follow these steps:

1. Choose Insert➜Tables➜PivotTable.

   The Create PivotTable dialog box appears.

2. If Excel doesn't correctly identify the range, change the Table/Range setting.

3. Specify a location for the PivotTable.

4. Click OK.

   Excel creates an empty pivot table and displays the PivotTable Fields task pane.

5. Drag the State field into the Rows section.

6. Drag the State field into the Values section.

Excel creates the pivot table, which shows the frequency of each state (see Figure 80-2).

	A	B	C	D	E	F	G
1	City	State		Row Labels	Count of State		
2	Bellevue	WA		CA	3150		
3	Simsbury	CT		TX	1745		
4	Washington	DC		NY	1191		
5	Campbell	CA		FL	1001		
6	Los Angelese	CA		IL	954		
7	Sterling	IL		NJ	816		
8	Bloomington	IN		PA	738		
9	Gastonia	NC		OH	723		
10	Chicago	IL		MI	652		
11	Wilmington	DE		WA	646		
12	New York	NY		VA	645		
13	San Jose	CA		MA	603		
14	Toledo	OH		GA	577		
15	New York	NY		NC	523		
16	Norman	OK		MD	517		
17	Longmeadow	MA		CO	408		
18	Boulder	CO		CT	388		
19	San Jose	CA		OR	369		
20	Winter Haven	FL		AZ	363		
21	Gainesville	FL		IN	348		
22	Ankeny	IA		MN	348		
23	Tacoma	WA		MO	300		
24	West Windsor	NJ		WI	291		

Figure 80-2: A quick pivot table shows the frequency of each state abbreviation.

This pivot table can be sorted, by using the Home➔Editing➔Sort & Filter command. In addition (as shown in Figure 80-3), you can even create a pivot chart to display the counts graphically. Just select any cell in the pivot table and choose PivotTable Tools➔Analyze➔Tools➔PivotChart.

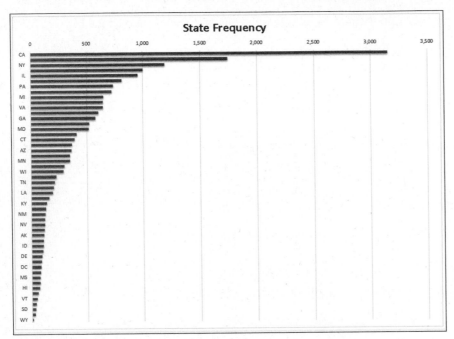

Figure 80-3: A few mouse clicks creates a chart from the pivot table.

Grouping Items by Date in a Pivot Table

One of the more useful features of a pivot table is the ability to combine items into groups. Grouping items is simple: Select them and choose PivotTable Tools➜Options➜Group➜Group Selection.

You can go a step further, though. When a field contains dates, Excel can create groups automatically. Many users overlook this helpful feature. Figure 81-1 shows a portion of a table that has two columns of data: Date and Sales. This table has 731 rows and covers dates between January 1, 2012, and December 31, 2013. The goal is to summarize the sales information by month.

	A	B	C	D
1	Date	Sales		
2	1/1/2012	3,830		
3	1/2/2012	3,763		
4	1/3/2012	4,362		
5	1/4/2012	3,669		
6	1/5/2012	3,942		
7	1/6/2012	4,488		
8	1/7/2012	4,416		
9	1/8/2012	3,371		
10	1/9/2012	3,620		
11	1/10/2012	4,548		
12	1/11/2012	5,493		
13	1/12/2012	5,706		
14	1/13/2012	6,570		
15	1/14/2012	6,333		
16	1/15/2012	6,101		
17	1/16/2012	5,289		
18	1/17/2012	5,349		
19	1/10/2012	5,814		
20	1/19/2012	6,501		
21	1/20/2012	6,513		
22	1/21/2012	5,970		
23	1/22/2012	5,791		
24	1/23/2012	5,478		

Figure 81-1: You can use the PivotTable feature to summarize the sales data by month.

Figure 81-2 shows part of a pivot table (in columns D:E) created from the data. Not surprisingly, it looks exactly like the input data because the dates haven't been grouped.

To group the items by month, right-click any cell in the Date column of the pivot table and select Group from the shortcut menu. You see the Grouping dialog box, shown in Figure 81-3. In the By list box, select Months and Years and verify that the starting and ending dates are correct. Click OK.

The Date items in the pivot table are grouped by years and by months (as shown in Figure 81-4).

Note

The Group command is available only if every item in the field is a date (or a time). Even a single blank cell will make it impossible to group by date.

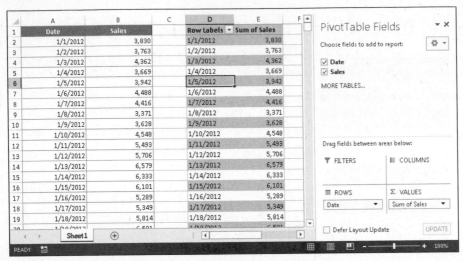

Figure 81-2: The pivot table, before grouping by months and years.

Figure 81-3: Use the Grouping dialog box to group items in a pivot table.

Note

If you select only Months in the Grouping list box, months in different years are combined. For example, the June item would display sales for both 2012 and 2013.

	A	B	C	D	E	F
1	**Date**	**Sales**		**Row Labels** ▼	**Sum of Sales**	
2	1/1/2012	3,830		⊟2012		
3	1/2/2012	3,763		Jan	167,624	
4	1/3/2012	4,362		Feb	137,825	
5	1/4/2012	3,669		Mar	214,896	
6	1/5/2012	3,942		Apr	100,872	
7	1/6/2012	4,488		May	158,005	
8	1/7/2012	4,416		Jun	117,649	
9	1/8/2012	3,371		Jul	295,248	
10	1/9/2012	3,628		Aug	518,966	
11	1/10/2012	4,548		Sep	612,673	
12	1/11/2012	5,493		Oct	699,854	
13	1/12/2012	5,706		Nov	863,085	
14	1/13/2012	6,579		Dec	970,441	
15	1/14/2012	6,333		⊟2013		
16	1/15/2012	6,101		Jan	974,625	
17	1/16/2012	5,289		Feb	969,696	
18	1/17/2012	5,349		Mar	1,081,596	
19	1/18/2012	5,814		Apr	983,306	
20	1/19/2012	6,501		May	1,044,322	
21	1/20/2012	6,513		Jun	930,076	
22	1/21/2012	5,970		Jul	961,557	
23	1/22/2012	5,791		Aug	938,433	
24	1/23/2012	5,478		Sep	975,503	
25	1/24/2012	6,564		Oct	948,120	
26	1/25/2012	6,642		Nov	950,493	
27	1/26/2012	7,083		Dec	906,389	
28	1/27/2012	6,468		**Grand Total**	**16,521,254**	
29	1/28/2012	6,801				
30	1/29/2012	5,651				

Figure 81-4: The pivot table, after grouping by months and years.

Notice that the Grouping dialog box contains other time-based units. For example, you can group the data into quarters. Figure 81-5 shows the data grouped by quarters and years.

	A	B	C	D	E	F
1	**Date**	**Sales**		**Row Labels** ▼	**Sum of Sales**	
2	1/1/2012	3,830		⊟2012		
3	1/2/2012	3,763		Qtr1	520,345	
4	1/3/2012	4,362		Qtr2	376,526	
5	1/4/2012	3,669		Qtr3	1,426,887	
6	1/5/2012	3,942		Qtr4	2,533,380	
7	1/6/2012	4,488		⊟2013		
8	1/7/2012	4,416		Qtr1	3,025,917	
9	1/8/2012	3,371		Qtr2	2,957,704	
10	1/9/2012	3,628		Qtr3	2,875,493	
11	1/10/2012	4,548		Qtr4	2,805,002	
12	1/11/2012	5,493		**Grand Total**	**16,521,254**	
13	1/12/2012	5,706				
14	1/13/2012	6,579				

Figure 81-5: The pivot table, after grouping by quarters and years.

Creating Pivot Tables with Multiple Groupings

If you've created multiple pivot tables from the same data source, you may have noticed that grouping a field in one pivot table affects the other pivot tables. Specifically, all the other pivot tables automatically use the same grouping. Sometimes, this is exactly what you want. Other times, it's not at all what you want. For example, you may want to see two pivot table reports: one that summarizes data by month and year, and another that summarizes the data by quarter and year.

The reason grouping affects other pivot tables is because all the pivot tables are using the same pivot table *cache*. Unfortunately, there's no direct way to force a pivot table to use a new cache. But there *is* a way to trick Excel into using a new cache. The trick involves assigning multiple range names to the source data.

For example, if your source range is named *Table1*, give the same range a second name: *Table2*. The easiest way to name a range is to use the Name box, to the left of the Formula bar. Select the range, type a name in the Name box, and press Enter. Then, with the range still selected, type a different name, and press Enter. Excel will display only the first name, but you can verify that both names exist by choosing Formulas➜Define Names➜Name Manager (see Figure 82-1).

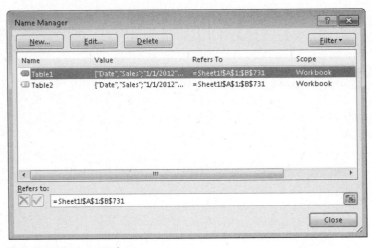

Figure 82-1: A range has two names.

When you create the first pivot table, specify *Table1* as the Table/Range in the Create PivotTable dialog box (see Figure 82-2). When you create the second pivot table, specify *Table2* as the Table/Range. Each pivot table will use a separate cache, and you can create groups in one pivot table, independent of the other pivot table.

Figure 82-2: Using a named range as the Table/Range.

You can use this trick with existing pivot tables. Make sure that you give the data source a different name. Then select the pivot table and choose PivotTable Tools➔Analyze➔Data➔Change Data Source. In the Change PivotTable Data Source dialog box, type the new name that you gave to the range. This will cause Excel to create a new pivot cache for the pivot table.

Figure 82-3 shows two pivot tables (with different groupings) created from the same data source. One pivot table is grouped by quarters and years, and the other is grouped by months and years.

	C	D	E	F	G	H	I
1		Row Labels ▼	Sum of Sales		Row Labels ▼	Sum of Sales	
2		⊟2012			⊟2012		
3		Qtr1	520,345		Jan	167,624	
4		Qtr2	376,526		Feb	137,825	
5		Qtr3	1,426,887		Mar	214,896	
6		Qtr4	2,533,380		Apr	100,872	
7		⊟2013			May	158,005	
8		Qtr1	3,025,917		Jun	117,649	
9		Qtr2	2,957,704		Jul	295,248	
10		Qtr3	2,875,493		Aug	518,966	
11		Qtr4	2,805,002		Sep	612,673	
12		**Grand Total**	**16,521,254**		Oct	699,854	
13					Nov	863,085	
14					Dec	970,441	
15					⊟2013		
16					Jan	974,625	
17					Feb	969,696	
18					Mar	1,081,596	
19					Apr	983,306	
20					May	1,044,322	

Figure 82-3: These pivot tables were created from the same data source, but use different groupings.

Using Pivot Table Slicers and Timelines

If you've worked with pivot tables, filtering data in a pivot table is fairly easy. Just click the filter button for a field, and remove the check mark from items that you don't want to see. This tip describes two ways to simplify pivot table filtering: slicers and timelines. These methods are most useful when the worksheet will be viewed by novices, or for those who prefer things very simple.

Using slicers

Figure 83-1 shows an unfiltered pivot table that summarizes bank account information by three fields: Customer Type (either New or Existing), Branch (either Central, North County, or Westside), and OpenedBy (either New Accts or Teller).

	A	B	C	D	E
1	Customer Type	(All)			
2					
3	Sum of Amount	Column Labels			
4	Row Labels	Central	North County	Westside	Grand Total
5	New Accts	2,047,032	1,487,516	861,511	4,396,059
6	CD	1,006,474	927,216	451,611	2,385,301
7	Checking	418,030	206,845	137,738	762,613
8	IRA	59,285	42,554	10,000	111,839
9	Savings	563,243	310,901	262,162	1,136,306
10	Teller	1,068,893	644,699	426,121	2,139,713
11	CD	352,911	210,695	196,938	760,544
12	Checking	384,373	185,671	155,257	725,301
13	IRA	9,095	91,820		100,915
14	Savings	322,514	156,513	73,926	552,953
15	Grand Total	3,115,925	2,132,215	1,287,632	6,535,772
16					

Figure 83-1: The normal way to filter items in a pivot table.

A *slicer* is an interactive control that makes it easy to apply simple filters to data in a pivot table. Figure 83-2 shows a pivot table with three slicers. Each slicer represents a particular field in the pivot table. In this case, the pivot table is displaying data for existing customers, opened by tellers at the Central branch.

The same type of filtering can be accomplished by using the field labels in the pivot table, but slicers are intended for those who might not understand how to filter data in a pivot table. Slicers can also be used to create an attractive and easy-to-use interactive *dashboard*.

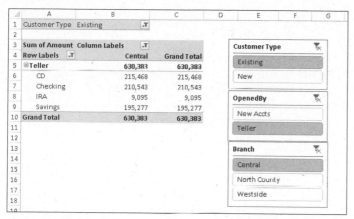

Figure 83-2: Using slicers to filter the data displayed in a pivot table.

To add one or more slicers to a worksheet, start by selecting any cell in a pivot table. Then choose Insert➜Filter➜Slicer. The Insert Slicers dialog box appears, with a list of all fields in the pivot table. Place a check mark next to the slicers you want, and then click OK.

Note

In Excel 2013, slicers aren't limited to pivot tables. You can also use slicers with a table (created with Insert➜Tables➜Table).

Slicers float on the worksheet's drawing layer, and they can be moved and resized. You can change the look and also specify multiple columns of buttons.

To use a slicer to filter data in a pivot table, just click a button in the slicer. To display multiple values, press Ctrl while you click the buttons. Press Shift and click to select a series of consecutive buttons.

To remove the effects of filtering by a particular slicer, click the icon in the slicer's upper-right corner.

Figure 83-3 shows a pivot table with two slicers to enable filtering the data (by State and by Month). In this case, the pivot table and pivot chart show only the data for California, Oregon, and Washington for the months of January through March. Slicers provide a quick-and-easy way to create an interactive chart.

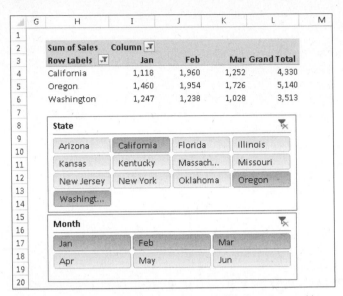

Figure 83-3: Using slicers to filter a pivot table by state and by month.

Using a timeline

A *timeline* is conceptually similar to a slicer, but this control is designed to simplify time-based filtering in a pivot table. Timelines are new to Excel 2013, and (unlike slicers) this feature is for pivot tables only.

A timeline is relevant only if your pivot table has a field that's formatted as a date. This feature does not work with times. To add a timeline, select a cell in a pivot table and choose Insert→Filter→Timeline. A dialog box appears listing all date-based fields. If your pivot table doesn't have a field formatted as a date, Excel displays an error.

Figure 83-4 shows a pivot table created from the data in columns A:E. This pivot table uses a timeline, set to allow date filtering by quarters. Click a button that corresponds to the quarter you want to view, and the pivot table is updated immediately. To select a range of quarters, press Shift while you click the buttons. Other filtering options (selectable from the drop-down in the upper-right corner) are Year, Month, and Day. In the figure, the pivot table displays data from the first two quarters of 2012.

You can, of course, use both slicers and a timeline for a pivot table. A timeline has the same type of formatting options as slicers, so you can create an attractive interactive dashboard that simplifies pivot table filtering.

	A	B	C	D	E	F	G	H	I	J	K
1	Ordered	Customer	Product	Units	TOTAL						
2	1/2/2009	Existing	Doodads	2	198.00			Customer			
3	1/2/2009	Existing	Sprockets	1	178.00		Products	Existing	New	Grand Total	
4	1/2/2009	Existing	Sprockets	1	178.00		Doodads	1,946	4,562	6,500	
5	1/2/2009	New	Snapholytes	1	188.00		Sprockets	38,870	64,418	103,289	
6	1/2/2009	New	Doodads	1	212.95		Snapholytes	0	20,868	20,868	
7	1/2/2009	New	Doodads	1	197.95		Grand Total	40,816	89,848	130,665	
8	1/3/2009	New	Sprockets	1	213.00						
9	1/3/2009	New	Sprockets	1	213.00						
10	1/4/2009	New	Doodads	2	206.95		Ordered				
11	1/4/2009	New	Doodads	1	186.95		Q1 - Q2 2012			QUARTERS	
12	1/4/2009	Existing	Doodads	2	198.00		2010 2011	2012			
13	1/4/2009	New	Sprockets	1	213.00		Q3 Q4 Q1 Q2 Q3 Q4 Q1 Q2 Q3 Q4				
14	1/5/2009	New	Doodads	1	212.95						
15	1/5/2009	New	Doodads	1	212.95						
16	1/6/2009	Existing	Doodads	1	178.00						
17	1/6/2009	Existing	Sprockets	2	183.00						
18	1/6/2009	New	Doodads	2	232.95						
19	1/7/2009	Existing	Doodads	1	178.00						
20	1/7/2009	Existing	Doodads	1	178.00						
21	1/7/2009	Existing	Sprockets	2	198.00						
22	1/7/2009	New	Snapholytes	1	188.00						
23	1/7/2009	New	Snapholytes	1	188.00						

Figure 83-4: Using a timeline to filter a pivot table by date.

PART VI

Charts and Graphics

A well-conceived chart can make a range of incomprehensible numbers make sense. The tips in this part deal with various aspects of chart making, and also covers topics related to other types of graphics.

Tips and Where to Find Them

Understanding Recommended Charts

One of the new features in Excel 2013 is Recommended Charts. Select your data, choose Insert➔ Charts➔Recommended Charts, and Excel responds by displaying the Recommended Charts of the Insert Chart dialog box (see Figure 84-1). This dialog box displays a preview of your data using several chart type options.

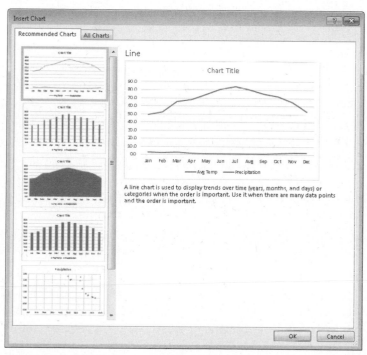

Figure 84-1: The Recommended Charts feature displays your data using several different chart types.

How does it work? According to the Excel Help:

Want us to recommend a good chart to showcase your data? Select data in your worksheet and click this button to get a customized set of charts that we think will fit best with your data.

Don't believe it. Excel uses some simple algorithms to make its suggestions, but don't expect any advanced artificial intelligence. In other words, you will probably never see a recommended chart that will make you say, "Why didn't *I* think of that!"

The recommended charts seem to be limited to the basic chart types: column charts, line charts, area charts, bar charts, pie charts, and scatter charts.

The recommendations don't seem to take the magnitude of the data into account. For example, if you select two data series that vary drastically in scale, a combination chart would be a good recommendation. But I've never seen Excel recommend a combination chart. Rather, it recommends a column or line chart in which one of the data series is so close to the axis that it may not even be visible.

Even when data is perfectly suited (and labeled) for a stock market chart, that chart is never recommended. But it does offer some recommendations that are clearly inappropriate.

But the recommended charts feature is not completely useless. For example, if a data series has more than eight data points, Excel will not recommend a pie chart. That's certainly good advice because pie charts are often used inappropriately to display too much data. Also, Excel will never recommend a 3D chart. That's also good advice because a 3D chart is almost never the best choice.

Excel's Recommended Charts feature is certainly a good idea, but the current implementation leaves much to be desired. The main problem is this feature is intended for novice users — and many of them will actually believe that a recommended chart is an appropriate way to present their data.

Bottom line: Don't trust Excel's chart recommendations, except for very simple data sets. Instead, take some time and become familiar with Excel's chart types. Strive for simplicity and clarity, and you won't be tempted to take bad advice from a computer program.

Customizing Charts

If you've ever been frustrated when trying to customize a chart, here's some good news: Excel 2013 makes this task easier than ever.

When you click on a chart in Excel 2013, you see three buttons at the upper-right of the chart. These buttons are the key to quick and easy chart customization.

Adding or removing chart elements

Figure 85-1 shows the options available when you click the Chart Elements button. Note that each item can be expanded to show additional options. To expand an item in the Chart Elements list, hover your mouse over the item and click the arrow that appears.

When you display the options for a button, hover the mouse over the item to get a preview of how the chart will look if you select (or deselect) an item.

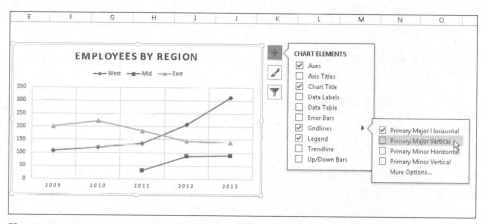

Figure 85-1: Options available from the Chart Elements button.

Modifying a chart style or colors

Figure 85-2 shows the options available when you click the Chart Styles button.

Notice that there's a two-item menu at the top: Style and Color. Click the Color item, and you can choose a different color palette for your chart.

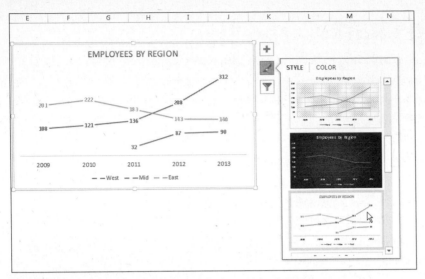

Figure 85-2: Options available from the Chart Styles button.

Filtering chart data

Options for the third button, Chart Filters, are shown in Figure 85-3. These options enable you to quickly hide one or more charts series or even data points within a chart series.

Note that previewing works differently for these options, and you must click the Apply button to see the effect of filtering.

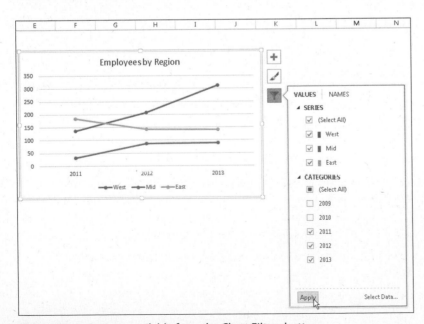

Figure 85-3: Options available from the Chart Filters button.

Making Charts the Same Size

If you have several embedded charts on a worksheet, you might want to make them all exactly the same size. Figure 86-1 shows a worksheet with four charts that would look better if they were all the same size and aligned.

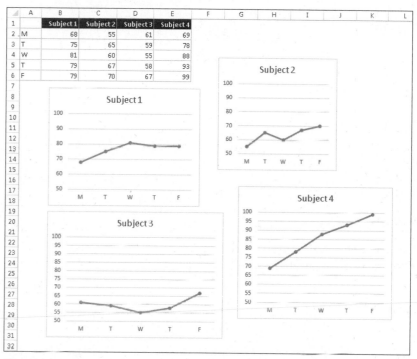

Figure 86-1: These charts would look better if they were all the same size.

To make all the charts the same size, first identify the chart that is already the size you want. In this case, you want to make all the charts the same size as the Subject 2 chart in the upper-right area.

1. Click the chart to select it.

2. Choose Chart Tools➜Format.

   You see the Height and Width settings in the Size group.

3. Make a note of the Height and Width settings.

4. Press Ctrl while you click the other three charts (so that all four are selected).

5. Choose Drawing Tools➜Format, enter the Height and Width settings that you noted in Step 3 and then click OK.

   The charts are now exactly the same size.

You can align the charts manually, or you can use the Chart Tools→Format→Arrange→Align commands. Figure 86-2 shows the result.

Note that if you Ctrl+click a chart, you select it as a graphic object so that you can use the arrow keys to move the chart. Using the arrow keys moves the chart one pixel at a time and allows more control than dragging it with your mouse.

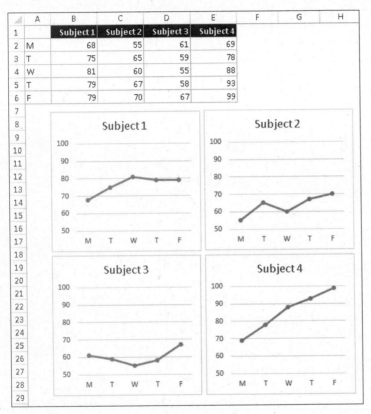

Figure 86-2: Four charts, resized and aligned.

Creating a Chart Template

If you find that you're continually making the same types of customizations to your charts, you can probably save some time by creating a template. Many users avoid this feature because they think that it's too complicated. Creating a chart template is actually very simple.

Figure 87-1 shows a highly customized chart that will be saved as a template so it can be used for future charts. This chart includes a shape and a text box, and both of these added elements are included in the template.

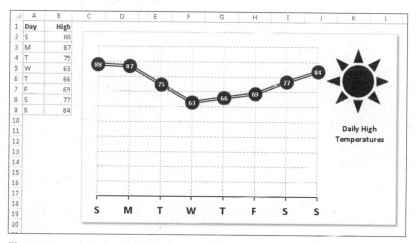

Figure 87-1: This chart will be saved as a template.

Creating a template

To create a chart template, follow these steps:

1. Create a chart to serve as the basis for your template.

   The data you use for this chart isn't critical, but for best results, it should be typical of the data that you will eventually plot with your custom chart type.

2. Apply any formatting and customizations that you like.

   This step determines the appearance of the charts created from the template.

3. Activate the chart; then right-click and choose Save as Template from the shortcut menu. (The Excel 2013 Ribbon doesn't have a command to create a chart template.)

   The Save Chart Template dialog box appears.

4. Provide a name for the template and click Save.

Chart templates are stored as `* .ctrx` files. You can create as many chart templates as you need.

Using a template

To create a chart based on a template you've created, follow these steps:

1. Select the data to be used in the chart.

2. Choose Insert→Charts→Recommended Charts.

   The Insert Chart dialog box appears.

3. At the top of the Insert Chart dialog box, choose the All Charts tab.

4. Choose Templates from the list on the left.

   Excel displays a preview image (using the selected data) for each custom template that has been created (see Figure 87-2).

5. Click the image that represents the template you want to use and click OK.

   Excel creates the chart based on the template you selected.

You can also apply a template to an existing chart. Select the chart and choose Chart Tools→ Design→Change Chart Type. That command displays a dialog box that's exactly the same as the Insert Chart dialog box. Choose the All Charts tab and then choose Templates from the list on the left.

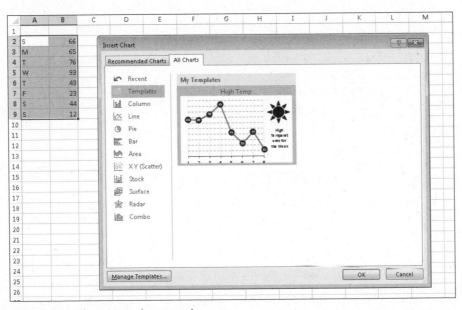

Figure 87-2: Choosing a chart template.

Creating a Combination Chart

A combination chart combines two chart types in a single chart. A combination chart may use a secondary vertical axis. In the past, creating a combination chart in Excel was relatively complicated and required some non-intuitive steps. Excel 2013 finally gets it right: creating a combination chart is easy.

Figure 88-1 shows a column chart with two data series: Temperature and Precipitation. Because these two measures have drastically different scales, the columns for the precipitation data are hardly visible. This is a good candidate for a combination chart.

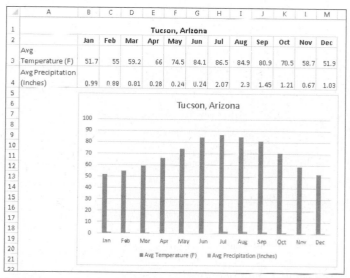

Figure 88-1: The two data series in this chart use drastically different scales.

Inserting a preconfigured combination chart

The following steps describe how to create a combination chart from the data in range A2:M4. The chart will display temperature as columns, and precipitation as a line. In addition, the precipitation series will use a secondary vertical axis.

1. Select the range A2:M4.

2. Choose Insert→Charts→Combo.

   This command expands to display three icons (see Figure 88-2). Hover your mouse over the icons, and you'll see a preview.

3. Choose the second icon: Clustered Column — Line on Secondary Axis.

   Excel creates the chart shown on Figure 88-3.

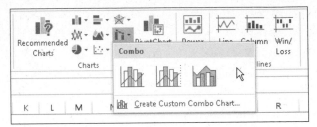

Figure 88-2: Excel proposes three preconfigured combination charts.

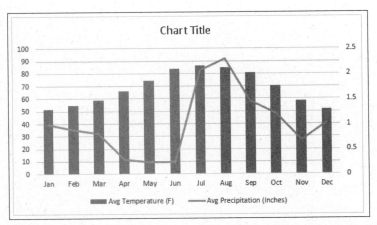

Figure 88-3: Excel created this combination chart with just a few mouse clicks.

The chart clearly shows both data series. The primary axis (on the left) is for the Avg Temperature series (columns). The secondary axis (on the right) is for the Avg Precipitation series (the line). You may want to add axis labels to make it easier to distinguish the two axes.

Customizing a combination chart

In some cases, none of the preconfigured combination charts will be exactly what you want. But creating a customized combination chart is a simple matter.

Choose Insert➜Charts➜Combo➜Create Custom Combo Chart, and the Insert Chart dialog box appears with the Combo section displayed (see Figure 88-4). Use the controls at the bottom of the All Charts tab of the Insert Chart dialog box to specify the chart type for each data series. Use the check boxes to indicate which (if any) of the series will use a secondary axis.

Figure 88-4: Use the controls at the bottom of this dialog box to customize a combination chart.

You have a great deal of control in customizing combination charts. But just because Excel allows you to create a certain combination chart doesn't mean it's a good idea. Figure 88-5 shows a custom combination chart that uses bars and columns — and it's not a good example of an effective chart.

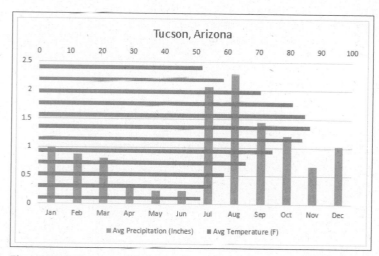

Figure 88-5: An example of a poorly conceived custom combination chart.

Handling Missing Data in a Chart

Sometimes, data that you're charting may be missing one or more data points. As shown in Figure 89-1, Excel offers three ways to handle the missing data:

➤ **Gaps:** Missing data is simply ignored, and the data series will have a gap. This is the default way missing data is handled in a chart.

➤ **Zero:** Missing data is treated as zero.

➤ **Connect Data Points with Line:** Missing data is interpolated, calculated by using data on either side of the missing point(s). This option is available for line charts, area charts, and XY charts only.

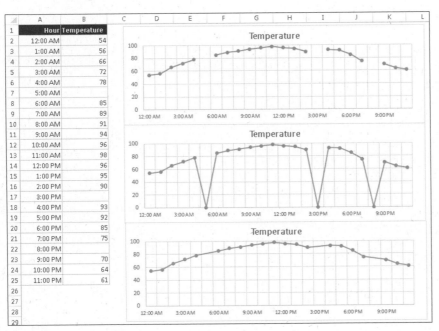

Figure 89-1: Three options for dealing with missing data.

To specify how to deal with missing data for a chart, choose Chart Tools➜Design➜Data➜Select Data. In the Select Data Source dialog box, click the Hidden and Empty Cells button. The Hidden and Empty Cell Settings dialog box appears, as shown in Figure 89-2. Make your choice in the dialog box.

The option that you choose applies to the entire chart, and you can't set a different option for different series in the same chart.

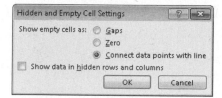

Figure 89-2: The Hidden and Empty Cell Settings dialog box.

Note

Normally, a chart doesn't display data that's in a hidden row or column. You can use the Hidden and Empty Cell Settings dialog box to force a chart to use hidden data, though.

Using High-Low Lines in a Chart

Excel supports a number of stock market charts, which are normally used to display stock market data. For example, you can create a chart that shows a stock's daily high, low, and closing prices. That particular chart type requires three data series.

But stock market charts aren't just for stock prices. Figure 90-1 shows a chart that depicts daily temperatures for a month. The vertical lines (called *high-low lines*) show the temperature range for the day.

This chart was created with a single command. I selected the range A3:D34, chose Insert→Charts→ Other Charts, and selected the High-Low-Close option. You can, of course, format the high-low lines any way you like. And you may prefer to have the average temperatures connected with a line.

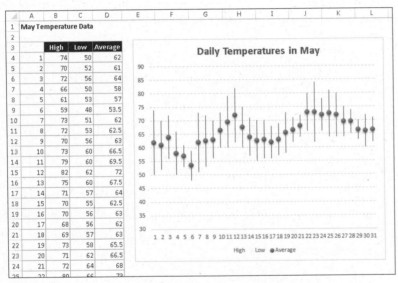

Figure 90-1: Using a stock market chart to plot temperature data.

When creating stock market charts, the order of the data for the chart series is critical. Because I chose the High-Low-Close chart type, the series must be arranged in that order. In this case, the "Close" data corresponds to Average temperatures.

Using Multi-Level Category Labels

Most users don't realize it, but when you create a chart, you can display multi-level category labels. You don't have to do anything special. Just select all of the data before you create the chart. Excel takes care of the details for you.

Figure 91-1 shows an example of a chart that uses two columns for the category labels. Here, the first level is the region, and the second level is the state. Notice that the Region labels in column A aren't repeated for each state. The blank regions cause the region name to appear once in the chart.

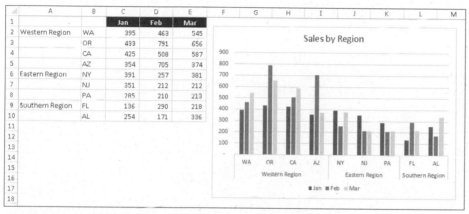

Figure 91-1: A chart that uses two columns for category labels.

Figure 91-2 shows another example, which uses three columns for the category axis labels. In this example, the additional lines of text are used to provide more information about each of the four branches.

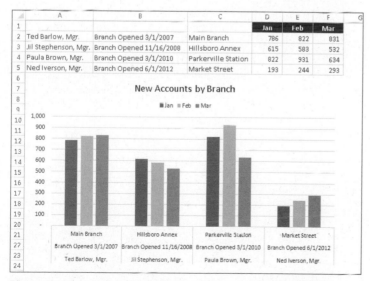

Figure 91-2: A chart that uses three columns for category labels.

You can apply formatting to the category axis labels, but the formatting is applied to all of the text. In other words, you can't apply different formatting for each level.

Figure 91-3 shows a variation of the previous example. After creating the chart with a multi-level category axis, I selected the category axis and pressed Ctrl+1 to display the Format Axis task pane. In the Axis Options→Labels section, I specified the Label Position to be High. I also deselected the Multi-level Category Labels option, which has the effect of making the lines closer together.

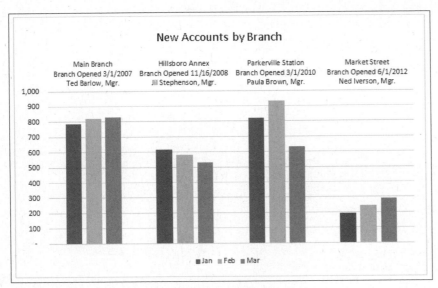

Figure 91-3: A chart that displays category labels at the top.

Linking Chart Text to Cells

When you create a chart, you may want to have some of the chart's text elements linked to cells. That way, when you change the text in the cell, the corresponding chart element is updated. You can even link chart text elements to cells that contain a formula. For example, you might link the chart title to a cell that contains a formula that returns the current date.

You can create a link to a cell for the chart title, the axis titles, and individual data labels.

1. Select the chart element that will contain the cell link.

2. Click the Formula bar.

3. Type an equal sign (=).

4. Click the cell that will be linked to the chart element.

5. Press Enter.

Figure 92-1 shows a chart title being linked to cell A1.

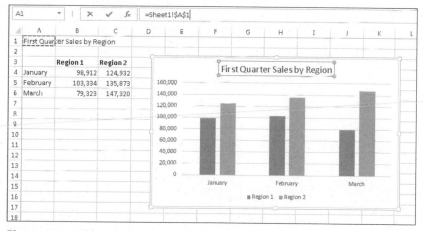

Figure 92-1: Adding a cell link to a chart title.

Note

Oddly, this technique doesn't work if the cell has a name. Excel displays an error claiming that the formula contains an error. If you must link the chart element to a named cell, override the name with the sheet name and cell address. For example:

```
=Sheet1!A12
```

In addition, you can add a linked text box (or a linked shape) to a chart:

1. Select the chart.

2. Choose Insert➜Text➜Text Box. Or choose Insert➜Illustrations➜Shapes and choose a shape that supports text.

3. Click inside the chart to add an empty text box (or shape).

4. Click the Formula bar.

5. Type an equal sign (=).

6. Click the cell that will be linked to the object.

7. Press Enter.

Freezing a Chart

Normally, an Excel chart uses data stored in a range. Change the data, and the chart is updated automatically. Usually, that's a good thing. But sometimes you want to "unlink" the chart from its data range to produce a *static* chart — a snapshot of a chart that never changes. For example, if you plot data generated by various what-if scenarios, you may want to save a chart that represents a baseline so that you can compare it with other scenarios. You can freeze a chart in two ways:

➤ Convert the chart to a picture.

➤ Convert the range references to arrays.

Converting a chart into a picture

To convert a chart to a static picture, follow these steps:

1. Create the chart as usual and format it the way you want.

2. Click the chart to activate it.

3. Choose Home➜Clipboard➜Copy➜Copy As Picture.

   The Copy Picture dialog box appears.

4. Accept the default settings and click OK.

5. Click any cell to deselect the chart.

6. Press Ctrl+V to paste the picture at the cell you selected in Step 5.

The result is a picture of the original chart. This chart can be edited as a picture, but not as a chart. In other words, you can no longer modify properties such as chart type and data labels. It's a dead chart — just what you wanted.

When you select the picture, Excel displays its Picture Tools contextual menu. You can use all of the tools in Picture Tools➜Format, plus those available in the Format Picture dialog box (displayed when you press Ctrl+1). Figure 93-1 shows a few examples of picture styles applied to a chart that was copied as a picture.

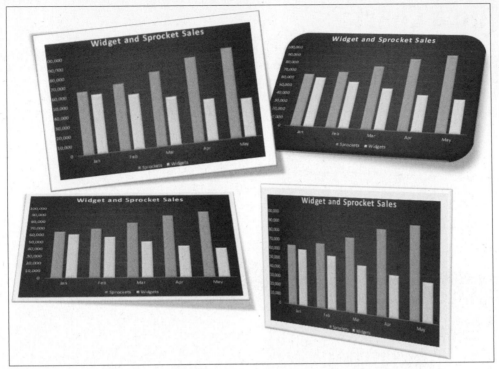

Figure 93-1: Applying picture styles to a chart that was copied as a picture.

Converting range references into arrays

The other way to unlink a chart from its data is to convert the SERIES formula range references to arrays. Follow these steps:

1. Activate your chart.

2. Click a chart series.

   The Formula bar displays the SERIES formula for the selected data series.

3. Click the Formula bar.

4. Press F9 and then press Enter.

Repeat these steps for each series in the chart.

Figure 93-2 shows a pie chart that has been unlinked from its data range. Notice that the Formula bar displays arrays, not range references. The original data SERIES formula was

```
=SERIES(,Sheet3!$A$1:$A$6,Sheet3!$B$1:$B$6,1)
```

The converted SERIES formula is

```
=SERIES(,{"Work","Sleep","Commute","Eat",
"Play Banjo","Other"},{8,7,2,1,3,3},1)
```

Note

Excel places a limit on the length of a SERIES formula. Therefore, this method may not work if the series consists of a large number of data points.

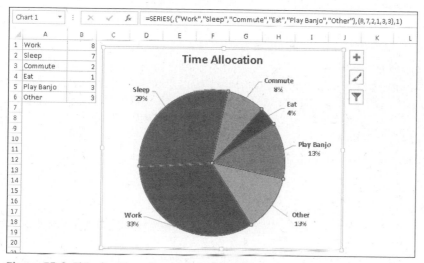

Figure 93-2: This chart is no longer linked to a data range.

Creating a Chart Directly in a Range

This tip describes two ways to display a bar chart directly in a range of cells:

➤ Using conditional formatting data bars

➤ Using formulas that display repeating characters

These "non-chart" charts often serve as a quick way to display lots of data graphically, without creating actual charts.

Using conditional formatting data bars

Using the data bars conditional formatting option can sometimes serve as a quick alternative to creating a chart. The data bars conditional format displays horizontal bars directly in the cell. The length of the bar is based on the value of the cell, relative to the other values in the range. When you adjust the column width, the bar lengths adjust accordingly. The differences among the bar lengths are more prominent when the column is wider.

Figure 94-1 shows results from a survey, using data bars to visualize the distribution for each survey item.

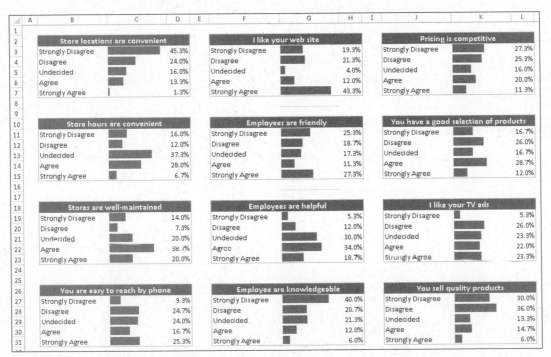

Figure 94-1: These tables use data bars conditional formatting.

To add data bars to a range, select the range and choose Home→Conditional Formatting→Data Bars and select one of the fill options.

Excel provides quick access to 12 data bar styles via Home→Styles→Conditional Formatting→Data Bars. For additional choices, click the More Rules option, which displays the New Formatting Rule dialog box. Use this dialog box to do the following:

➤ Show the bar only (hide the numbers).

➤ Specify Minimum and Maximum values for the scaling.

➤ Change the appearance of the bars.

➤ Specify how negative values and the axis are handled.

➤ Specify the direction of the bars.

Using formulas to display repeating characters

Figure 94-2 shows an example of a chart created by using formulas.

	Month	Employees	Graphic
3	January	60	*******************************
4	February	64	*********************************
5	March	62	********************************
6	April	67	***********************************
7	May	71	************************************
8	June	72	**************************************
9	July	77	***
10	August	79	**
11	September	79	**
12	October	80	***
13	November	81	**
14	December	89	***

Figure 94-2: A histogram created directly in a range of cells.

Column D contains formulas that incorporate the rarely used REPT function, which repeats a text string a specified number of times. For example, the following formula displays five asterisks:

```
=REPT("*",5)
```

In the example shown in Figure 94-2, cell D3 contains this formula, which was copied down the column:

```
=REPT("*",C3/2)
```

Notice that the formula divides the value in column B by 2. This is a way to scale the chart. Instead of displaying 60 asterisks, the cell displays 30 asterisks. For improved accuracy, you can use the ROUND function:

```
=REPT("*",ROUND(C3/2,0))
```

Without the ROUND function, the formula *truncates* the result of the division (disregards the decimal part of the argument). For example, the value 67 in column B displays 33 characters in column D. Using ROUND rounds up the result to 34 characters.

You can use this type of graphical display in place of a column chart. As long as you don't require strict accuracy (because of rounding errors), this type of nonchart might fit the bill.

Figure 94-3 shows some other examples that use different characters and fonts. The chart that displays the solid bars (beginning in row 39) uses the pipe character of the Script font. On most keyboards, the pipe character is generated when you press Shift+backslash. The formula in cell D39 is

```
=REPT("|",C39/2000)
```

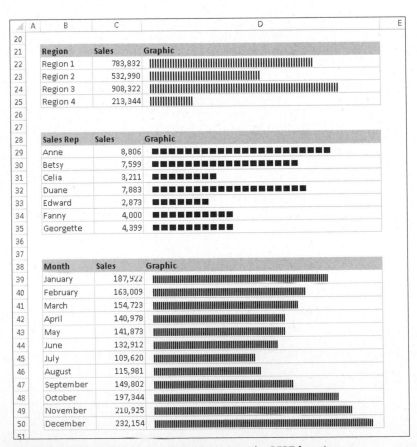

Figure 94-3: Examples of in-cell charting using the REPT function.

The example in Figure 94-4 uses formulas in columns F and H to graphically depict monthly budget variances by displaying a series of characters. You can then easily see which budget items are under or over budget. This pseudo bar chart uses the character n, which appears as a small square in the Wingdings font.

The key formulas are

```
F3: =IF(D3<0,REPT("n",-ROUND(D3*100,0)),"")
G3: =A3
H3: =IF(D3>0,REPT("n",-ROUND(D3*-100,0)),"")
```

	A	B	C	D	E	F	G	H	I
1									
2	Month	Budget	Actual	Pct. Diff		Under Budget		Exceeded Budget	
3	Jan	300	311	3.7%			Jan		
4	Feb	300	343	14.3%			Feb		
5	Mar	300	305	1.7%			Mar		
6	Apr	350	351	0.3%			Apr		
7	May	350	402	14.9%			May		
8	Jun	350	409	16.9%			Jun		
9	Jul	500	421	-15.8%			Jul		
10	Aug	500	454	-9.2%			Aug		
11	Sep	500	474	-5.2%			Sep		
12	Oct	500	521	4.2%			Oct		
13	Nov	500	476	-4.8%			Nov		
14	Dec	500	487	-2.6%			Dec		
15									

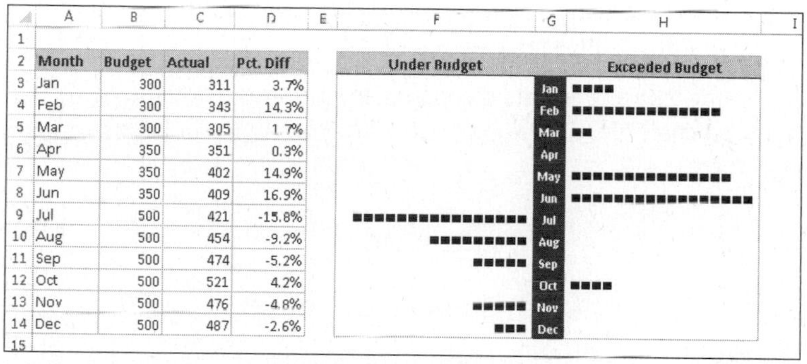

Figure 94-4: Displaying monthly budget variances by using the REPT function.

For this example, follow these steps to set up the bar chart after entering the preceding formulas:

1. Assign the Wingdings font to cells F3 and H3.

2. Copy the formulas down columns F, G, and H to accommodate all the data.

3. Right-align the text in column E and adjust any other formatting.

Depending on the numerical range of your data, you may need to change the scaling. Experiment by replacing the 100 value in the formulas. You can substitute any character you like for the n in the formulas to produce a different character in the chart.

Creating Minimalistic Charts

Effective charts don't always have to be complicated. In fact, simpler charts that convey a clear message are almost always preferable to more complex charts.

This tip presents some simple charts that demonstrate various ways to provide a different visual experience, compared to the standard chart types. The point is to help you realize that, with a bit of creativity, you can create charts that don't look like everyone else's charts.

Simple column charts

Figure 95-1 shows four charts, each of which uses only one data point. This data could be displayed in a single chart, but using four charts provides a different, cleaner look.

These are very minimalistic charts. The only chart elements displayed are the single data point series, the data label for that data point, and the chart tile (displayed on the left, and rotated). The single column fills the entire width of the plot area.

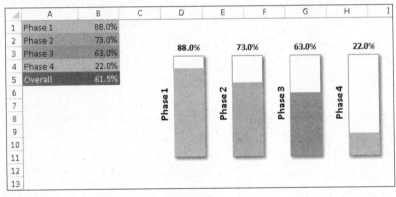

Figure 95-1: Four minimalistic column charts.

Simple pie charts

Figure 95-2 shows the same data, plotted as four pie charts. These charts were adjusted such that the angle of the first slice is 0 degrees. That step makes it easy to make comparisons across the four charts.

The chart titles are linked to the cells in column E (see Tip 92). Each title is generated with a formula that uses the original data. For example, the formula in cell E2 is

```
=A2&" ("&TEXT(B2,"0%")&")"
```

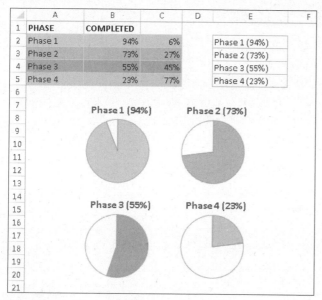

Figure 95-2: Four pie charts.

Simple line charts

Figure 95-3 shows four line charts, with all chart elements removed except for the series and the data labels. Importantly, all four charts use the same vertical scale values (0 through 50). If you allowed Excel to calculate the scale bounds, comparisons among the charts would be difficult.

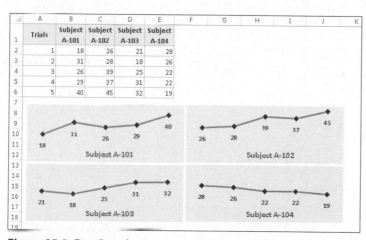

Figure 95-3: Four line charts.

Using four charts makes it very easy to spot trends. The alternative, four series in a single chart, is shown in Figure 95-4.

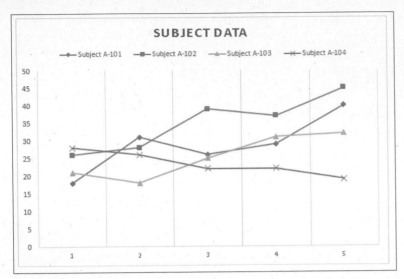

Figure 95-4: A line chart with four series.

Note

Another option is to use Sparkline graphics — perhaps the ultimate in minimal charts. Sparklines are small graphics that display directly in a cell.

A gauge chart

Figure 95-5 shows a chart based on a single cell. It's a pie chart set up to resemble a gauge. Although this chart displays only one value (entered in cell B1), it actually uses three data points (in A4:A6).

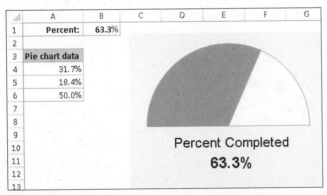

Figure 95-5: This chart resembles a speedometer gauge and displays a value between 0 and 100 percent.

One slice of the pie — the slice at the bottom — always consists of 50 percent. I rotated the pie so that the 50-percent slice was at the bottom. Then I hid that slice by specifying No Fill and No Border for the data point. The other two slices are apportioned based on the value in cell B1. The formula in cell B4 is

```
=MIN(B1,100%)/2
```

This formula uses the MIN function to display the smaller of two values: either the value in cell B1 or 100 percent. It then divides this value by 2 because only the top half of the pie is relevant. Using the MIN function prevents the chart from displaying more than 100 percent.

The formula in cell A5 simply calculates the remaining part of the pie — the part to the right of the gauge's *needle:*

```
=50%-A4
```

The chart's title (Percent Completed) was moved below the half-pie. A linked text box displays the percent completed value in cell B1.

Applying Chart Data Labels from a Range

Excel 2013 introduced a feature that's been on the wish lists of many users for at least 15 years: the ability to specify an arbitrary range to be used as data labels for a series.

Figure 96-1 shows an XY scatter chart that uses data labels stored in a range to identify the data points. In previous versions of Excel, adding these data labels had to be done manually, or with the assistance of a macro.

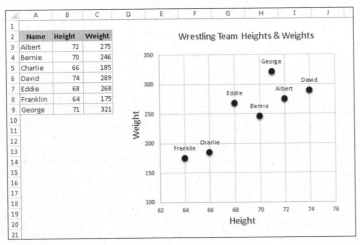

Figure 96-1: Excel 2013 can add data labels from an arbitrary range.

To specify data labels from a range:

1. Activate the chart and select the series that will contain data labels.

2. Click the Chart Elements icon (to the right of the chart) and add data labels.

   Excel displays default data labels for the series.

3. Select the data labels and press Alt+1 to display the Format Data Labels task pane.

4. In the Label Options section of Format Data Labels task pane, deselect any check boxes that are selected and select the Values from Cells check box.

   The Data Label Range dialog box appears, as shown in Figure 96-2.

5. Specify the range that contains the labels and click OK.

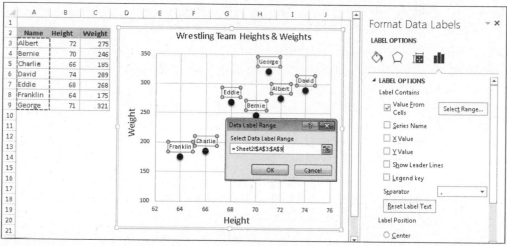

Figure 96-2: Specifying a range to be used as data labels.

Note

When the data labels are placed on the chart, you can fine-tune the location of each one, if necessary. Click one data label to select them all; then click a single data label and drag it to its new position.

Grouping Charts and Other Objects

If you create a number of charts, you may want to be able to work with them all as a group. For example, move them all, or resize them all. The solution is to group the charts into a single object.

Grouping charts

Start by creating the charts that you'd like to group and then arrange and size them as you like. Then press Shift and click each chart. When the charts are selected, right-click any one of them and choose Group→Group.

Figure 97-1 shows six charts that have been grouped. The group name (*Group 14*) appears in the Name box.

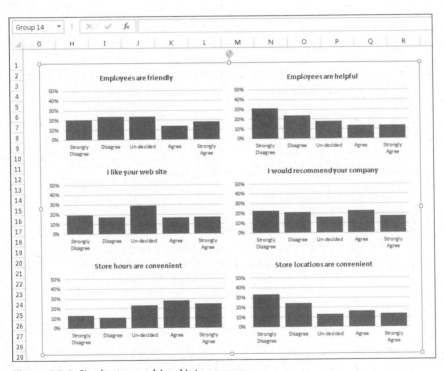

Figure 97-1: Six charts, combined into a group.

To move the entire group, click anywhere in the group and drag.

Note If the group is already selected when you click and drag, you will select a particular chart in the group and change its position. Most of the time, this is not what you want. Press Ctrl+Z to undo.

To resize the entire group, click anywhere in the group to select the group. Then drag any of the resizing handles that appear in the group's outline.

Figure 97-2 shows the grouped charts after I resized the entire group.

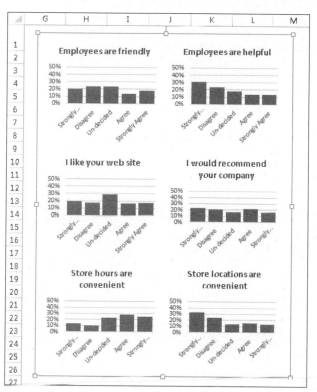

Figure 97-2: Grouped charts, after resizing the group.

Even though charts are grouped, you can still work with a particular chart in a group — and charts that are in a group can still be moved and resized individually. To work with a single chart in a group, click anywhere in the group to select the group; then click the chart you want to work on.

To ungroup the objects in the group, right-click anywhere in the group and choose Group➡ Ungroup.

Grouping other objects

You can combine various types of objects into a group. Figure 97-3 shows a group that consists of a shape (which serves as the background), a text box, and a chart. Figure 97-4 shows the group after I resized it to change the proportions. Resizing a group is much easier than resizing three separate objects.

Note   **When combining objects that overlap, you'll often need to adjust the stack order. Right-click an object and use the Bring to Front or Send to Back commands.**

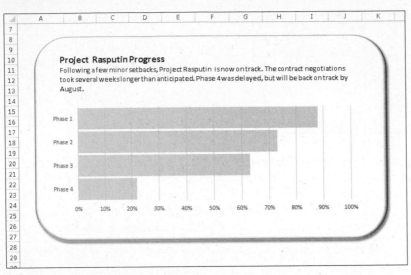

Figure 97-3: Three objects in a group.

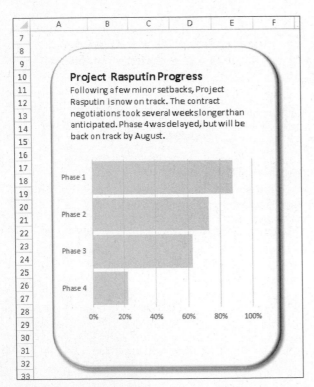

Figure 97-4: The object group, after resizing.

Taking Pictures of Ranges

Excel makes it easy to convert a range of cells into a picture. The picture can either be a *static* image (it doesn't change if the original range changes) or a *live* picture (which reflects changes in the original range). The range can even contain objects, such as charts or shapes.

Creating a static image of a range

To create a snapshot of a range, start by selecting a range of cells and then press Ctrl+C to copy the range to the Clipboard. Then choose Home→Clipboard→Paste→Other Paste Options→Picture (U). The result is a graphic image of the original range, pasted on top of the original range. Just click and drag to move the picture to another location. When you select this image, Excel displays its Picture Tools context menu — which means that you can apply some additional formatting to the picture.

Figure 98-1 shows a range of cells (B2:E9), along with a picture of the range after I applied one of the built-in styles from the Picture Tools→Format→Picture Styles gallery. It's a static picture, so changes made within the range B2:E9 aren't shown in the picture.

Note

If you want to include a graphic that shows information from another (non-Excel) window, choose Insert→Illustrations→Screenshot. You can capture an entire window or just a portion of a window (by choosing Screen Clipping). The copied information is pasted as a picture in the active worksheet.

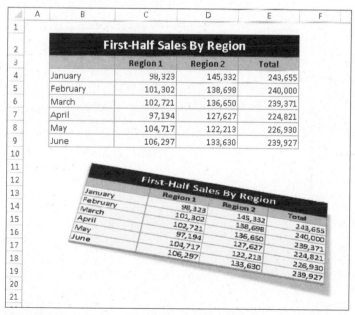

Figure 98-1: A picture of a range, after applying some picture formatting.

Creating a live image of a range

To create an image that's linked to the original range of cells, select the cells and press Ctrl+C to copy the range to the Clipboard. Then choose Home→Clipboard→Paste→Other Paste Options→Linked Picture (I). Excel pastes a picture of the original range, and the picture is linked — if you make changes to the original, those changes are shown in the linked picture.

Notice that when you select the linked picture, the Formula bar displays the address of the original range. You can edit this range reference to change the cells that are displayed in the picture. To unlink the picture, just delete the formula on the Formula bar.

As with an unlinked picture, you can use Excel's Picture Tools context menu to modify the appearance of the linked picture.

You can also cut and paste this picture to a different worksheet, if you like. Doing so makes it easy to refer to information on a different sheet.

Figure 98-2 shows a linked picture of a range placed on top of a shape, which has lots of interesting formatting capabilities. Placing a linked picture on top of a shape is a good way to make a particular range stand out.

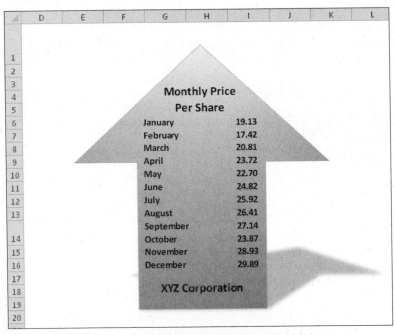

Figure 98-2: A linked picture of a range, placed on top of a shape.

Saving a range as a graphic image

If you need to save a range as a graphic image, the best approach is to use one of several screen capture programs that are available. This type of software makes it easy to capture complete windows or just a portion of a window. After you capture the screen, click a button to save it as a graphics image in the format you choose (GIF, PNT, TIF, and so on).

If you don't have a screen capture program, you probably have some other type of graphics software. When you copy a range of cells, that range is stored on the Windows Clipboard in several different formats. One of those formats is a graphic image. Therefore, you can copy a range, activate your graphics software, and press Ctrl+V to paste the range as a graphic. Then save the graphics file in your desired format.

Figure 98-3 shows a range after it was copied and pasted into a freeware program named IrfanView.

Clipboard01 - IrfanView

File   Edit   Image   Options   View   Help

Month	Region-1	Region-2	Region-3	Region-4
January	5,960	5,467	6,195	5,868
February	5,002	5,759	5,025	5,307
March	5,074	5,266	5,891	6,275
April	6,454	6,004	5,853	5,787
May	6,377	6,434	5,350	5,554
June	5,172	5,783	5,141	5,902
July	5,361	5,054	5,620	5,497
August	5,206	6,063	5,568	5,618
September	6,328	5,638	5,681	5,586
October	5,364	6,488	5,841	6,245
November	6,201	5,474	6,430	6,458
December	5,326	6,031	5,973	6,131
Total	67,825	69,461	68,568	70,228

418 x 281 x 24 BPP   Not a file   100 %   Not a file / 344.70 KB   Not a file

Figure 98-3: A range of data, ready to be saved as a graphic image.

Copying a range is a what-you-see-is-what-you-get thing. For example, if the selected range contains a chart, the chart will also appear in the image.

Cross-Ref

For another method to save a range as a graphic image, see Tip 101.

Changing the Look of Cell Comments

Cell comments are useful for a variety of purposes. But sometimes you just get tired of looking at the same old yellow rectangle. This tip describes three tricks that you can use to make your comments stand out:

➤ Format a comment.

➤ Change the shape of a comment.

➤ Add an image to a comment.

Note

All of these changes require that the cell comment is visible. If the comment isn't visible, right-click the cell and choose Show/Hide Comments from the shortcut menu.

Setting up your Quick Access toolbar

The operations described in this tip require commands that aren't normally available in the Ribbon when a comment is selected. So the first step is to add three commands to your Quick Access toolbar:

1. Right-click the Quick Access toolbar and choose Customize Quick Access Toolbar.

   The Customization section of the Excel Options dialog box appears.

2. From the Choose Commands From drop-down list, select All Commands.

3. In the list on the left, select Format Shape and then click the Add button.

4. In the list on the left, select Change Shape and then click the Add button.

5. In the list on the left, select Picture Fill and then click the Add button.

6. Click OK to close the Excel Options dialog box.

After you complete these steps, your Quick Access toolbar has three new icons.

Formatting a comment

To change the formatting of a comment, Ctrl+click the comment (to select it as a shape) and then click the Format Shape icon in your Quick Access toolbar, or you can press Ctrl+1. Either of these actions displays the Format Comment dialog box. This dialog box has eight tabs that enable you to change just about any aspect of the comment.

Figure 99-1 shows a normal cell comment, and the same comment after changing the font, alignment, fill color, text color, and border width and style.

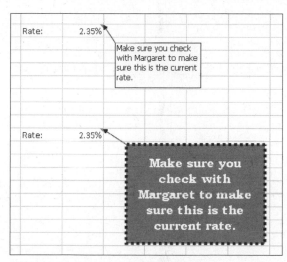

Figure 99-1: A normal cell comment and a comment with different formatting.

Changing the shape of a comment

Comments don't have to display as a rectangular box. Figure 99-2 shows a cell comment, after applying a different shape.

To change the shape of a comment, Ctrl+click the comment (to select it as a shape). Click the Change Shape button on the Quick Access toolbar and choose a new shape for the comment from the Shape gallery.

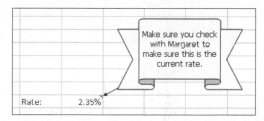

Figure 99-2: A cell comment that uses a nonstandard shape.

Adding an image to a cell comment

Most users don't realize it, but a cell comment can display an image. The image can reside in a file or can come from the Office.com Clip Art collection. You can't use shapes or clip art images that are copied to the Clipboard.

To add an image to a comment, Ctrl+click the comment to select it as a shape and then click the Picture Fill icon in the Quick Access toolbar. Excel displays the Insert Pictures dialog box, in which you can select or search for an image.

Figure 99-3 shows a comment that contains a clip art image. Using an image in a comment increases the size of your workbook, so keep that in mind before you go overboard with images.

Figure 99-3: Displaying an image in a cell comment.

Enhancing Images

A set of features that you might overlook is image enhancement. These tools allow you to modify and enhance images that you insert on a worksheet. This doesn't mean you can uninstall your favorite image editing software, but you may be surprised at the type of enhancements you can perform without even leaving Excel.

To embed an image on a worksheet, choose Insert➜Illustrations➜Pictures (for an image stored on your hard drive) or Insert➜Illustrations➜Online Pictures (to search for and retrieve an image from an online source).

When you select an embedded image, use the tools in the Picture Tools➜Format➜Adjust group to work it. The tools include the following:

> ➤ **Remove Background:** Makes it very easy to remove an extraneous background from a photo.

> ➤ **Corrections:** Sharpen or soften the image or adjust the brightness and contrast.

> ➤ **Color:** Adjust the color saturation and color tone or convert the image to use just a few colors.

> ➤ **Artistic Effects:** Apply some Photoshop-like filters to the image.

> ➤ **Compress Pictures:** Make your images smaller.

> ➤ **Change Picture:** Substitute a different image for the selected image.

> ➤ **Reset Picture:** Undo all modifications you've made.

In most cases, you get a live preview of the effect when you move your mouse pointer over the icon. Just click to apply it. For more control over the enhancements, right-click the image and choose Format Picture. Then use the controls in the Format Picture task pane to adjust the parameters.

Figure 100-1 shows a photo before and after I removed the background. The parts of the image that are removed become transparent. This feature works surprisingly well.

Figure 100-1: The result of using the Remove Background command.

Figure 100-2 shows a clipart image before and after I applied the Pencil Grayscale effect.

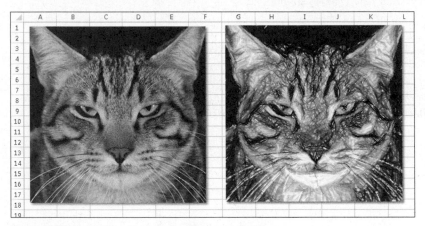

Figure 100-2: Applying an artistic effect to a photo.

Even if you have no need to adjust images, you might enjoy playing around with these features when you need a break from number crunching.

Saving Shapes, Charts, and Ranges as Images

Excel supports quite a few types of graphics, but it doesn't provide a way to save the graphic as a separate file for use in another program. For example, you may want a separate PNG or GIF file created from a chart, a shape, SmartArt, or even a range pasted as a picture (see Tip 98).

Although Excel doesn't provide a direct way to export a graphic, here's a useful trick you can use. First, a bit of set-up work is required:

1. Right-click the Quick Access toolbar and choose Customize the Quick Access Toolbar.

    The Quick Access Toolbar tab of the Excel Options dialog box appears.

2. In the upper-left drop-down control, choose Commands Not in the Ribbon.

3. In the list box, scroll down and select Web Options and then click the Add button.

4. In the list box, select Web Page Preview and click the Add button.

5. Click OK to close the Excel Options dialog box.

    Your Quick Access toolbar now has two new buttons.

Here's how to use these tools to export graphic objects (including charts) from a worksheet.

1. Make sure that your graphics appear the way you want.

2. Click the Web Page Preview button in the Quick Access toolbar.

    A copy of your workbook is converted to an HTML file and is displayed in your default browser.

3. In the browser, right-click a graphic object, choose Save Image As, and specify a location for the file.

    Your browser may have a different, but equivalent, command. Or you can just drag the graphic image to your desktop.

If the quality of the images in your browser is lacking, click the Web Options button in your Quick Access toolbar. The Web Options dialog box is shown in Figure 101-1.

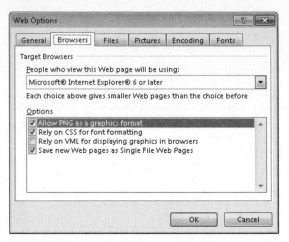

Figure 101-1: The Web Options dialog box.

In the Web Options dialog box, click the Browsers tab and make sure Allow PNG as a Graphics Format is enabled. If graphics don't appear in your browser at all, remove the check mark from Rely on VML for Displaying Graphics in Browser. Next, click the Pictures tab and choose the 120 Pixels Per Inch option. Click OK and do the web preview again. You should see higher-quality graphics (transparent PNG files).

▶ Index

Symbols

#DIV/0! error message, 130

#REF! error message
    avoiding display of, 90–91
    displaying in name lists, 28, 30

* wildcard character, 194

? wildcard character, 195

~ search character, 195

A

absolute references. *See also* formulas
    identifying with dollar signs, 87
    in mixed references, 88–89
    relative versus, 87
    usefulness of, 88

add-ins
    file format for, 37
    Inquire, 132–134
    XDATE, 111–112

Add-Watch dialog box, 83

Advanced Text Import Settings dialog box, 154

age calculations, 108–109

AGGREGATE function, 125–127

alignment
    adjusting by indenting, 48–49
    defaults for text and numbers, 48
    font substitution, avoiding, 72–74

analysis tools, 132

apostrophes
    including in worksheet names, 93
    preceding credit card numbers with, 168

appearance. *See also* formatting
    fonts, adjusting with, 75
    ranges, converting into tables, 205–206
    shading, adjusting with, 62–64

array formulas
    curly braces, using with, 2
    lookups, using with, 103

arrays
    AGGREGATE function, replacing with, 125
    concatenation, using with, 103
    curly braces, using with, 2

formulas, entering properly, 114, 123
    IFERROR function, using with, 124
    limitations of, 207
    lists, generating with, 27–28
    multicell formulas, creating, 174–175
    nonblank cells, finding with, 117
    range references, converting into, 258–259

asterisk (*) wildcard character, 194

audio
    proofing data with, 196
    text-to-speech feature, enabling, 196
    voice qualities, adjusting with, 197

AutoComplete, 211

AutoCorrect, propagating formulas with, 210

AutoFill
    date series, creating with, 152
    filling range with, 151
    lists, creating for, 153
    predicting values with, 152–153
    table of data types, 153

autofit, issues with merged cells, 45

AutoRecover
    autosave intervals, setting, 21
    recovering unsaved workbooks with, 20–21
    saved versions of current workbooks, using, 20

autosave
    AutoRecover, using with, 20
    intervals, setting, 21

AutoSum button (alt+=), 85–86

AVERAGE function, inserting with AutoSum button, 85

AVERAGEIF function, 220

B

bar charts, creating directly in ranges
    condition formatting data bars, 260–261
    formulas, using to display, 261–263
    with repeating characters, 261

bullet lists
    additional columns, creating with, 60–61
    characters for, creating, 60
    numbered lists, using for, 60–61
    SmartArt, creating with, 61
    wrap-text formatting, using with, 60

More great Excel guides from Mr. Spreadsheet!

Need to know more about Excel? John Walkenbach has it covered.

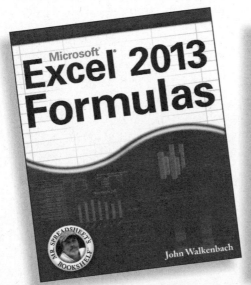

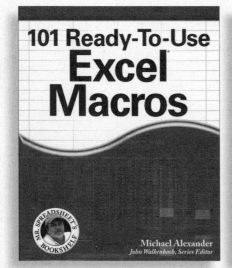
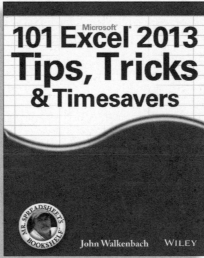
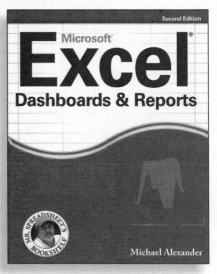